RECIPES

from

HOME

THE DROVER FAMILY FARM IN BERLIN, WISCONSIN, 1910

FOREWORD BY CALVIN TRILLIN

RECIPES

from

HOME

DAVID PAGE
and
BARBARA SHINN

ARTISAN NEW YORK

This book is dedicated to the fields and waters of America, over which we have journeyed with family, friends, each other, and alone. Nothing has taught us more about cooking than the simple bounty of the land.

Published by Artisan
A Division of Workman Publishing, Inc.
708 Broadway
New York, New York 10003-9555
www.artisanbooks.com

Library of Congress Cataloging-in-Publication Data
Page, David
Recipes from Home/David Page and Barbara Shinn.
p. cm.
ISBN 1-885183-99-2
1. Cookery, American. 2. Home Restaurant.
I. Shinn, Barbara. II. Title.

TX715 .S55816 2000
641.5973—dc21   00-029960

Printed in Great Britain by Butler & Tanner, Frome, London, and New York

10 9 8 7 6 5 4 3 2 1

BOOK DESIGN BY DANIA DAVEY

THE PAGES AND DROVERS

NAPOLEON
AND
VERNA PAGE

JULIUS, SR.
AND
JOSEPHINE DROVER

EARLE (BUD) PAGE ——————— FELICIA DROVER
JULIUS DROVER, JR.

JoANNE PAGE
PATRICK PAGE
DAVID PAGE ————————————
ELIZABETH PAGE
CHRISTOPHER PAGE

THE SHINNS AND McCALLS

CLIFTON, SR.
AND
LEILA SHINN

JOHN (BUD), SR.
AND
KATHRYN McCALL,

JOHN (BUD) McCALL, III
KAY McCALL
CLIFTON SHINN, JR ——————— WILMA McCALL
BARBARA SHINN

LEE SHINN
KATHLEEN SHINN
CLIFTON SHINN, III
JOHN SHINN
BARBARA SHINN ——————————

ACKNOWLEDGMENTS

We would like to offer our sincerest gratitude to the many people who, although they may not all be mentioned by name in the text of the book, have been a presence in the writing of it throughout. You have inspired us, taught us, and guided us as we journey onward.

A warm thank-you to the Page and Shinn families, who have always found encouraging words, even during the unpredictable times. You have supported us with your love through our moves from coast to coast, through opening a restaurant, planting a vineyard, and writing this book. Thank you for a family environment where history and a love of the land are passed from generation to generation. And a special thank-you to Chris Page, David's brother, who bravely moved to New York City from Wisconsin to manage Home Restaurant while we planted Shinn Vineyard and completed this book.

Much fondness to our friends with whom we cook. Whether we cook in our kitchen or yours, the meals are always memorable. We would like to especially mention chef Daniel Malzhan, who first put a knife in David's hand and allowed him to think freely about ingredients and cooking. Daniel's focused and imaginative approach to cooking lives in our food today. Robert Stehling, chef and owner of Hominy Grill, who taught us how to "put food by." We will always remember our late-night canning marathons in the kitchen of Home Restaurant. Maybe someday you will give us your ginger jelly recipe. And Amelia Bucci and Paul Camardo, of Bucci's Restaurant, who cook and live with gusto, you have taught us to do the same.

Gratitude to our mentors. Thank you for finding the wonder in American cookery and writing about it.

To the brave James Beard. There might not be "American cuisine" without his insight and insistence.

To M.F.K. Fisher, who gave David the poignant advice to "feed as many people as you can."

To Amelia Simmons, who wrote the first American cookbook in 1796, giving us a glimpse of the eighteenth-century American kitchen.

To Edna Lewis, for sharing her life through the seasons on her family farm. Her cookbook *A Taste of Country Cooking* taught us how to go home.

To Calvin Trillin, who continually makes us laugh and want to fry it up in a pan. You taught us how to drink up the life of a town and take a little home with us.

To Raymond Sokolov, food historian, for your comprehensive tracking of American ingredients around the world and back.

To Betty Fussell, who has traveled through American kitchens and "has heard America cooking."

Thank you to our many food purveyors for Home Restaurant. You have grown us special produce, selected the best prime meats, and sent us fresh local fish: Guy Jones of Blooming Hill Farms, Mark Dunau of Mountain Dell Farm, and John the Greek for your outstanding produce. Benny at Florence Meat Market and Eddie and Joe at Faicco's Pork Store for your perfect meats. John of Eden Brook Farms for sending us the most beautiful trout not caught with a fly. And Amy Scherber of Amy's Breads for delivering her crusty country sourdough to our door every day come rain or shine.

And to our purveyors on the North Fork of Long Island: Charlie at the Southold Fish Market for giving us not only fish but several good fish stories. And the farm stands that line our roads: Latham's for produce,

Wickham's for stone fruits, and Sang Lee Farms for fabulous lettuces and herbs.

We could not fail to mention our past and present Home Restaurant staff, who tirelessly cook and wait tables. You somehow brave it through hot summer days at the stove and cold winter nights at the garden tables. We especially thank pastry chef Melissa Murphy for working closely with David in the development of some of the dessert recipes in this book. Nor can we forget our customers at Home. You bring a little more home to Home, and we hope that you take a little bit of Home with you when you leave.

Thank you to everyone at Artisan, who took this book from a twinkle in our eyes to what it is today. Thank you to Peter Workman for having taken on two people who couldn't write and letting us make this book. From the depths of our hearts, thank you to Ann Bramson, who molded, melded, and welded this book into something that made sense to us all. Thank you to Deborah Weiss Geline for personally taking the book under her wing and keeping it moving forward. Thank you to Irene Sax for her editorial expertise and Dania Davey for her design.

Finally, sincere gratitude to our friends on the North Fork who graciously give us advice, guidance, and courage in farming. You have unselfishly opened your doors to us. To Eric Fry and Sam McCullough of Lenz Winery. Kip and Susan Bedell, Dave Thompson, and Donna Rudolph of Bedell Cellars. Charles and Ursula Massoud of Paumanok Vineyard. Joyce and Bob Pellegrini of Pellegrini Vineyards. Wojtec Majewski of Martha Clara Vineyard. Marty and Carol Sidor of Sidor Farms. And a special thank you to Butch Rowehl of Rowehl Farms for showing us the rhythm and art of farming.

CONTENTS

by *Calvin Trillin*

I wish I could say that my first meal at Home, the restaurant that David Page and Barbara Shinn established a few blocks from where I live in Greenwich Village, reminded me of eating at home—the home I grew up in, that is, which is what midwesterners who live in New York often mean when they use that word. David and Barbara both grew up in the Midwest, and they carried memories of its bounties—not to speak of its recipes—as they crossed the country to California and eventually to Manhattan. I must report, though, that my immediate response to eating at Home was relief that none of those recipes were my mother's. I have admitted that at our midwestern dinner table my father's customary question after sampling the green beans was not "When were these picked?" but "What brand are these?" Since he was a grocer who regularly brought home canned goods that had lost their labels, my mother sometimes couldn't answer the question.

Within a few years of Home's opening, there were half a dozen first-rate restaurants on Cornelia Street, a single block between Fourth and Bleecker. A midwesterner in the Village who got a bit homesick could cheer himself up with the thought that on one block, a short stroll away, he could find a trattoria or a fish house or a bistro beyond the dreams of most midwestern cities. And at the center of the restaurant row, literally and figuratively, was Home; I used to refer to David as the mayor of Cornelia Street. For most of us, eating at a place where the chef makes not only his own salami but his own ketchup brings on a feeling that is not precisely nostalgia. "Think of it," I have sometimes said, while downing some of David's roasted mushroom soup or garlic potato cakes. "This is what eating at home could have been like!"

INTRODUCTION

When we opened Home Restaurant in 1993, we had one goal: to have a place where people could go to eat well, feel good, and to touch base with where they came from—a home away from home. Home Restaurant is located in the West Village, an old part of New York City with narrow meandering streets, gently aged townhouses, and great food markets. When we saw an ad in *The New York Times* for "a cozy 34-seat West Village restaurant with a 30-seat garden, perfect for an aspiring chef or a couple who want to do their own thing," we knew we had found it.

In the early 1990's, Cornelia Street, where the restaurant is, was lined with vacant storefronts, and people rarely traveled down the street, especially after dark. Undaunted, David would stand by the front door in his chef's coat, greeting our neighbors as they came home from work. We also handed out home-baked cookies, and soon, our neighbors began coming to dinner. We knew that a neighborhood is something that has to be nourished to thrive and within a couple of years other restaurants had opened. Now Cornelia Street buzzes every night with hungry diners.

We are often asked how we decided on the name Home. The inspiration came from the "dean of American cookery," James Beard, a teacher and cookbook author. When asked to define American cooking, he retorted, "American food is anything you eat at home." A simple thought that encompasses many big ideas. For us, home is a place, a time, and a relationship among many different people. Our cooking is too.

Home is on a tiny side street in a tiny area of the city, and it is only nine and a half feet wide—with one of the smallest kitchens in the city, about as big as many "home" kitchens. But in tiny places big things often happen.

Our childhood memories of our kitchens are rich with good cooking, warmth, and extended family conversations. Both of our mothers fed big families three meals a day out of cramped quarters and were able to maintain a peaceful environment. The several family recipes that we have included in this book commemorate those times.

We met in California in 1988, when David had been cooking in Bay Area restaurant kitchens for nine years. While in California, we witnessed the remarkable transformation of American cooking, a transformation that would affect many cuisines around the world. We had literally fallen off the midwestern hay wagon and were in awe of the unusual ingredients available to us. We were not alone. The appearance of tender young lettuces, local farmstead cheeses, and never-seen-before produce was inspiring chefs in every California kitchen. Looking back, we see our time in the Bay Area as an awakening—our eyes were opened and our palates followed.

Soon we grew restless in California and decided to journey eastward. We packed our pickup truck with the essentials: cast-iron skillets, good hiking boots, and a stack of maps with no itinerary. For six weeks we managed to stay off the interstate highways, driving on roads that were more often dirt than paved, seeking out community barbecues, small town parades, and local farmers' markets. Afternoons we hiked through forests, where David would disappear and emerge with handfuls of foraged mushrooms or berries. We camped out every night, cooking dinner over a campfire. These experiences confirmed that America was indeed beautiful and bountiful. And it was our home.

At that time, the final frontier was New York City. After years of discovering American cookery, we finally opened our own restaurant. We never thought we would dig such deep roots in the East, but we have, and not only in New York City but on the North Fork of Long Island. When we discovered the bounty of this tiny preserved agricultural area ninety miles east of New York City, we knew we had found another place to call home.

The North Fork is surrounded by the Peconic Bay, the Atlantic Ocean, and Long Island Sound. These bodies of water insulate it from the cold, making it possible to harvest tomatoes in November and to fully ripen vinifera grapes for world-class wines. More days of sun there than anywhere on the Northeast seaboard sustain an agricultural area that is over four hundred years old.

On the North Fork, we were able to realize one more of our dreams—the planting of Shinn Vineyard. With twenty-two acres of farmland, we grin when we realize that we have returned to our midwestern farming roots. We have restored an 1890 farmhouse and barn that will soon be our winery and look forward to the evening we can serve our own wine at our table.

Perhaps we feel at home on the East Coast because we grew up enjoying four distinct seasons. The passage from autumn to winter gives the land a needed rest. In the spring, when the land, seized from freezing, thaws and drinks in melted snow and rainwater, we witness Mother Nature's preparation for the arduous growing season ahead.

Time is metered by these events. When we are at a farm stand and see asparagus, radishes, chives, mint, and sprouts, we say, "This is spring." As the tomatoes turn deep red and juicy sweet, we know "this is summer." As our winemaker friends prepare their barrels for harvest, "It's fall."

We are fortunate to have personal relationships with the people who grow our food and make our wine. In New York City, Benny, our butcher at Florence Meat Market, has beautiful prime meats. Our pork comes from Eddie and Joe at Faicco's down the street. Our produce comes from two upstate farmers, Mark and Guy, and from John, a local produce dealer. Our artisanal breads are baked by Amy at Amy's Breads. Out on the North Fork our fish supplier, Charlie, has pulled up oysters out of his oyster beds and we have eaten them on the spot. At Latham's and Wickham's farm stands, a progression of outstanding produce comes forth throughout the summer and fall. We even get to taste grapes on the vine in the fall, follow their progress from barrel to bottle, and finally see that wine on the list at Home Restaurant. And our lives are enriched by these relationships. To walk on a plowed field, then see it planted, then see it produce, and then use its gifts to feed as many people as we can is an experience we cherish. We know that this is the time of our life.

This book is a collection of these experiences, past and present. The family recipes are part of our memories. Our soups are reminiscent of campfire cooking, our salad and vegetable recipes of California. New York City has cemented our love of perfect prime meats. Long Island, with its fresh seafood, great wine, and homegrown vegetables, has brought yet more good cooking to our kitchen. We hope that by cooking from these pages, you will remember a bit of your own family kitchen and bring a little taste of home to your table.

the PANTRY

BASIC CONDIMENTS

Scallion Mustard   4

Roasted Garlic Mustard   5

Cranberry Mustard   6

Sweet Beet Mustard   7

Golden Beet Mustard Sauce   8

Homemade Mayonnaise   9

Apricot Ketchup   10

Famous Tomato Ketchup   11

Home Barbecue Sauce   13

Mustard Barbecue Sauce   14

FLAVORED BUTTERS

Basil Butter   16

Roasted Garlic–Bourbon Butter   17

Strawberry Butter   17

Sweet Lemon Butter   18

Maple-Bourbon Butter   18

DRIED AND ROASTED TOMATOES

Overnight Tomatoes   19

Roasted Tomato Sauce   20

HERB PURÉES AND PESTOS

Basil Purée   21

Walnut Pesto   22

Sunflower Seed Pesto   23

Mint Pesto   24

Ramp and Mint Pesto   25

LAGNIAPPE

Home Spice Mix   26

Seasoned Bread Crumbs   27

BASIC CONDIMENTS

When we look at the roots of American cookery, we see

an abundance of mustards, ketchups, mayonnaises, but-

ters, and barbecue sauces. All the recipes for these vary

widely in their ingredients and techniques, which leads us

to believe that most of them were family recipes. Today,

the ready availability and variety of condiments on the

supermarket shelf make it easy to forget that no mass-

produced condiment can compare to one created to your

own palate. We love to make our own to dress our sand-

wiches, appetizers, and main dishes.

Scallion Mustard

Berlin, Wisconsin, had a mustard factory that made Uncle Phil's Mustard, and it was on every grocery shelf and in every kitchen cabinet in central Wisconsin. It was good, spicy, and not at all sweet. When we decided to make our own mustard, David felt as though he were going home: another Berliner making mustard. This spread has a pleasant green hue from all the scallions in it. We slather it on roast beef sandwiches when we want to add a kick between the bread slices.

½ bunch scallions
⅛ teaspoon kosher salt
¼ cup Dijon mustard
½ cup olive oil
About 2 tablespoons water
Kosher salt and freshly ground black pepper to taste

Cut roots and green tops off the scallions and set the greens aside. Fill a 2-quart saucepan with water, add the ⅛ teaspoon kosher salt, and bring it to a boil. Blanch the scallion greens for 1 minute, drain, rinse under cold water to stop them from cooking, and pat dry. Coarsely chop the scallion greens. Combine the scallion greens, the white parts, and the mustard in a food processor or blender and purée. With the machine running, slowly add the olive oil and blend until it is completely incorporated. Slowly add enough water to thin the mustard to your desired consistency. Season with salt and pepper. The mustard can be stored in the refrigerator for up to 1 week.   **MAKES ABOUT 1 CUP**

Roasted Garlic Mustard

We've made this garlic-lovers' mustard for years and served it with Chicken Sausage with Lemon and Parsley (page 273) and our homemade salami (page 277).

¼ cup Roasted Garlic Purée (see below)
1 tablespoon sherry wine vinegar
1 tablespoon honey
1 teaspoon crushed yellow mustard seeds (see Note)
¾ cup whole-grain Dijon mustard
1 teaspoon minced fresh thyme
Kosher salt and freshly ground black pepper to taste

Whisk together the garlic purée, vinegar, honey, and mustard seeds in a medium bowl. Fold in the mustard and thyme. Season with salt and pepper. The mustard can be stored in the refrigerator for up to 1 week.

MAKES 1 1/4 CUPS

N O T E : Crush mustard seeds with a mortar, or put them between sheets of waxed paper and roll with a rolling pin.

to make roasted garlic purée It's a great luxury to have garlic purée around. We use it in soups or stews or salad dressings, we paint it on chicken breasts, and we spread it on bread. It's also really easy to make. Cut the tops off several heads of garlic, rub the heads with olive oil, place in a baking dish, and roast at 375°F for an hour. Let cool. When you can handle the heads, press the soft garlic out of the skins into a small dish. It keeps well in the fridge, covered with a little oil, but if you're like us, you'll use it up quickly.

Cranberry Mustard

This is delicious served with duck, game birds, venison, and, of course, the Thanksgiving turkey. Just put a crock of it out on the table and watch it disappear.

1 cup water

2 cups cranberries, rinsed and picked over

2 tablespoons granulated sugar

2 tablespoons honey

1 tablespoon olive oil

1 tablespoon unsalted butter

1 small red onion, thinly sliced

1 tablespoon red wine vinegar

1 tablespoon Dijon mustard

Kosher salt and freshly ground black pepper to taste

Bring the water to a boil in a 2-quart saucepan. Add the cranberries, sugar, and honey. Reduce the heat to low and simmer until all the cranberries have popped, about 5 minutes. Remove from the heat. Heat the olive oil and butter in an 8-inch nonreactive skillet over medium heat. Add the onions and cook until golden brown and tender, 8 to 10 minutes. Add the vinegar and mustard and cook for 5 minutes longer.

Transfer this mixture, along with the cranberries, to a food processor or blender and purée. Season with salt and pepper. Strain through a fine-mesh strainer. The mustard can be stored in the refrigerator for up to 1 week.

MAKES 2 CUPS

Sweet Beet Mustard

We can't resist buying beets during the summer months and inevitably end up with leftovers. This is a perfect way to use them. Thick and spicy, it's good with Simply Roasted Chicken (page 211).

¾ cup diced roasted beets (see below),
  ½-inch dice
¼ cup Dijon mustard
1 teaspoon red wine vinegar
½ teaspoon minced garlic
½ teaspoon minced shallots
1 teaspoon honey
½ cup olive oil
2 tablespoons water
Kosher salt and freshly ground black pepper to taste

Purée the roasted beets, mustard, vinegar, garlic, shallots, and honey in a food processor or blender. With the machine running, slowly add the olive oil and blend until it is completely incorporated. Slowly add the water until it is completely incorporated. Season with salt and pepper and strain through a fine-mesh strainer. The mustard can be stored in the refrigerator for up to 1 week.

MAKES 1 1/2 CUPS

to roast beets To roast beets, wrap them in aluminum foil and put them in a 350°F oven for 45 minutes to 1 hour, or until tender. Open the foil. As soon as the beets cool down enough to handle, you'll be able to rub the skins off with a damp cloth.

Golden Beet Mustard Sauce

Because of its thin consistency, this is a sauce, not a proper mustard. We like to serve it alongside pan-seared tuna or salmon, an arugula or dandelion green salad, and, continuing the theme, roasted red beets.

¾ cup peeled and diced golden beets
   (½-inch dice)
¼ cup dry white wine
¼ cup water
1 tablespoon apple cider vinegar
1 teaspoon granulated sugar
⅛ teaspoon yellow mustard seeds
2 garlic cloves, peeled
1 fresh bay leaf
1 fresh thyme sprig
1 tablespoon Dijon mustard
¼ cup olive oil
Juice of ½ lemon
Kosher salt and freshly ground black pepper to taste

Place the beets, wine, water, vinegar, sugar, mustard seeds, garlic, bay leaf, and thyme in a 4-quart saucepan over medium-low heat. Simmer uncovered until the beets and garlic are cooked through, 8 to 10 minutes. Remove the bay leaf and thyme sprig and discard them.

Transfer the mixture, along with the mustard, to a food processor or blender and purée until it is smooth. With the machine running, slowly add the olive oil and lemon juice. The sauce should be pourable; if it is too thick, thin it with a little warm water. Season with salt and pepper. The mustard can be stored in the refrigerator for up to 1 week.   MAKES 1 1/2 CUPS

golden beets With their delicate mellow flavor, golden beets are also pretty. They have another advantage too: There's no red coloring to stain your hands, clothes, and kitchen counter.

Homemade Mayonnaise

As children, we grew up in households where it mattered whether your refrigerator contained a jar of Hellmann's mayonnaise or Miracle Whip. David's family used Miracle Whip, while Barbara's used Hellmann's. Now, of course, we think the flavor of homemade is unrivaled.

1 large egg yolk
2 teaspoons Dijon mustard
1 teaspoon fresh lemon juice
1 cup canola oil
⅛ teaspoon cayenne pepper
Kosher salt and freshly ground black pepper to taste

Whisk together the egg yolk, mustard, and lemon juice in a large stainless-steel bowl. Add a few drops of the oil and continue whisking. Gradually add the oil in a thin stream while continuing to whisk. Stop every few seconds and check that all the oil has been incorporated. Season with the cayenne and salt and pepper. Store in the refrigerator for up to 2 weeks.   **MAKES 1 1/2 CUPS**

GARLIC MAYONNAISE Add 2 teaspoons minced garlic before adding the seasonings.

ROASTED GARLIC MAYONNAISE The creaminess of roasted garlic melds deliciously with mayonnaise. We like to serve this as a dipping sauce with an assortment of freshly cut vegetables, or in a potato salad. Add 2 tablespoons Roasted Garlic Purée (page 5) to the mayonnaise before adding the seasonings.

BASIL MAYONNAISE Add ¼ cup minced fresh basil before adding the seasonings.

TOMATO MAYONNAISE Add ¼ cup puréed Overnight Tomatoes (page 19) before adding the seasonings.

ROASTED RED PEPPER MAYONNAISE Add ¼ cup Red Pepper Sauce (page 112) before adding the seasonings.

emulsions When you make mayonnaise, you're creating an emulsion, blending two liquids together that don't ordinarily combine. James Beard used his mother's recipe, which called for beating the oil into the egg yolks with a silver fork on a flat dish, and he claimed this mayonnaise could be cut with a knife. A whisk and stainless-steel bowl work well, but if speed is of the essence, probably the easiest method is to use a food processor.

Apricot Ketchup

We encourage a return to a time when many different fruits and vegetables were used to make ketchup. We especially like to serve this ketchup with Spiced Pork Chops (page 255) and, when we add ½ cup Dijon mustard to it, Smoked Duck Breasts (page 230).

1 cup dried apricots (about ½ pound)
1½ cups water
¾ cup dry white wine

¼ cup tarragon vinegar

1 small shallot, minced

2 garlic cloves, minced

¼ teaspoon ground ginger

¼ teaspoon cayenne pepper

⅛ teaspoon ground allspice

⅛ teaspoon ground turmeric

⅛ teaspoon ground cardamom

3 tablespoons honey

Kosher salt and freshly ground black pepper to taste

Place the dried apricots, water, wine, vinegar, shallots, garlic, ginger, cayenne, allspice, turmeric, and cardamom in a 4-quart saucepan. Simmer uncovered until the apricots are softened, about 15 minutes. Remove from the heat and let cool.

Transfer the apricot mixture to a food processor or blender and purée until smooth. Strain the purée through a fine-mesh strainer into a bowl. Stir in the honey and season with salt and black pepper. Thin the ketchup with water if it seems too thick. Store in the refrigerator for up to 1 week.   **MAKES ABOUT 2 1/2 CUPS**

Famous Tomato Ketchup

Our homemade ketchup is the only one served at our restaurant. After all, the motto at Home Restaurant is "Fine Wine. Fine Ketchup." New customers can seem a bit suspicious, but just one taste and they're dunking their onion rings into it and even spreading it on bread.

Americans have an inferiority complex about ketchup. Europeans tell us we put it on everything, and we feel embarrassed. Then one day we decide, "Right, ketchup. And what's wrong with that?" It's a really historic condiment that went through lots of changes until Heinz defined its taste as being tomato-based. We think ours is one of the best.

2 large onions, sliced about ⅔ inch thick

2 tablespoons olive oil

1 cup red wine vinegar

⅓ cup plus 1 tablespoon (packed) dark brown sugar

10 garlic cloves, peeled

¼ cup capers with their brine

¼ cup Tabasco sauce

1 tablespoon Home Spice Mix (page 26)

¾ teaspoon mild paprika

¾ teaspoon ground cinnamon

¾ teaspoon ground allspice

¾ teaspoon ground ginger

¾ teaspoon dried oregano

¾ teaspoon freshly ground black pepper

¾ teaspoon ground cardamom

3 (28-ounce) cans whole tomatoes

2 (12-ounce) cans tomato paste

Kosher salt and freshly ground black pepper to taste

Preheat the broiler.

Toss the onion slices with the olive oil and broil them until charred, about 8 minutes on each side.

Put the onions and all the remaining ingredients in a deep heavy nonreactive pot. Simmer uncovered over low heat for about 3 hours, stirring every 15 minutes to break up the tomatoes and to keep the ketchup from sticking to the bottom of the pot. The mixture will thicken.

Purée the ketchup in batches in a food processor or blender. If the puréed ketchup seems too thin, return it to the pot and simmer until it is as thick as you like it. This ketchup keeps well refrigerated for up to 4 weeks.

MAKES 3 QUARTS

Home Barbecue Sauce

This is our version of the classic tomato-based midwestern barbecue sauce. We marinate chicken or ribs in it before we grill them, then brush on extra sauce while they're cooking to keep the meat moist.

¼ cup olive oil

2 medium yellow onions, cut into ½-inch dice

¼ cup chopped garlic

1 cup apple cider vinegar

10 pounds plum tomatoes, peeled, seeded, and chopped

3 tablespoons capers

1 cup Worcestershire sauce, preferably homemade
(page 249)

½ cup soy sauce

¼ cup (packed) dark brown sugar

1 tablespoon dried oregano

1 tablespoon cayenne pepper

1½ teaspoons ground ginger

Kosher salt and freshly ground black pepper to taste

Heat the olive oil in a large nonreactive pot over medium heat. Add the onions and brown them until quite dark, 15 to 18 minutes. Add the garlic and vinegar and simmer until the liquid is reduced by two thirds. Add the tomatoes, capers, Worcestershire, soy, sugar, oregano, cayenne, and ginger; simmer uncovered until the mixture begins to thicken, about 1 hour. Stir the sauce often to prevent scorching.

Transfer one quarter of the sauce to a food processor or blender and purée, then stir the purée back into the remaining sauce. Season with salt and pepper. Cool the sauce, then transfer to a glass jar. The sauce will keep in the refrigerator for up to 3 weeks. **MAKES ABOUT 2 QUARTS**

a winter barbecue When a deep January freeze has us in its grasp, we thwart it by throwing a winter barbecue. We slather a pork tenderloin with this sauce, roast it in the oven, and savor the caramelized sauce twice as much as we would if it were July and we could barbecue all the time.

Mustard Barbecue Sauce

This Southern-style mustard-based barbecue sauce is one of our favorites. Marinate pork chops, chicken, or salmon in it, then brush on more while you're grilling. The mustard and honey become deliciously caramelized in the heat, giving you an excuse to lick your fingers throughout the meal.

2 tablespoons whole-grain Dijon mustard

2 tablespoons red wine vinegar

1 tablespoon honey

2 tablespoons Home Spice Mix (page 26)

2 tablespoons minced fresh herbs, such as thyme, oregano,
   and/or parsley

2 garlic cloves, minced

1 tablespoon mild paprika

1 serrano chile, minced

1 cup olive oil

Kosher salt and freshly ground black pepper to taste

Purée the mustard, vinegar, honey, spice mix, herbs, garlic, paprika, and chile in a food processor or blender. With the machine running, slowly add the olive oil. Season with salt and pepper. The sauce will keep tightly covered in the refrigerator for several days, but we like to use it right away.   MAKES 2 CUPS

barbecue pride The first time we tasted Southern barbecue sauce, which is made with vinegar or mustard, was a revelation. Being Yankee, and, therefore, used to the tomato-based smoky sauce, we kept quiet through the meal. But we enjoyed observing the fierce conflict that erupted among the Southerners over which of their generations-old recipes was the only correct one.

FLAVORED BUTTERS

Basil Butter

Basil butter is wonderful spread on hot corn on the cob or dropped onto a steaming mound of mashed potatoes. Because butters freeze so well, you can roll the finished mixture into a log, wrap it in waxed paper, and put it in the freezer, where it will keep for several months.

8 tablespoons (1 stick) unsalted butter, softened

1 tablespoon minced shallots

1 tablespoon minced fresh chives

2 teaspoons minced garlic

1 teaspoon minced lemon zest

10 large basil leaves

Kosher salt and freshly ground black pepper to taste

Purée all the ingredients in a food processor until smooth. **MAKES 3/4 CUP**

ROASTED RED PEPPER BUTTER Substitute ½ cup diced roasted red pepper (see page 112) for the basil and add ¼ teaspoon cayenne pepper and you have a terrific butter that's a natural with grilled tuna.

Roasted Garlic–Bourbon Butter

Try this with boiled new potatoes or roasted pork loin.

8 tablespoons (1 stick) unsalted butter, softened

2 tablespoons Roasted Garlic Purée (page 5)

1 tablespoon minced shallots

1 tablespoon whole-grain Dijon mustard

1 tablespoon minced fresh thyme

2 teaspoons honey

2 teaspoons bourbon

Kosher salt and freshly ground black pepper to taste

Purée all the ingredients in a food processor until smooth. **MAKES 3/4 CUP**

Strawberry Butter

We like to make sweet flavored butters to go with biscuits, scones, sweet breads, pancakes, and waffles.

½ pint fresh strawberries, hulled and sliced

2 tablespoons granulated sugar

1 teaspoon fresh lemon juice

1 teaspoon vanilla extract

8 tablespoons (1 stick) unsalted butter, softened

Pinch of kosher salt

Place the strawberries, sugar, lemon juice, and vanilla in a 2-quart saucepan over low heat and simmer until the strawberries are softened and the sugar dissolved, 5 to 6 minutes. Let cool.

Purée the strawberry mixture with the butter in a food processor until smooth. Season with the salt.

MAKES 1 1/2 CUPS

Sweet Lemon Butter

A sweet accompaniment to biscuits, scones, and muffins.

8 tablespoons (1 stick) unsalted butter, softened

2 tablespoons fresh lemon juice

2 tablespoons granulated sugar

1 tablespoon honey

2 teaspoons minced lemon zest

1 teaspoon vanilla extract

1 tablespoon minced fresh mint

Pinch of kosher salt

Place the butter in a medium bowl.

    Heat the lemon juice, sugar, honey, lemon zest, and vanilla in a small saucepan over low heat until the sugar is dissolved, about 1 minute. Let cool, then fold the lemon mixture into the butter. Fold in the mint and season with the salt.   **MAKES ABOUT 1 CUP**

Maple-Bourbon Butter

Melt this on French toast or pancakes.

8 tablespoons (1 stick) unsalted butter, softened

2 tablespoons pure maple syrup

2 tablespoons finely chopped pecans

1 tablespoon Kentucky bourbon

Pinch of kosher salt

Place the butter in a medium bowl.

    Gently heat the syrup, pecans, and bourbon in a small saucepan over low heat for 1 minute. Let cool, then fold the bourbon mixture into the butter. Season with the salt.   **MAKES 3/4 CUP**

DRIED AND ROASTED TOMATOES

Overnight Tomatoes

This slow-drying method makes use of the flood of tomatoes that come to ripeness all at once in late summer. If
you cover them with olive oil and put them in an airtight
container, they'll keep in the fridge for up to two weeks.
We purée them for sauces, use them whole on sandwiches, slice them into salads, and chop them up to use as
a garnish on soup and on sliced fresh mozzarella with
basil leaves.

5 pounds ripe plum tomatoes
½ cup extra virgin olive oil
10 assorted fresh herb sprigs, such as summer savory,
   oregano, basil, thyme, and/or rosemary
3 garlic cloves, slivered
2 teaspoons kosher salt
2 teaspoons granulated sugar
Freshly ground black pepper to taste

Preheat the oven to 175°F. Place wire racks in two
18 x 12-inch baking sheets.

Cut the tomatoes lengthwise in half and scoop out the
seeds. Place the tomatoes in a large bowl, add the rest of
the ingredients, and toss to coat with the oil. Place the
tomatoes cut side up on the wire racks. Scatter any herbs
and garlic left behind in the bowl over the top. Slowly dry
the tomatoes in the oven until shriveled but still some-
what moist, 6 to 8 hours, or overnight.

MAKES ABOUT 5 CUPS

continued

OVERNIGHT TOMATO–BALSAMIC DRESSING
In a medium bowl, whisk 1 cup diced Overnight
Tomatoes, 1 cup olive oil, ¼ cup minced scallions, 3 tablespoons balsamic vinegar, and kosher salt and freshly
ground black pepper to taste.

Roasted Tomato Sauce

We roast tomatoes to accentuate their sweetness and add
a bit of smoky flavor. When tomatoes are roasted, their
acidity is lessened and they take on a much mellower
character. It's similar to what happens when you roast a
whole head of garlic, and it becomes buttery in texture
and taste. You can serve this sauce with pasta or fish, and
we like it with Garlic Potato Cakes (page 122) as well.

4 large ripe tomatoes (about 1½ pounds),
  cored and quartered
6 garlic cloves, peeled
2 tablespoons olive oil
1 tablespoon chopped fresh oregano

Preheat the oven to 425°F.

Combine all the ingredients in a baking dish. Roast
until the tomatoes and garlic are very soft, 18 to 20 minutes. Purée in a food processor or blender until smooth.
Reheat before serving.   MAKES 2 1/2 CUPS

HERB PURÉES AND PESTOS

We first learned to make pesto with basil, but there are many other interesting preparations, especially if you've got a lot of fresh herbs whose flavor you want to concentrate. We use these pestos tossed with pasta, as a garnish on grilled fish or meat, on pizzas, and in soup. We don't really like to freeze pesto, but we do admit to feeling grateful when we happen to find some herb pesto in the freezer on a December day.

Basil Purée

Most people think the best way to preserve basil is to make pesto out of it. Although it's a good idea, we like to save most of our basil unadulterated by garlic and cheese, so we simply purée it with a little olive oil.

4 cups (tightly packed) fresh basil leaves
2 cups olive oil, plus extra if storing
Kosher salt and freshly ground black pepper to taste

Place the basil in a food processor or blender. With the machine running, slowly add the oil, processing to a purée. Season with salt and pepper. The purée can be covered with a little olive oil and refrigerated for up to 3 weeks or frozen for up to 3 months. MAKES ABOUT 3 CUPS

varieties of basil When we go to the farm stands in June, there are large bunches of basil in jugs of water; as the summer progresses, the fragrant bunches get thicker and taller, until they begin to resemble bunches of flowers. After we've sniffed our way through cinnamon basil, opal basil, Thai basil, and lemon basil, we often arrive home with more than we know what to do with.

Walnut Pesto

When fall arrives and we're still bringing home basil from the market, we like to use walnuts instead of pine nuts in pesto. This is delicious with game and game birds, especially quail, squab, or duck.

4 cups (tightly packed) fresh basil leaves
2 garlic cloves, peeled
¾ cup olive oil, plus extra if storing
½ cup grated pecorino Romano, Parmesan,
  or Dry Jack cheese
½ cup toasted and chopped walnuts
Kosher salt and freshly ground black pepper to taste

Purée the basil and garlic in a food processor or blender. With the machine running, slowly pour in the olive oil. Add the cheese and nuts and purée until smooth. Season with salt and pepper. The pesto can be covered with a little olive oil and stored in the refrigerator for up to 1 week or in the freezer for up to 1 month. If you are freezing the pesto, don't add the walnuts until just before using.

MAKES 2 CUPS

Sunflower Seed Pesto

This pesto is unique in that it substitutes sunflower seeds for the traditional pine nuts. We also use a little sorrel in this recipe. It has a slightly lemony flavor that gives this pesto a kick. This pesto is great on tomatoes and pasta as well as a garnish for grilled fish and shellfish. If you like, you can add a little grated hard cheese to this recipe.

½ cup sunflower seeds, lightly toasted

2 cups (tightly packed) fresh basil leaves, coarsely chopped

1 cup (tightly packed) sorrel leaves, coarsely chopped

2 garlic cloves, minced

¾ cup olive oil

Kosher salt and freshly ground black pepper to taste

Purée the sunflower seeds, basil, sorrel, and garlic in a food processor or blender. With the machine running, slowly pour in the olive oil and process until smooth. Season with salt and pepper. The pesto can be covered with a little olive oil and stored in the refrigerator for up to 1 week or in the freezer for up to 1 month. If you are freezing the pesto, don't add the seeds until just before using. **MAKES 2 CUPS**

Mint Pesto

Summer mint is as abundant as summer basil, and we like to combine the two in a refreshing sauce that we often serve with Roast Leg of Lamb with Red Wine Sauce (page 264).

2 cups (tightly packed) fresh basil leaves
2 cups (tightly packed) fresh mint leaves
2 garlic cloves, minced
¾ cup olive oil, or more if needed
½ cup grated pecorino Romano, Parmesan,
   or Dry Jack cheese
¼ cup pistachio nuts
Kosher salt and freshly ground black pepper to taste

Purée the basil, mint, and garlic in a food processor or blender. With the machine running, slowly pour in the olive oil. Add the cheese and nuts and purée until smooth. If the pesto seems too thick, add a little additional oil and purée until smooth. Season with salt and pepper. The pesto can be covered with a little olive oil and stored in the refrigerator for up to 1 week or in the freezer for up to 1 month. If you are freezing the pesto, don't add the cheese and nuts until just before serving.

MAKES ABOUT 2 CUPS

m i n t There are even more varieties of mint than there are of basil, but most of what we get is either peppermint or spearmint. Mint is one of those herbs that works just as well in sweet fruit compotes as it does with savory lamb, carrots, and white beans.

Ramp and Mint Pesto

Ramps, a member of the onion family that looks something like scallions and are sometimes called wild leeks, appear on hillsides throughout the country in the early spring. Stronger than cultivated leeks, with garlicky hot-pepper flavor, they make a delicious pesto that we use as a condiment or, without the cheese, as a marinade for meat that will go on the grill.

½ teaspoon kosher salt

1 pound ramps, rinsed and coarsely chopped

2 cups (tightly packed) fresh basil leaves

1 cup (tightly packed) fresh mint leaves

2 tablespoons minced garlic

2 cups olive oil

1 cup grated Parmesan cheese

1 cup pine nuts, toasted

Kosher salt and freshly ground black pepper to taste

Bring a 2-quart saucepan filled with water to a boil. Add the ½ teaspoon kosher salt and ramps and blanch for 1 minute. Drain and rinse under cold running water to stop the cooking. Pat the ramps dry.

Purée the ramps, basil, mint, and garlic in a food processor or blender. With the machine running, slowly pour in the olive oil. Add the cheese and nuts and purée until smooth. Season with salt and pepper. The pesto can be covered with a little olive oil and stored in the refrigerator for up to 1 week or in the freezer for up to 1 month; if you are freezing the pesto, don't add the cheese and nuts until just before using. MAKES 4 CUPS

LAGNIAPPE

Home Spice Mix

We use this spice mix as if it were salt and pepper. Since it's included in quite a few of our recipes, we always keep a large stash on hand. When you toast the spices, be careful that they don't burn. You'll know that they're done when a toasty, nutty aroma rises out of the pan.

⅓ cup cumin seeds
⅓ cup coriander seeds
⅓ cup yellow mustard seeds

Heat a skillet over medium heat until hot. Add the cumin seeds and toss occasionally until lightly toasted, about 1 minute. Transfer to a plate to cool, and repeat with the coriander seeds and then the mustard seeds.

When the spices are cool, coarsely grind them together in a spice grinder or in a mortar with a pestle.

MAKES 3/4 CUP

s p i c e   g r i n d e r Since whole spices keep their flavor longer than those that are preground, it's worthwhile buying them whole, but you'll need to have a coffee grinder that's used just for spices. If you don't, you could wind up with an odd-tasting morning brew.

Seasoned Bread Crumbs

We always have seasoned bread crumbs on hand. They add a welcome crunch when you use them to coat pan-fried fish or pork loin, to top baked casseroles, and to sprinkle on pasta instead of the expected grated cheese.

6 slices crusty bread, cut into 1-inch cubes (about 2 cups)

4 tablespoons (½ stick) unsalted butter

4 garlic cloves, minced

3 tablespoons minced fresh herbs, such as basil, parsley, thyme, or oregano

½ teaspoon kosher salt

¼ teaspoon freshly ground black pepper

Preheat the oven to 300°F.

Spread the cubes of bread on a baking sheet and toast them in the oven until golden; about 15 minutes.

Place the butter, garlic, and herbs in a small saucepan and heat over low heat until the butter is melted.

Toss the toasted bread with the butter mixture in a large bowl and sprinkle with the salt and pepper. Process the bread in 2 batches in a food processor until you have fine crumbs. Sift the crumbs through a mesh strainer and process the larger crumbs again until all are fine. (If you do not have a food processor, crush the bread on the baking sheet with a rolling pin.)   **MAKES 1 CUP**

to peel garlic The fastest and easiest way to peel garlic is to lay the clove on a chopping board, lay the side of a large knife blade over it, and smash down on the blade with your fist, crushing the garlic clove and releasing it from its papery peel. Then go ahead and mince the garlic.

SOUPS,

CHOWDERS,

and STOCKS

COLD-WEATHER SOUPS

In late autumn, a north wind sweeps across the water from Connecticut and lands in the backyard of our house on the bluffs overlooking Long Island Sound. At times the house is surrounded by gusts for days in a row. The winds continue their noisy growl throughout the night, lulling us to sleep and making us thankful for the good roof over our heads. When the days are at their shortest and the cold orange moon rises in the evening, we warm up by making soup together.

Roasted Mushroom Soup

Now that a variety of cultivated "wild" mushrooms—
cepes, chanterelles, morels, etc.—can be found in markets throughout the year, it's tempting to prepare this
soup in all seasons. We particularly enjoy it in the autumn,
however, when the harvest wanes, the leaves drop, and
the fall mushroom season begins. If you can get true wild
mushrooms foraged from woods and forests, then by all
means use them: Their earthy flavor is incomparable.

1 tablespoon unsalted butter
½ cup minced yellow onion
½ cup minced celery
2 garlic cloves, minced
½ pound fresh mushrooms, such as cremini, shiitake,
*   or portobello, roasted (see page 110)*
4 cups chicken stock, preferably homemade (page 54)
1 tablespoon Worcestershire sauce, preferably homemade
*   (page 249)*
2 tablespoons dry sherry
Kosher salt and freshly ground black pepper to taste

Melt the butter in a large soup pot over medium heat.
Add the onion, celery, and garlic and cook until the vegetables are softened, about 5 minutes. Add the roasted
mushrooms, chicken stock, and Worcestershire; simmer
for 15 to 20 minutes. Add the sherry and simmer for
5 minutes longer.

Purée the soup in a food processor or blender until
smooth. Return the purée to the pot, season with salt and
pepper, and simmer over medium-low heat until heated
through. Serve hot.   **SERVES 4**

Red Bean and Saffron Soup

This was the first recipe we printed on the cards we send out as a restaurant newsletter. Customers still come in clutching the cards and saying, "We made this and it was great."

1 pound dried red kidney beans

2 quarts chicken stock, preferably homemade (page 54), plus more if needed

2 cups orange juice

6 to 8 saffron threads, crushed

2 slices bacon, cut into ½-inch dice

1 medium red onion, cut into ½-inch dice

1 red bell pepper, cut into ½-inch dice

2 ribs celery, cut into ½-inch dice

6 garlic cloves, chopped

½ cup sherry vinegar

2 tablespoons minced fresh tarragon

¼ cup minced scallions

Kosher salt and freshly ground black pepper to taste

Cover the beans with plenty of water in a large bowl and let soak for 5 to 7 hours, or overnight. Drain and rinse.

Place the beans, chicken stock, orange juice, and saffron in a large soup pot and bring to a simmer.

Meanwhile, cook the bacon, onions, red peppers, celery, and garlic in a medium skillet over medium heat until the vegetables are softened, about 5 minutes. Deglaze the skillet with ¼ cup of the vinegar.

Add the mixture to the simmering beans and simmer until the beans are very tender, about 1½ hours.

Purée the soup in a food processor or blender until it is smooth. Return the soup to the pot and heat through.

continued

Add the remaining ¼ cup vinegar, the tarragon, and scallions. Season with salt and pepper. If the soup seems too thick, adjust the consistency with a little stock or water. Serve hot. **SERVES 6**

Smoked Turkey, Cabbage, and Barley Soup

When the weather turns cold, we want to eat things that are a little richer and a little fuller, like this soup. It's autumn, it's cabbage time, and we're beginning to think about turkey now that the holidays are coming up. There's a lot of meat on turkey drumsticks, and they're packed with flavor. They impart the same kind of old-time quality as ham or bacon or ham hocks, but are a little lighter to cook with.

¼ teaspoon kosher salt

⅓ cup pearl barley

2 tablespoons unsalted butter

2 tablespoons olive oil

2 cups peeled and diced carrots (¼-inch dice)

1½ cups diced celery (¼-inch dice)

1 medium yellow onion, cut into ¼-inch dice

3 garlic cloves, minced

2 smoked turkey drumsticks

2 teaspoons crushed yellow mustard seeds

2 fresh bay leaves

2 fresh thyme sprigs

6 cups water

1 (12-ounce) bottle medium-bodied beer

2 cups halved fresh cremini mushrooms

½ head savoy cabbage, cored and cut into large pieces

2 tablespoons minced fresh parsley

1 tablespoon minced fresh sage

Kosher salt and freshly ground black pepper to taste

Place 2 cups water and the kosher salt in a 2-quart saucepan and bring to a gentle boil. Add the barley and simmer until it is tender, 30 to 40 minutes. Drain and set aside.

Heat the butter and oil in a large soup pot over medium heat. Add the carrots, celery, onions, and garlic and cook until they are softened, about 5 minutes. Add the turkey legs, mustard seeds, bay leaves, and thyme and cook for 2 minutes longer. Add the water and beer and simmer for 35 minutes. Remove from the heat.

Remove the turkey legs and let cool, then pull off and coarsely chop the turkey meat. Return the turkey to the pot, add the mushrooms and cabbage, and simmer for 15 minutes. Add the parsley and sage and season with salt and pepper. Serve hot.   SERVES 6

Black Bean Soup with Ham and Sherry

Black bean soup comes in two styles. The whole-bean version is traditional in the South. It often contains a ham bone, and it is seasoned with dry sherry and a little cayenne pepper. The Latin American style found in the Southwest and California is often puréed and flavored with fresh jalapeño chile and cilantro. Both are delicious.

continued

1 cup dried black beans

2 tablespoons unsalted butter

½ cup diced yellow onion (¼-inch dice)

½ cup diced celery (¼-inch dice)

½ cup peeled and diced carrots (¼-inch dice)

2 teaspoons minced garlic

2 quarts chicken stock, preferably homemade (page 54),
* or water*

1 smoked ham hock

1 fresh bay leaf

½ teaspoon cayenne pepper

2 tablespoons dry sherry

Kosher salt and freshly ground black pepper to taste

Bring the black beans and 2 cups water to a gentle boil in a small saucepan. Remove the pan from the heat, cover, and let stand for 1 hour. Drain and rinse the beans.

Melt the butter in a large soup pot over low heat. Add the onion, celery, carrots, and garlic and slowly cook until the vegetables are softened. Add the stock, beans, ham hock, bay leaf, and cayenne. Simmer until the beans are tender, about 1½ hours. Remove from the heat.

Remove and discard the bay leaf. Remove the ham hock and let cool, then remove and shred the meat. Purée one quarter of the bean mixture in a food processor and return it to the soup. Stir in the shredded ham, and the sherry, bring to a simmer, and simmer for 10 minutes. Season with salt and pepper and serve hot.   SERVES 4 TO 6

Black Bean Soup with Chiles and Cilantro

1 cup dried black beans

2 tablespoons unsalted butter

½ cup diced yellow onion (¼-inch dice)

½ cup diced celery (¼-inch dice)

½ cup peeled and diced carrots (¼-inch dice)

½ cup chopped tomatoes

1 tablespoon minced jalapeño chile

2 teaspoons minced garlic

2 quarts chicken stock, preferably homemade (page 54),
*   or water, plus more if needed*

1 fresh bay leaf

2 tablespoons fresh lemon juice

Kosher salt and freshly ground black pepper to taste

¼ cup minced scallions

2 tablespoons minced fresh cilantro

¼ cup sour cream

Bring the black beans and 2 cups water to a gentle boil in a small saucepan. Remove the pan from the heat, cover, and let stand for 1 hour. Drain and rinse the beans.

Melt the butter in a large soup pot over low heat. Add the onion, celery, carrots, tomatoes, chile, and garlic. Slowly cook until the vegetables are softened. Add the stock and bay leaf. Simmer until the beans are tender, about 1½ hours.

Remove the bay leaf and purée the soup in a food processor or blender until it is smooth. Return the soup to the pot, add the lemon juice, and season with salt and pepper. If the soup is too thick, add a little stock or water. Heat the soup through. Ladle it into 4 soup bowls and garnish with the scallions, cilantro, and sour cream.

SERVES 4

Death Valley Soup When I was in my early

twenties, I went to Death Valley with Tim, a photogra-

pher friend. We lived in a sky-blue Chevy pickup, slept

out under the stars, and subsisted on a lot of soup because

between us, we had $1.50 a day for food. A cut-up potato,

a few vegetables, and some chicken stock filled up our

bowls and warmed us as the cold approached. Not only

was it satisfying, but we never tired of it. When I got back

to San Francisco, I missed the satisfaction of assembling

and sharing a meal—and, in less than a year, I was cooking

for Tim's brother Daniel, a chef in a San Francisco restau-

rant, and decided that cooking was my home.   —DAVID

Split Pea Soup

The flavor of split pea soup brightens up when you add an acid such as lemon juice or vinegar. We think the dark beer and mint add another level of complexity to the soup, one of our winter mainstays.

2 quarts chicken stock, preferably homemade (page 54),
*   or water, plus more if needed*
½ pound green split peas
1 smoked ham hock
1 fresh bay leaf
2 tablespoons plus 1 teaspoon minced fresh mint
1 tablespoon unsalted butter
1 cup diced celery (¼-inch dice)
1 cup diced yellow onions (¼-inch dice)
3 garlic cloves, minced
1 cup dark beer
2 tablespoons sherry vinegar
1 teaspoon Dijon mustard
Kosher salt and freshly ground black pepper to taste

Combine the stock, peas, ham hock, bay leaf, and 1 teaspoon of the mint in a large soup pot and simmer over medium-low heat until the peas soften, about 1 hour.

Remove the ham hock and let cool, then remove and shred the meat.

Meanwhile, melt the butter in an 8-inch skillet over medium heat. Add the celery, onions, and garlic and cook until the vegetables are softened, about 5 minutes. Deglaze with the beer and cook until the beer is reduced by half.

Transfer this mixture to a food processor or blender, add half the cooked peas, and purée until smooth. Stir the purée into the rest of the peas, add the ham, and simmer for 30 minutes. If the soup seems too thick, adjust the consistency with a little stock or water. Whisk in the vinegar and mustard and season with salt and pepper. Ladle the hot soup into soup bowls and garnish with the remaining 2 tablespoons mint. **SERVES 4**

split peas Sometimes called field peas, these yellow and green peas are grown especially for drying. After they're dried, they're split along a natural seam, making it unnecessary to presoak them as you would dried beans.

White Bean and Rosemary Soup

One of the most comforting dishes we prepare, it can be doubled or tripled to serve at several meals over several days. This is what we do when the weather turns stormy and we know we'll be staying close to home.

1 cup dried white beans, such as navy beans

2 quarts water, plus more if needed

2 tablespoons unsalted butter

¾ cup diced celery (¼-inch dice)

¾ cup peeled and diced carrots (¼-inch dice)

½ cup diced onion (½-inch dice)

1 teaspoon minced garlic

1 fresh bay leaf

2 fresh thyme sprigs

Kosher salt and freshly ground black pepper to taste

2 tablespoons chopped fresh parsley

1 tablespoon chopped fresh rosemary

1 teaspoon minced lemon zest

Bring the white beans and 2 cups of the water to a boil in a medium saucepan. Remove the pan from the heat, cover, and let stand for 1 hour. Drain and rinse the beans.

Melt the butter in a large soup pot over medium heat. Add the celery, carrots, onion, and garlic and cook until the vegetables are softened, 5 to 6 minutes. Add the beans, water, bay leaf, and thyme. Simmer until the beans are tender, 45 minutes to 1 hour.

Remove and discard the bay leaf and the thyme sprigs. If the soup seems too thick, adjust the consistency with a little water. Season with salt and pepper. Ladle the hot soup into soup bowls and garnish with the chopped parsley, rosemary, and lemon zest.   SERVES 4

Roasted Tomato Soup

We make chilled tomato soups all summer, but when the air turns cold, we like this robust version. Have it for lunch with a grilled cheese sandwich (pages 295 to 297) or serve it at the start of a Sunday supper of Simply Roasted Chicken (page 211) and Yukon Gold Mashed Potatoes (page 116).

2 pounds ripe plum tomatoes, halved

6 garlic cloves, peeled

3 fresh thyme sprigs

3 tablespoons olive oil

3 cups chicken or vegetable stock, preferably homemade
   (page 54 or 63)

Kosher salt and freshly ground black pepper to taste

4 fresh sage leaves

continued

Preheat the oven to 450°F.

Toss the tomatoes with the garlic, thyme, and olive oil. Spread the tomatoes evenly on a baking sheet and roast them for 20 minutes. Let the tomatoes cool, then remove the thyme sprigs and slip the skins off the tomatoes.

Purée the tomatoes, garlic, and stock in a food processor until smooth. Transfer the purée to a soup pot and simmer over medium-low heat until it is heated through. Season with salt and pepper. Ladle into bowls and serve hot, with the sage leaves torn over the tops.   SERVES 4

roasted tomatoes Roasting tomatoes helps bring out their natural sweetness. That means winter plum tomatoes can be as rich-tasting as summer's crop. Take a look at our recipe for Overnight Tomatoes (page 19).

Bay Scallop Chowder with Sweet Cream and Leeks

When we moved to the East Coast, we began cooking with fresh bay scallops. Smaller than sea scallops, they are sweet and buttery and usually are in season for only a short time. Our local scallops come from the Peconic Bay, a body of water at the eastern end of Long Island, between the North and South forks about ninety miles from New York City. They come into season in October. If you can't find bay scallops, substitute sea scallops.

Celebrate scallop season by serving this chowder with Chopped Spring Vegetable Salad (page 72), some homemade Oyster Crackers (page 310), and a slice of Toasted Angel Food Cake (page 370) for dessert.

1½ pounds bay scallops

1½ cups peeled and diced white potatoes (½-inch dice)

2 tablespoons unsalted butter

1½ cups thinly sliced leeks

¾ cup dry white wine

¾ cup clam juice or Fish Stock (page 61)

3½ cups heavy cream

Kosher salt and freshly ground black pepper to taste

2 tablespoons chopped fresh parsley

1 teaspoon mild paprika

Look for the tough muscle on the side of each scallop, which it uses to attach itself to the shell, and remove the muscle by peeling it away from the body of the scallop with your fingers.

Place the potatoes in a medium pot of salted water. Bring to a boil and cook for about 3 minutes. Drain and set aside.

Melt the butter in a large soup pot over medium-low heat. Add the leeks and gently cook until they are softened and tender, about 3 minutes. Add the wine and clam juice and boil over medium-high heat until reduced by half, about 15 minutes. Add the cream, reduce the heat, and simmer for 15 to 20 minutes, stirring occasionally. Add the potatoes and simmer for 3 to 4 minutes. Add the scallops and simmer for 3 minutes longer; do not boil. The scallops should be just heated through. Season with salt and pepper and ladle into soup bowls. Garnish with the chopped parsley and paprika.   SERVES 6

WARM-WEATHER SOUPS

Our warm-weather soups are lighter and brighter than their cold-weather counterparts. Chilled soups perk up appetites that have been dulled by the heat. But by some magic, hot chowders manage to cool us off too, just what we want to eat on a sultry night in July.

Blackfish and Asparagus Soup

Blackfish reappear after their winter hibernation at around the same time we see the first asparagus, so it seemed natural to combine the two in a delicate broth. Blackfish are never really plentiful, though; if you can't find them, you can use monkfish, bass, or snapper instead.

FOR THE STOCK

Bones and head from a 4- to 5-pound blackfish

2 tablespoons unsalted butter

2 tablespoons olive oil

2 cups diced onions (⅛-inch dice)

1½ cups diced fennel (⅛-inch dice)

¾ cup peeled and diced carrots (⅛-inch dice)

1 tablespoon minced garlic

1 fresh bay leaf

2 fresh thyme sprigs

3 cups chopped tomatoes

4 cups water

2 cups dry white wine

2 tablespoons olive oil

2 tablespoons unsalted butter

1 cup diced onions (¼-inch dice)

1 cup diced leeks (¼-inch dice)

2 pounds blackfish fillets, cut into 2- to 3-inch pieces

1½ cups sliced asparagus (cut into ½-inch lengths)

Kosher salt and freshly ground black pepper to taste

2 tablespoons chopped fresh herbs, such as parsley,

   rosemary, thyme, and/or chives

For the stock, soak the bones and head of the blackfish in several changes of cold water. Drain and rinse well.

Heat the butter and oil in a large soup pot over medium-low heat. Add the onions, fennel, carrots, garlic, bay leaf, and thyme and cook gently until the vegetables are softened, about 5 minutes. Add the fish bones and head and cook for 2 minutes. Add the tomatoes, water, and wine, bring to a simmer, and simmer for 25 minutes. Strain the stock through a fine-mesh strainer; you should have about 2 quarts. Set aside.

Heat the olive oil and butter in a large soup pot over medium-low heat. Add the onions and leeks and gently cook until softened, 5 to 7 minutes. Add the fish stock and simmer. Add the blackfish and asparagus and simmer until the fish is just cooked through, about 3 minutes. Season with salt and pepper. Ladle into soup bowls and garnish with the herbs.   SERVES 6 TO 8

blackfish Also known as tautogs, blackfish are most abundant in the fall and spring. Their hearty taste, due to their rich diet of clams, oysters, and other shellfish, their sturdy texture, and their low price make them a good choice for soups. Ask your fish market for skinned fillets, and also for the bones and head for your stock.

Chilled Tomato Soup

This uncooked chilled tomato soup, inspired by gazpacho, is chunky with the squash, zucchini, peppers, and tomatoes we get from the farm stand. We serve it really cold, in prechilled bowls.

4 pounds very ripe tomatoes

3 tablespoons red wine vinegar

1 tablespoon granulated sugar

1 teaspoon cayenne pepper

½ cup diced red onion (⅛-inch dice)

½ cup diced summer squash (⅛-inch dice)

½ cup diced zucchini (⅛-inch dice)

½ cup diced red bell pepper (⅛-inch dice)

¼ cup olive oil

Kosher salt and freshly ground black pepper to taste

2 tablespoons chopped fresh parsley or summer savory

Core and coarsely chop the tomatoes in a food processor, purée the tomatoes, in batches, until smooth. Place a large strainer over a large bowl and press the tomatoes through the strainer. Add the vinegar, sugar, and cayenne to the purée and mix thoroughly. Stir in the diced vegetables and olive oil and season with salt and pepper. Refrigerate for at least 1 hour.

Serve chilled, garnished with the fresh herbs.

SERVES 4

Chilled Tomato Soup
with Shellfish Salad

On a summer night, this soup can be our whole supper, followed by just a fresh ripe peach. The soup is fairly spicy because of the serranos—small, pointed chiles that start out green and turn red and then yellow as they ripen. We find them in Latin groceries and, increasingly, in supermarket produce departments, but if we can't get them, we use jalapeños.

6 large vine-ripened tomatoes, quartered

6 tablespoons olive oil

4 garlic cloves, peeled

2 serrano chiles, chopped

Kosher salt and freshly ground black pepper to taste

1 cup dry white wine

¼ cup fresh lemon juice

24 bay scallops, tough side muscle removed

12 littleneck clams, scrubbed

12 mussels, scrubbed and debearded

1 cup loosely packed small, young lettuce leaves

6 to 8 small fresh mint leaves, thinly slivered

Preheat the oven to 400°F.

Toss together the tomatoes, 3 tablespoons of the olive oil, the garlic, and chile in a large bowl. Transfer this mixture to a large baking dish and roast for 25 minutes. Let cool, then transfer the mixture to a food processor or blender and purée until smooth. Strain the soup into a large bowl, season with salt and pepper, and refrigerate for at least 1 hour.

continued

Bring the wine and 2 tablespoons of the lemon juice to a simmer in a 10-inch nonreactive skillet. Add the scallops, cover the skillet, and steam them until they are just cooked through, about 3 minutes. Transfer the scallops to a bowl. Add the clams and mussels to the skillet, cover it, and steam them until they open. Remove the clams and mussels; reserve the cooking liquid. Remove most of the clams and mussels from their shells, saving 4 of each in the shell for the garnish, and add the shucked clams and mussels to the scallops.

Whisk together half of the reserved cooking liquid (discard the rest), the remaining 3 tablespoons olive oil, and the remaining 2 tablespoons lemon juice in a small bowl.

Toss the shucked shellfish and greens with just enough of this dressing to coat and place in the center of 4 chilled large soup bowls. Ladle the chilled soup around the salad and garnish the bowls with the clams and mussels still in their shells and the mint.   SERVES 4

to cook with peppers To tell how hot a chile is, take a fingernail and scratch a little bit off the top near the stem to taste it. Then finely chop the pepper and add it a little bit at a time to the pot. I try to be careful, by tasting and retasting as I go. Sometimes you can add chiles very carefully to soup or salsa and it's fine, but when you go back and taste it an hour later, you find the heat has exploded. I believe that a light hand with a variety of chiles makes for more interesting and complex flavors. Try experimenting with dry chiles as well as fresh.

—DAVID

Chilled Cantaloupe Soup
with Minted Yogurt

Once melon season hits, it comes in with such abundance that local farm stands have to wheel in extra carts to hold all the fruit. We use cantaloupe to make a clean, delicate purée that we serve at brunch in chilled soup bowls. We've played around with garnishes, scattering our soup one time with blueberries, another time with mint leaves and sour cream, and, once, even drizzling it with red chili oil.

1 medium cantaloupe, halved, seeded, peeled, and cut
into ½-inch dice
½ cup dry Riesling wine
2 tablespoons apple cider vinegar
2 teaspoons granulated sugar
1 teaspoon kosher salt
¼ cup plain yogurt
1 tablespoon minced fresh mint

Place the cantaloupe, wine, vinegar, sugar, and salt in a food processor or blender and purée until smooth. Refrigerate for at least 1 hour.

Stir together the yogurt and mint in a small bowl. Pour the soup into 4 chilled bowls and garnish each serving with a dollop of the minted yogurt.   SERVES 4

riesling   Riesling is one of the many grape varieties grown on Long Island and upstate New York. Pour a chilled glass to drink with this soup, and you'll find you like its balance of fruit and acidity with the sweet-and-tart cantaloupe and yogurt.

Roasted Red Bell Pepper Soup

Leave a green bell pepper on the vine to ripen fully, and it turns red and sweet. The yellow, orange, and purple peppers, however, are entirely different varieties and have their own individual flavor characteristics. When roasted, red bell peppers have a wonderful sweet, smoky taste.

2 tablespoons unsalted butter

½ cup diced red onion (¼-inch dice)

½ cup diced fennel (¼-inch dice)

1 teaspoon minced garlic

8 large red bell peppers, roasted (see page 112)
  and coarsely chopped

2 tablespoons red wine vinegar

6 cups chicken stock, preferably homemade (page 54),
  plus more if needed

¼ teaspoon cayenne pepper

Kosher salt and freshly ground black pepper to taste

4 fresh fennel or dill sprigs

Melt the butter in a medium pot over medium heat. Add the red onion, fennel, and garlic and gently cook until the vegetables are softened, about 5 minutes. Add the roasted peppers and cook for 3 minutes. Add the vinegar and cook for 1 minute. Add the chicken stock and cayenne, reduce the heat, and simmer for 20 minutes.

Purée the soup in a blender or food processor until it is smooth. Return the soup to the soup pot; if the soup seems too thick, adjust the consistency with a little stock or water. Simmer over medium-low heat until it is heated through. Season with salt and pepper. Ladle into bowls and garnish with the fennel.   SERVES 4

Clam and
Sweet Corn Chowder

Every year at the chowder contest in Greenport, Long Island, we are saddened to note that there are fewer New England–style white chowders entered in the contest. We are both white chowder fans, and we make ours with littlenecks, one of the smallest of the hard-shell clams, which are usually under two inches across. Be sure they are alive when you buy them; their shells should be closed tightly. Use them the same day you purchase them.

5 slices bacon, diced (¼-inch dice)

1 small yellow onion, cut into ¼-inch dice

1 medium leek, cut into ¼-inch dice

3 ribs celery, cut into ¼-inch dice

2 garlic cloves, minced

1 fresh bay leaf

3 fresh thyme sprigs

4 cups Vegetable-Corn Stock (page 63)

3 ears sweet corn, kernels cut off the cobs (see Note)

3 cups peeled and diced white potates (½-inch dice)

36 littleneck clams, shucked and chopped, or

    2 (8-ounce) jars chopped clams, drained

1 cup heavy cream

Kosher salt and freshly ground black pepper to taste

2 tablespoons chopped fresh parsley

2 teaspoons paprika

continued

Cook the bacon in a large soup pot over medium heat until crisp. Pour off all but 2 tablespoons of the fat and add the onions, leeks, celery, garlic, and bay leaf to the pot. Continue to cook over medium heat until the vegetables are softened, 4 to 5 minutes. Add the thyme, stock, corn, and potatoes and simmer until the potatoes are tender, 7 to 10 minutes.

Add the clams and cream and simmer until the clams are warmed through, 2 to 3 minutes. Season with salt and pepper. Ladle the hot soup into bowls and garnish with the parsley and paprika.   SERVES 6

NOTE: If you don't have the stock on hand, reserve the corn cobs for making it.

Manhattan Clam Chowder

New Englanders believe mixing clams and tomatoes in chowder is an abomination. We think it's a useful way to use fresh summer produce. In our recipe, we use cherrystone clams, one step up in size from littlenecks. Cherrystones have good flavor and a meatier texture.

4 dozen cherrystone clams, scrubbed

2 tablespoons olive oil

2 tablespoons unsalted butter

3 cups diced yellow onions (¼-inch dice)

2 cups diced celery (¼-inch dice)

2 tablespoons minced garlic

¾ cup diced poblano chiles (⅛-inch dice)

¾ cup diced yellow bell peppers (¼-inch dice)

3 cups peeled, seeded, and chopped tomatoes

2½ cups dry white wine

4 cups water

2 cups diced and peeled sweet potatoes (¼-inch dice)

1 cup diced carrots (¼-inch dice)

¾ cup fresh sweet corn kernels

Kosher salt and freshly ground black pepper to taste

3 tablespoons freshly chopped herbs, such as thyme,
    oregano, and/or marjoram

Put 3 cups water and the clams in a wide shallow pan, cover the pan, and steam the clams over medium-high heat until they open, 5 to 7 minutes. Remove the clams from their shells and put aside. Strain and reserve the cooking liquid.

Heat the olive oil and butter in a large soup pot over medium heat. Add the onions, celery, and garlic and cook until the vegetables are softened, about 4 minutes. Add the poblanos and yellow peppers and cook for 5 minutes.

Add the tomatoes, 2½ cups of the cooking liquid from the clams, the wine, and water and simmer for 10 minutes. Add the sweet potatoes, carrots, and corn and simmer until tender, about 10 minutes. Add the clams and simmer for 3 to 4 minutes. Season with salt and pepper, and ladle into soup bowls. Garnish the chowder with the chopped herbs. **SERVES 6 TO 8**

STOCKS

Well-made stock should sum up all the ingredients in one

sip, and using homemade stocks instead of water can turn

an ordinary dish into one that's exceptional. That's why

we always have several different stocks on hand, either

fresh in the refrigerator or tucked away in the freezer.

Chicken Stock

Good cooking is easy when you use good ingredients, and the trick to full-flavored chicken stock is using full-flavored chicken. Use hormone-free chickens that have been fed a healthy grain diet and allowed some legroom in the barnyard.

¼ cup olive oil

2 cups diced celery (½-inch dice)

2 cups diced onions (½-inch dice)

2 cups diced carrots (½-inch dice)

½ pound fresh mushrooms, sliced

1 medium leek, cut into ½-inch dice

4 garlic cloves, peeled

5 pounds chicken bones (backs, necks, and wings
　　work best), rinsed and drained

1 gallon cold water

1 cup loosely packed celery leaves

1 fresh thyme sprig

2 fresh bay leaves

12 black peppercorns

Heat the olive oil in a large heavy stockpot over medium heat. Add the celery, onions, carrots, mushrooms, leeks, and garlic and gently cook until the vegetables are softened, about 5 minutes. Add the chicken bones, water, celery leaves, thyme, bay leaves, and peppercorns. Bring the liquid to a boil. Skim off the impurities that float to the top, reduce the heat, and simmer uncovered for 2 hours.

Strain the stock through a cheesecloth-lined or fine-mesh strainer and cool uncovered to room temperature; cover and refrigerate. The stock will keep for up to 2 months in the freezer or up to 7 days in the refrigerator.

MAKES 3 QUARTS

for deeper flavor You don't have to roast the bones before you make chicken stock, but if you do, you'll get a richer flavor. Roast them in a shallow pan in a 400°F oven for 30 to 45 minutes, spooning off the fat occasionally. Then proceed with the recipe.

GRANDMOTHER PAGE WITH MY DAD, BUD, 1945

On Sundays, Grandmother Page would

make chicken noodle soup, simmering and reducing her

chicken stock while she rolled out egg noodles. I would

watch her attentively as she kneaded the eggs into the

flour with her hands, rolled the dough out, cut it into

noodles, and hung them on a clothes rack to dry. She'd

cook them in the simmering pot of soup just before the

family sat down to eat.   —DAVID

Grandmother Page's
Egg Noodles

1½ cups all-purpose flour, plus more if needed
3 large eggs, beaten

Place the flour in a mound on a clean work surface and make a deep well in the center. Add the eggs to the well, being careful not to break the well. Gently stir the eggs with a fork, gradually mixing in the flour. When the eggs are completely incorporated into the flour, bring the dough together and begin to knead it; you may need to add a little more flour as you go along. Knead the dough until it becomes slightly elastic, about 10 minutes. The dough should spring back when you poke your finger into it. Wrap the dough in plastic wrap and let it rest for 30 minutes before rolling it out. (The dough can be refrigerated at this point for up to 2 weeks.)

Cut the dough into 4 equal pieces. If you have a pasta machine, roll out the dough into thin sheets. Then cut into noodles. Or, to make the noodles by hand, roll out each piece as thin as possible, adding a little flour to keep it from sticking. Be sure to keep the dough in a rectangular shape. Fold the top and bottom edges to the center and then fold this in half. Cut the dough into thin noodles with a sharp knife. Separate the noodles and dust with a little flour. Either cook the noodles immediately in salted boiling water or dry them on a clothes rack for later use. **SERVES 3 TO 4**

Beef or Veal Stock

Beef bones make a robust, deeply flavored stock that adds zest to soups and sauces. Veal bones make a more delicate stock that's useful for lighter preparations.

5 pounds beef or veal bones

2 cups diced celery (½-inch dice)

2 cups diced carrots (½-inch dice)

2 cups diced yellow onions (½-inch dice)

½ pound fresh mushrooms, sliced

1 medium leek, cut into ½-inch dice

4 garlic cloves, peeled

3 tablespoons tomato paste

1 gallon cold water

1 cup dry red wine

2 fresh bay leaves

12 black peppercorns

1 fresh thyme sprig

Preheat the oven to 400°F.

Roast the bones on a baking sheet for 30 to 45 minutes, occasionally removing the accumulated fat and turning the bones, being careful not to burn them.

Scatter the celery, carrots, onions, mushrooms, leeks, and garlic over the bones, then spread the tomato paste over them, and continue to roast until the vegetables are browned, about 20 minutes.

Transfer the bones and vegetables to a large heavy stockpot and add the water, wine, bay leaves, pepper-corns, and thyme. Bring the stock to a boil over medium heat. Skim off the impurities that float to the top, reduce the heat, and simmer uncovered for 4 to 5 hours.

Strain through a cheesecloth-lined or fine-mesh strainer and cool uncovered to room temperature; cover and refrigerate. The stock will keep up to 2 months in the freezer or up to 7 days in the refrigerator.

MAKES 3 QUARTS

tomato paste One of the great inventions of the twentieth century is tomato paste in tubes. Now you no longer have to throw out a can of tomato paste after you've used only a couple of tablespoonsful to coat bones or enrich a sauce.

Lamb Stock

We use this lamb stock as the braising liquid in wintry stews. And on a cold night, we'll just reheat the broth, correct the seasoning, and float in some barley, wild rice, and vegetables cut into very small dice. Or we'll use a cup of it to make a little sauce with a leg of lamb's drippings in the bottom of the roasting pan.

The next time you roast a leg of lamb, put the leftover big bone in the freezer. Then, when you have time, take it out and make stock. If you want a lighter taste for summer dishes, leave out the tomato paste.

continued

5 pounds lamb bones

1 small leek, cut into ½-inch dice

2 cups diced carrots (½-inch dice)

2 cups diced celery (½-inch dice)

2 cups diced yellow onions (½-inch dice)

6 garlic cloves, peeled

3 tablespoons tomato paste

1 gallon cold water

1 cup dry red wine

2 fresh bay leaves

10 black peppercorns

3 fresh thyme sprigs

Preheat the oven to 400°F.

Roast the bones on a baking sheet for 30 to 45 minutes, occasionally removing the accumulated fat and turning the bones, being careful not to burn them.

Scatter the leeks, carrots, celery, onions, and garlic over the bones, then spread the tomato paste over them and continue to roast until the vegetables are browned, about 20 minutes.

Transfer the bones and vegetables to a large heavy stockpot and add the water, wine, bay leaves, peppercorns, and thyme. Bring the stock to a boil over medium heat. Skim off the impurities that float to the top, reduce the heat, and simmer uncovered for 4 to 5 hours.

Strain through a cheesecloth-lined or fine-mesh strainer and cool uncovered to room temperature; cover and refrigerate. The stock will keep up to 2 months in the freezer or up to 7 days in the refrigerator. **MAKES 3 QUARTS**

Fish Stock

If you buy fish only in fillets, you'll never have bones for making stock, which is wonderful to use in sauces, soups, and dressings. For the clearest flavor, use white-fleshed fish such as cod, bass, halibut, or flounder, and make sure the bones are extremely fresh. Start with cold water for a crystal-clear stock. Let it come to a boil, skim off the foam that has come to the surface, and then immediately lower the heat to a bare simmer; don't let it continue to boil.

5 pounds white fish bones, such as flounder, bass,
  and/or cod
2 tablespoons unsalted butter
2 cups diced leeks (½-inch dice)
2 cups diced onions (½-inch dice)
2 cups diced celery (½-inch dice)
½ pound fresh mushrooms, sliced
1 shallot, sliced
1 cup dry white wine
1 gallon cold water
1 fresh bay leaf
1 fresh thyme sprig
12 black peppercorns

Remove any gills and entrails from the fish bones and thoroughly rinse the bones under cold water. Put the bones in a large pot, add cold water to cover, and let soak for 3 to 4 hours, changing the water several times. Drain well.

continued

Melt the butter in a large heavy stockpot over medium-low heat. Add the leeks, onions, celery, mushrooms, and shallots and gently cook until the vegetables are softened, about 5 minutes. Add the wine and cook until slightly reduced. Add the water, fish bones, bay leaf, thyme, and peppercorns. Bring to a boil. Skim off the impurities that float to the top, reduce the heat, and simmer uncovered for 25 minutes.

Strain the stock through a cheesecloth-lined or fine-mesh strainer and cool uncovered to room temperature; cover and refrigerate. The stock will keep for up to 2 months in the freezer or up to 3 days in the refrigerator.

MAKES 4 QUARTS

no fish stock? If you don't have fish stock on hand, substitute the little bottles of clam juice. They work fine, as long as you're careful about adding salt.

Vegetable-Corn Stock

We love the sweet rich flavor of this vegetable stock. Seasoned with salt and pepper, it can substitute for chicken stock when you're feeding vegetarians, or be used to lighten dressings for summer salads, like one we make with fresh tomatoes and a sprinkling of corn kernels.

3 ears sweet corn

6 cups cold water

1 cup dry white wine

1 cup diced celery (½-inch dice)

1 cup diced carrots (½-inch dice)

1 cup diced yellow onions (½-inch dice)

1 small leek, white and green parts cut into ½-inch dice

4 garlic cloves, peeled

½ small bunch fresh parsley

10 black peppercorns

4 fresh basil leaves

3 fresh thyme sprigs

1 fresh bay leaf

Cut the kernels from the corn and save them for another use. (They can be frozen for up to 3 months.) Cut the cobs into thirds.

Place all the ingredients in a large heavy stockpot over medium heat and bring to a boil. Skim off the impurities that float to the top, reduce the heat, and simmer uncovered for 1½ hours.

Strain through a cheesecloth-lined or fine-mesh strainer and cool uncovered to room temperature; cover and refrigerate. The stock will keep for 2 months in the freezer or 3 to 5 days in the refrigerator.   **MAKES 5 CUPS**

Mushroom Stock

Because of their earthy flavor, mushroom stocks are a fine substitute for meat stocks. They're also a thrifty way to use the mushroom stems that are usually discarded. Use whatever mushrooms are available. At the restaurant, we use an assortment of cremini, portobello, and shiitake mushrooms and stems.

½ cup dried porcini mushrooms

½ cup dry red wine

2½ quarts quartered fresh mushrooms and stems

1 cup diced celery (½-inch dice)

1 cup diced carrots (½-inch dice)

1 cup diced yellow onions (½-inch dice)

1 small leek, cut into ½-inch dice

4 garlic cloves, peeled

¼ cup olive oil

2½ quarts cold water

1 fresh bay leaf

8 black peppercorns

1 fresh thyme sprig

Preheat the oven to 400°F.

Soak the dried mushrooms in the red wine in a small bowl until softened (see Note).

Meanwhile, toss the fresh mushrooms, celery, carrots, onions, leeks, and garlic with the olive oil in a large bowl. Spread the vegetables out on a large baking sheet and roast until they begin to brown, about 30 minutes.

Pour the water into a large heavy stockpot and place the pot over medium heat. Add the wine and porcini mushrooms, the roasted mushrooms and vegetables, the bay leaf, peppercorns, and thyme. Bring to a boil. Skim off the impurities that float to the top, reduce the heat, and simmer uncovered 1½ hours.

Strain through a cheesecloth-lined or a fine-mesh strainer and cool uncovered to room temperature; cover and refrigerate. The stock will keep for up to 2 months in the freezer or up to 7 days in the refrigerator.

MAKES 2 QUARTS

NOTE: Dried mushrooms add deep tones of flavor to a broth. They're usually covered with boiling water to rehydrate them, and then the water is strained through cheesecloth or coffee filters and added to the pot. When we make mushroom stock, we use red wine for soaking instead and strain the entire pot.

Mushrooms Years ago, while living in California,

I learned that morel mushrooms grew in the Stanislaus

National Forest and that they grew particularly well in

pine forests in the spring that have been burned by forest

fires in the previous summer. With David Miles, a friend

visiting from Vermont, I set out for the Stanislaus

National Forest with modest expectations. I had never

foraged there, but I had a good understanding of what we

should be looking for. Within a few hours of arriving, we

had scouted a likely spot to hunt, and in what seemed like

an instant later we were gathering more morels than

we'd seen in our lifetimes.

After two days of foraging, we returned to Berkeley

and arrived at the kitchen door of the Chez Panisse

restaurant with well over one hundred pounds of morels.

Alice Waters, the chef and owner, was reputed to pay the

best price for quality morels. Twenty minutes later, after

having sold the mushrooms, we were escorted by Alice to

the dining room, where we sat down to an incredible

lunch highlighted by a lovely pasta dish studded with

morels and asparagus. —DAVID

SALADS,

FRESH RELISHES,

and SLAWS

SALADS AND FRESH RELISHES

Chopped Spring Vegetable Salad 72

Spring Sprout Salad 73

Simple Radish Salad 76

Summer Three-Bean and Radish Salad 76

The Simplest Tomato Salad 78

Tomato-Cucumber Salad 79

Sweet Corn, Red Onion, and Basil Relish 80

Pineapple Ambrosia Relish 81

Warm Frisée Salad with
Blue Cheese and Apples 82

Parsley Salad with Country Ham and
Overnight Tomatoes 84

Chicken Salad with Blue Cheese and Apple 85

SLAWS

Savoy Cabbage and Carrot Slaw 87

Classic Cabbage Slaw 88

Fennel and Apple Slaw 89

Fennel and Tangerine Slaw 90

Celery and Celery Root Slaw 91

Artichoke and Turnip Slaw 92

Smoked Trout and Jicama Slaw 93

Grandmother Shinn's Coleslaw Dressing 95

SALADS
AND FRESH RELISHES

It was when we were living in California in the eighties that our eyes were opened to how vast the salad choices were beyond that midwestern inquiry of "Russian, blue cheese, or oil and vinegar?" In part, it was the quality of the vegetables, fruits, and greens available all year round. It was also the freedom of experimentation that produced salads and fresh relishes that were dynamic in flavor and visually exciting.

Now that we live on the East Coast, where the seasons are more pronounced, we make salads of sprouts and radishes in the spring, relish our tomatoes in the summer, and love warm salads on a winter's night.

Chopped
Spring Vegetable Salad

Chopped salads are a splendid way to toss together all we've brought home from the farm stand.

2 teaspoons kosher salt

1 cup sliced asparagus (cut into ½-inch lengths)

1 cup sliced snap peas (cut into ½-inch lengths)

1 cup sliced green beans (cut into ½-inch lengths)

½ cup diced leeks (¼-inch dice)

½ cup peeled and diced young carrots (¼-inch dice)

1 cup peeled, seeded, and diced cucumber (½-inch dice)

½ cup thinly sliced radishes

½ cup radish sprouts

1 cup chopped sorrel leaves

2 teaspoons minced shallots

1 tablespoon Dijon mustard

1 teaspoon fresh lemon juice

1 cup extra virgin olive oil

Kosher salt and freshly ground black pepper to taste

Fill a large pot with water, add the kosher salt, and bring it to a boil. Fill a large bowl with ice water.

Blanch the asparagus and peas in the boiling water until tender, 1 to 2 minutes. Remove them from the boiling water and plunge them into the ice water; let cool in the ice water for about 2 minutes, then remove, drain well, and place them in a large bowl. Blanch the beans, leeks, and carrots until tender, 2 to 3 minutes. Remove them from the boiling water and plunge them into the ice water; let cool in the ice water for about 2 minutes, then remove and drain well. Add them to the bowl with the other vegetables. Add the cucumber, radishes, and sprouts to the bowl.

Purée the sorrel, shallots, mustard, and lemon juice in a food processor. With the machine running, slowly add the olive oil until it is incorporated. Season with salt and pepper. Add the dressing to the vegetables and toss together. Serve immediately.   SERVES 4

Spring Sprout Salad

The secret of this salad, beyond freshness, is having as many kinds of sprouts as you can. We buy them at the Union Square Greenmarket in Manhattan, where one of the farmers brings in bins of radish, sunflower, broccoli, alfalfa, and bean sprouts and gives out free tastes and cooking suggestions to the Saturday-morning shoppers. We like this as an appetizer for a fish dinner.

4 cups assorted sprouts, such as radish, sunflower,
  broccoli, and/or bean
1 head Belgian endive
3 tablespoons olive oil
1 teaspoon mustard oil (see Note)
¼ teaspoon minced garlic
8 (½-inch-thick) slices crusty bread
½ cup Grandmother McCall's Salad Dressing
  (recipe follows)
Kosher salt and freshly ground black pepper to taste

Preheat the oven to 350°F.

Place the sprouts in a large bowl, separating and fluffing the strands as you do so. Slice the endive leaves crosswise into 1-inch pieces and add them to the sprouts.

continued

Whisk together the olive oil, mustard oil, and garlic in a small bowl. Brush both sides of the bread with the oil mixture and place the slices on a baking sheet. Toast in the oven, turning once, until golden, about 10 minutes.

Add the salad dressing to the sprout mixture and toss. Season with salt and pepper and serve with the toasts.

SERVES 4

NOTE: Mustard oil can be readily found in Indian grocery stores. If you have trouble finding it, you can substitute ½ teaspoon dry mustard in the recipe.

sprouts These crunchy threads are the shoots growing from germinated seeds and beans. Choose bright, crisp-looking sprouts that have no brown edges, and keep them in the refrigerator for no more than a day or so.

GRANDMOTHER MCCALL, UNCLE BUD,
WILMA (BARBARA'S MOM), AND AUNT KAY,
IN MARGATE, NEW JERSEY, 1935

GRANDMOTHER McCALL'S
❖ SALAD DRESSING ❖

This is an old-fashioned sweetened tomato dressing that's been passed from mother to daughter in my family. A nice alternative to today's vinaigrettes, it has changed slightly from generation to generation as tastes changed or ingredients became outdated. Although this is the contemporary incarnation with modern ingredients, we still call it Grandma's dressing. —BARBARA

1 cup extra virgin olive oil

½ cup red wine vinegar

2 tablespoons balsamic vinegar

1 tablespoon Worcestershire sauce, preferably homemade
   (page 249)

1 tablespoon granulated sugar

1 teaspoon Dijon mustard

1 tablespoon minced onion

1 garlic clove, minced

½ teaspoon mild paprika

1 teaspoon kosher salt

½ teaspoon freshly ground black pepper

1 fresh bay leaf

1 cup diced fresh tomatoes (¼-inch dice)

Whisk together the olive oil, both vinegars, the Worcestershire, sugar, mustard, onion, garlic, paprika, salt, and pepper in a medium bowl. Add the bay leaf and tomatoes and stir until combined. The dressing can be stored for up to 1 month in the refrigerator; remove the bay leaf before using.   **MAKES 3 CUPS**

Simple Radish Salad

We both love the peppery taste of radishes. They come in many varieties, and in sizes from spring's cherry-sized bites to autumn's enormous daikons. All share a crispness and mustard flavor that wake up the appetite: good reason why restaurant relish trays used to include radishes along with their celery, olives, and pickled vegetables. Here's a recipe that doesn't push radishes off to the side of the plate, but keeps them front and center.

1 bunch radishes (about 8), thinly sliced

1 small red onion, thinly sliced

2 tablespoons minced fresh chives

1 tablespoon red wine vinegar

1 tablespoon fresh lemon juice

¼ cup extra virgin olive oil

Kosher salt and freshly ground black pepper to taste

Combine the radishes and red onions in a medium bowl.

Whisk the chives, vinegar, lemon juice, olive oil, and salt and pepper together in a small bowl. Pour the dressing over the radishes and onion and toss together. Let stand for 30 minutes before serving.　　　**SERVES 4**

Summer Three-Bean and Radish Salad

Although the traditional three-bean combination is green beans, wax beans, and kidney beans, this variation with fresh Romanos instead of kidney beans is very dear to us because we made it for our wedding barbecue.

½ teaspoon kosher salt

½ pound Romano beans, trimmed

½ pound yellow wax beans, trimmed

½ pound green beans, trimmed

¼ pound red radishes, thinly sliced

¾ cup olive oil

¼ cup red wine vinegar

2 tablespoons fresh thyme leaves

1 tablespoon Dijon mustard

1 tablespoon coarsely ground yellow mustard seeds

1 tablespoon minced shallot

Kosher salt and freshly ground black pepper to taste

Fill a large pot with water, add the ½ teaspoon kosher salt and bring it to a boil. Fill a large bowl with ice water.

Blanch the beans until they are tender, 3 to 5 minutes. Drain and plunge them into the ice water. Let them cool for about 2 minutes, then drain well. Combine the beans and radishes in a large bowl.

Whisk together the olive oil, vinegar, thyme, mustard, mustard seeds, and shallots in a small bowl. Add the dressing to the salad, toss together, and season with salt and pepper. Serve right away, or chill for 1 to 2 hours.

SERVES 6

green beans Beans come in many varieties, from slender French haricots verts to broad, flat Italian Romanos to narrow yard-long Asian beans. In spring and early summer, when they're young enough to bend and snap, they make wonderful eating with no cooking at all; later in the season, the pods toughen, and you'll have to blanch them to use them in a salad.

The Simplest Tomato Salad

To those of us who love tomatoes, summers are remembered as a good tomato year or a bad tomato year. In the beginning of July, just before it's time to begin tomato harvesting, we talk about past seasons when the tomato plants were so prolific that we wished we could ask them to slow down a bit. Then we shake our heads, remembering the years when the farm stands had only a sparse few.

The best way to enjoy a tomato is to eat it right off the vine on a hot summer afternoon. Failing that, ripe tomatoes are most delicious when tossed with vinegar, oil, and fresh herbs.

2 very ripe tomatoes, cut into wedges or slices
8 medium fresh basil leaves, torn in half
2 tablespoons balsamic vinegar
5 tablespoons olive oil
Kosher salt and freshly ground black pepper to taste

Toss all the ingredients together in a medium bowl. Let stand for 10 to 20 minutes before serving.   SERVES 2

balsamic vinegar True balsamic vinegar is made from boiled-down must, the nonfermented juice of freshly crushed grapes. It must be aged for at least 12 to 25 years and can cost as much as $250 for a small bottle. Ordinary balsamic, which this recipe calls for, is usually wine vinegar with some caramel added for sweetness. It varies in quality and price. If you like the sweetness of balsamic, you may also like sherry vinegar.

Tomato-Cucumber Salad

This salad relies on perfectly vine-ripened tomatoes, a warm summer evening, good friends, and conversation.

2 large English cucumbers (see Note)
2 teaspoons kosher salt
4 cups seeded and diced vine-ripened tomatoes
¼ cup thinly sliced red onion
¼ cup chopped fresh mint leaves
5 tablespoons extra virgin olive oil
3 tablespoons fresh lemon juice
Kosher salt and freshly ground black pepper to taste

Peel the cucumbers and cut them lengthwise in half. Scrape out the seeds with a teaspoon, then slice the cucumbers crosswise into ¼-inch-wide crescents. Toss the cucumbers with the 2 teaspoons kosher salt in a colander and let them drain for 30 minutes.

Combine the cucumbers, tomatoes, onion, and mint in a large bowl. Whisk together the olive oil and lemon juice in a small bowl, add the dressing to the tomato mixture, and toss together. Season with salt and pepper. Cover and refrigerate briefly; serve slightly chilled.   SERVES 6

NOTE: As most cucumbers grow, their seeds become bigger and more bitter and therefore should be scraped out and discarded. English cucumbers (sometimes called hothouse or gourmet cukes) are nearly seedless even when they grow to be over a foot long, but we still scrape out the seeds.

Sweet Corn, Red Onion, and Basil Relish

Although relishes are often made to be canned, we like fresh relishes and serve them cold to set off the main course of the meal. This one is wonderful with grilled fish, for example.

3 ears sweet corn

3 tablespoons red wine vinegar

1 medium red onion, minced

2 garlic cloves, minced

1 pound plum tomatoes, diced (½-inch dice)

½ tablespoon ground cumin, preferably freshly ground

½ tablespoon ground coriander, preferably freshly ground

½ tablespoon ground yellow mustard seeds

¼ cup chopped fresh basil

3 tablespoons olive oil

Kosher salt and freshly ground black pepper to taste

Cut the kernels from the cobs.

Bring the vinegar to a simmer in a small nonreactive saucepan over low heat. Add the red onions and garlic and simmer until they are softened, 3 to 5 minutes. Add the corn and cook 2 minutes more. Transfer the mixture to a large bowl and let cool completely.

Add the rest of the ingredients to the onions and toss together well. Let macerate for 15 minutes and serve.

SERVES 6

vinegar Vinegar is a potent refresher, restoring the vim we lose during prolonged bouts with heat. Home cures have included it for centuries. My grandmother used to drink a weak solution of cider vinegar and ice water on the hottest summer days, saying it was her only protection against dehydration. —BARBARA

Pineapple Ambrosia Relish

This is a variation on southern fruit ambrosia, which is always served as a dessert. We decided to create a savory version that's actually a relish, to serve with sausages, roasted meat, and fish. In winter, when fresh fruit is scarce, pineapple brings a bright tropical flavor to the table.

1 cup diced fresh pineapple (½-inch dice)

2 medium oranges, peeled, seeded, and cut into
  ½-inch dice

¼ cup diced red onion (¼-inch dice)

1 scallion, thinly sliced

2 fresh sage leaves, cut into thin ribbons

2 tablespoons fresh lemon juice

1 tablespoon light rum

Combine all the ingredients in a large bowl and toss them together. Cover and refrigerate for 30 minutes. Serve slightly chilled. SERVES 6 TO 8

Warm Frisée Salad with Blue Cheese and Apples

On fall evenings, we often make this warm salad, whose dressing takes on a wonderful aroma once it's heated. It is important to use greens that are firm in texture so that they retain their character when heated. Here we use frisée, which is a curly type of chicory, but other firm greens, such as spinach, mustard greens, and kale, will do as well. Spiced Pork Chops (page 255), Red Cabbage and Apples (page 105), and Baked Apples (page 405) for dessert complete a fall menu.

6 tablespoons Mustard-Thyme Dressing (recipe follows)
1 tart green apple, such as Granny Smith, cored and
  thinly sliced
½ pound frisée, torn into 3-inch lengths
¼ cup crumbled Maytag blue cheese or other rich,
  creamy blue cheese

Heat 3 tablespoons of the dressing in a 10-inch nonreactive skillet over low heat. Add the apple slices and warm through, about 1 minute. Add the frisée and the remaining 3 tablespoons dressing, toss, and continue heating and tossing for 1 minute. Add the blue cheese and combine. Serve immediately. **SERVES 4**

maytag blue Maytag cheese is made in Newton, Iowa, and yes, it's the same family that makes the washing machines. The son of that company's founder raised dairy cattle as a hobby, and when his sons inherited the herd, they decided to make them pay their way. With the cooperation of scientists at Iowa State University, they produced their first wheels of blue cheese in 1941.

❖ MUSTARD-THYME DRESSING ❖

2 tablespoons Dijon mustard

1 tablespoon minced shallots

1 teaspoon mustard powder

1 teaspoon ground yellow mustard seeds

¾ cup olive oil

¾ cup vegetable oil

1 tablespoon chopped fresh thyme

Kosher salt and freshly ground black pepper to taste

Place the mustard, shallots, mustard powder, and mustard seeds in a food processor and purée until smooth. With the machine running, drizzle in the olive oil and then the vegetable oil. If the mixture is too thick, thin it with a couple drops of water. Transfer the dressing to a bowl and fold in the thyme. Season with salt and pepper. This dressing can be stored covered in the refrigerator for up to 1 week.   **MAKES 2 CUPS**

Parsley Salad with Country Ham and Overnight Tomatoes

Until we encountered James Beard's parsley salad, we had always thought of parsley only as the curly greenery that was stuck into the nooks and crannies of a roast bird or paired with cherry tomatoes as a garnish. We serve this mix of greens and salty ham, deeply flavored tomatoes, and lemony dressing as a first course to a big meal.

¾ cup cubed bread (½-inch cubes)

8 cups loosely packed fresh flat-leaf parsley leaves

½ cup Overnight Tomatoes (page 19), thinly sliced

¼ cup grated Wisconsin Asiago or other hard cheese, such
*   as pecorino Romano or Parmesan (see Note)*

½ cup olive oil

2 tablespoons fresh lemon juice

2 garlic cloves, minced

Kosher salt and freshly ground black pepper to taste

4 paper-thin slices Smithfield country ham, prosciutto,
*   or other good-quality cured ham*

Preheat the oven to 350°F.

Place the bread on a baking sheet and toast it in the oven, shaking the pan occasionally, until golden, 10 to 12 minutes.

Combine the parsley, tomatoes, cheese, and croutons in a large bowl. Whisk together the olive oil, lemon juice, and garlic in a small bowl, pour the dressing over the parsley mixture, and toss together. Season with salt and pepper.

Place the ham on 4 salad plates and spoon a portion of the salad on top of each slice. Serve immediately.

SERVES 4

NOTE: You don't have to use Wisconsin Asiago—there's plenty of Asiago made in the Veneto and Friuli regions of Italy—but we prefer the native product. It's a little harder and sharper, it doesn't have the tiny holes of the imported brand, and, besides, it tastes like home.

Chicken Salad with Blue Cheese and Apple

This creamy, spicy salad can be served surrounded by dressed salad greens or used to fill a sandwich.

4 cups shredded cooked chicken (see Note)
½ cup diced celery (¼-inch dice)
½ cup diced green apple (½-inch dice)
1 tablespoon Home Spice Mix (page 26)
2 teaspoons minced fresh thyme
½ cup crumbled blue cheese, such as Maytag blue
  or Roquefort
2 tablespoons sour cream
1 tablespoon green Tabasco (jalapeño) sauce

Toss together the chicken, celery, apple, spice mix, and thyme in a large bowl.

Gently stir together the blue cheese, sour cream, and Tabasco sauce in a small bowl. Add the blue cheese dressing to the chicken mixture and gently toss them together. Serve immediately.   **SERVES 6**

NOTE: When we need cooked chicken for a recipe, we roast it. It's fine to boil or steam the chicken, but roasting is just as easy and adds flavor. Just season it with salt and pepper, stuff it with fresh herbs, and put it in a hot oven (see page 211).

salads, fresh relishes, and slaws

SLAWS

We use a lot of slaws in the restaurant; they're always crisp
and so lively with vinegar that they just naturally go with
rich foods like an oyster po'boy or a meaty pork chop.

Slaws are typically made with savoy cabbage, red cabbage, or common green cabbage, but the fact is that you
don't even need cabbage. You can use many other vegetables and even fruits, as long as they will hold up well in
the dressing. Whether this is a simple mix of oil and vinegar or made creamy with the addition of mayonnaise,
sour cream, buttermilk, or yogurt, the dressing is what
holds the slaw together, giving it flavor and character.
Vinegar, besides adding its own sharp flavor, softens the
vegetables and allows the other seasonings to permeate
them. If you're in a hurry, you can toss a slaw together
and serve it right away. But if you have time, let it marinate in the dressing for up to one hour so the vegetables
will become a little softer and the flavors a little deeper.

Savoy Cabbage
and Carrot Slaw

On fall mornings, when the cabbages are as big as bowling balls, the pale sun washes over the heads and the cabbage field becomes a bulbous landscape: You've never seen a prettier shade of green. Red cabbages are a whole other kind of artwork, their scarlet heads looking like meteors from outer space. The ruffly texture and sweet, delicate flavor of savoy cabbage makes a wonderful slaw, but other varieties work as well.

2 tart green apples, such as Granny Smith

2 tablespoons fresh lemon juice

4½ cups shredded savoy cabbage (about 1 small head)

1½ cups peeled and matchstick-size cut carrots

½ cup minced scallions

3 tablespoons apple cider vinegar

3 tablespoons apple cider

3 tablespoons olive oil

1½ tablespoons Home Spice Mix (page 26)

2 tablespoons chopped fresh parsley

Kosher salt and freshly ground black pepper to taste

Core the apples and cut into matchstick-size pieces. Place in a large bowl and immediately toss with the lemon juice. Add the cabbage, carrots, and scallions and combine.

Whisk together the vinegar, cider, olive oil, and spice mix in a small bowl. Add the dressing to the cabbage mixture and toss. Refrigerate for 1 to 2 hours.

Add the parsley to the slaw and toss once more. Season with salt and pepper and serve slightly chilled. **SERVES 6**

Classic Cabbage Slaw

This classic slaw is wonderful with fried fish, Mom Page's Skillet-Fried or Oven-Fried Chicken (page 213 or 215), or barbecued ribs. Of all the slaw recipes, this is our mainstay.

1 tablespoon kosher salt

4 cups shredded green cabbage

1 cup peeled and shredded carrots

¾ cup minced scallions

1½ tablespoons apple cider vinegar

1 tablespoon granulated sugar

1 tablespoon sour cream

½ teaspoon celery seeds

½ teaspoon caraway seeds

Kosher salt and freshly ground black pepper to taste

Dissolve the 1 tablespoon kosher salt in 2 cups water in a large bowl. Add the cabbage and soak for 30 minutes.

Rinse the cabbage and drain well. Return it to the bowl and combine with the carrots and scallions.

Whisk together the vinegar, sugar, sour cream, and celery and caraway seeds in a small bowl. Add the dressing to the cabbage and toss together. Season with salt and pepper. Refrigerate the slaw for 1 to 2 hours. Serve slightly chilled.   SERVES 6

shredding cabbage Two tools that make shredding an easy task are a Japanese mandoline and a Benriner cutter. Both are available in specialty houseware and cooking stores everywhere, allowing even the amateur slaw maker to shred vegetables quickly and perfectly. Of course, a sharp knife or the shredding side of a box grater work as well.

Fennel and Apple Slaw

Italians use shredded fennel in salads, sometimes with thin-sliced artichokes and Parmesan. We think that its delicate licorice flavor goes well with tart green apples.

3 tart green apples, such as Granny Smith, cored and cut
  into matchsticks
2 small fennel bulbs, cut into matchsticks
1 small red onion, thinly sliced
¼ cup extra virgin olive oil
2 tablespoons fresh lemon juice
Kosher salt and freshly ground black pepper to taste
2 tablespoons chopped fresh parsley

Toss together the apples, fennel, and red onions in a large bowl.

Whisk together the olive oil and lemon juice in a small bowl, add to the apple mixture, and toss together. Season with salt and pepper. Let stand at room temperature for 20 minutes.

Add the parsley to the slaw and toss once more. Serve immediately.   **SERVES 6**

fennel White with the faintest touch of green, fennel is a chubby bulb that has long stalks and graceful, feathery leaves. When it's served raw, it's crunchy and has a faintly licorice taste. When it's braised, it becomes tender, and the licorice all but disappears.

Fennel and Tangerine Slaw

We make this for those crisp early-winter months when we walk down Bleecker Street and notice the first tangerines in the markets and realize that Christmas is right around the corner.

1 medium fennel bulb, thinly sliced

1 medium red onion, thinly sliced

2 tangerines or 3 clementines

¼ cup olive oil

2 tablespoons fresh lemon juice

2 tablespoons minced fresh chives

Kosher salt and freshly ground black pepper to taste

Combine the fennel and red onions in a large bowl. Peel and segment the tangerines and add them to the fennel mixture.

Whisk together the olive oil, lemon juice, and chives, add to the fennel mixture, and toss together. Season with salt and pepper. Serve immediately or refrigerate for up to 1 hour.   SERVES 4

tangerines and clementines Tangerines are sweet, easily peeled, and full of seeds; clementines are smaller and often seedless. Ten years ago, we had never heard of clementines, but now they turn up in the market every November. Use either one in this midwinter slaw.

Celery and
Celery Root Slaw

One of the strangest looking vegetables in the market, knobby brown celery root (also called celeriac or celery knob) has the crisp texture of a turnip and tastes like a cross between potatoes and celery. Because it discolors when it's exposed to the air, drop the peeled or shredded pieces into acidulated water, what cooks call the lemony or vinegar-tart water that's used to keep some foods from turning brown when they're exposed to the air.

1 cup thinly sliced celery
1 cup peeled and thinly sliced celery root
   (cut into matchsticks)
1 cup thinly sliced red bell peppers
1 cup thinly sliced savoy cabbage

2 tablespoons olive oil
1 tablespoon apple cider vinegar
1 teaspoon Home Spice Mix (page 26)
Kosher salt and freshly ground black pepper to taste
2 tablespoons chopped fresh parsley

Combine the celery, celery root, red peppers, and cabbage in a large bowl.

Whisk together the olive oil, vinegar, and spice mix in a small bowl. Add the dressing to the cabbage mixture and toss together. Season with salt and pepper. Let stand at room temperature for 20 to 30 minutes.

Add the parsley to the slaw and toss once more. Serve immediately or refrigerate for up to 1 hour. **SERVES 6**

Artichoke and Turnip Slaw

This unusual combination of ingredients makes a terrific winter salad to serve with seafood. On occasion we've also added slices of our homemade salami (page 277) and turned it into a lunch main dish.

4 raw artichoke hearts, sliced paper-thin

4 small turnips, peeled and sliced paper-thin (see Note)

1 tart green apple, such as Granny Smith,
*   cored and cut into matchsticks*

6 tablespoons olive oil

3 tablespoons fresh lemon juice

Kosher salt and freshly ground black pepper to taste

1 tablespoon minced fresh chives

1 tablespoon minced fresh thyme

1 tablespoon minced fresh parsley

Combine the artichokes, turnips, and apples in a large bowl.

Whisk together the olive oil and lemon juice in a small bowl, add to the turnip mixture, and toss together. Season with salt and pepper. Let the slaw stand for 30 minutes at room temperature.

Add the chives, thyme, and parsley to the slaw and toss once more. Serve immediately or refrigerate for up to 1 hour.   SERVES 6

NOTE: You'll find two kinds of turnips in the market, small white ones tinged with purple and big yellow ones that are actually rutabagas. Use the small white turnips here. They're easy to peel and slice and add a good snap to the slaw.

Smoked Trout
and Jicama Slaw

You can't get much further from the cabbage slaw made with Miracle Whip that we grew on with than this elegant appetizer.

1 (14- to 16-ounce) whole smoked trout

1 tart green apple, such as Granny Smith, cored and
  thinly sliced

1 small jicama, peeled and thinly sliced

4 red radishes, thinly sliced

1 small red onion, thinly sliced

1 tablespoon fresh lemon juice

FOR THE DRESSING

¼ cup sour cream

2 tablespoons apple cider vinegar

¾ cup olive oil

2 teaspoons honey

3 green scallion tops, blanched and chopped

1 teaspoon minced fresh ginger

¼ cup buttermilk

Kosher salt and freshly ground black pepper to taste

Carefully remove the skin and bones from the trout and flake the flesh. Combine the apples, jicama, radishes, red onions, and fish in a bowl. Toss with lemon juice.

In a food processor or blender, mix the sour cream with the vinegar. With the machine running, add the olive oil in a thin stream until incorporated. Add the honey, scallions, ginger, and buttermilk and purée until smooth. Season with salt and pepper. If necessary, thin with a little warm water. Toss together the dressing and slaw, adjust seasonings, and serve at once.   SERVES 4

A FAMILY NIGHT, 1952: GRANDMOTHER McCALL IN
THE MIDDLE, AUNT KAY AND UNCLE BRUCE (LEFT),
AND MOM AND DAD (RIGHT)

As far as we can tell, this recipe has been in the

Shinn family for at least a hundred and twenty years. It

comes from Barbara's father's grandmother, and it's prob-

able that her mother taught it to her. The creaminess of

the dressing makes the slaw a rich treat, and it can also be

used as a dressing for potato salad.

Grandmother Shinn's Coleslaw Dressing

2 large eggs

½ cup apple cider vinegar

3 tablespoons granulated sugar

½ teaspoon dry mustard

½ teaspoon kosher salt

¼ teaspoon freshly ground black pepper

2 tablespoons sour cream

Whisk the eggs in a medium bowl until fluffy. Gradually whisk in the vinegar a little at a time. Add the sugar, mustard, salt, and pepper; whisk until uniformly combined.

Transfer the mixture to a 2-quart saucepan and place it over medium-low heat. Heat slowly, stirring constantly, until the mixture reaches a gentle boil. Continue cooking and stirring until the mixture thickens, about 1 minute. Cool, then stir in the sour cream. Store in the refrigerator for up to 2 days. **MAKES 2 CUPS; SERVES 4 TO 6**

VEGETABLES

VEGETABLES

There are few places in this country where freshly grown vegetables *cannot* be found, whether at sprawling farmers' markets, small ethnic inner-city produce stands, road-side farm stands, or friends' gardens.

Wherever we are, we especially love mornings at the local farmers' markets, seeking out what they have to offer. Many times the farmers lure us into conversations that turn to local politics and gossip, which gets us home with much more to chew on than a supply of fresh vegetables. On the North Fork of Long Island where we now live, we are lucky to have farmers that grow unusual vegetables along with the standards. We have a surprising diversity of shell beans, tomatoes, lettuces, and orchard fruits, all of which translate into delicious meals.

However, perhaps the simplest and most rewarding source of vegetables is our friends' backyard gardens. Nothing tastes as good as something grown by a friend.

Artichokes Steamed with Lemon and Thyme

We were driving along Highway 1 in California the first time we saw a field of artichokes growing like tall thistles, so beautiful it took our breath away. The first time you cook artichokes, you can't believe how small the proportion of food is to what you bought. We use the hearts puréed in mashed potatoes or in sauces for fish. We use them whole, steamed, chilled, and (with the center and choke dug out) filled with Artichoke and White Bean Dip (page 157). And we serve whole artichokes hot with Garlic Mayonnaise (page 9).

6 medium artichokes
½ lemon
2 fresh thyme sprigs
2 tablespoons fresh lemon juice
1 teaspoon kosher salt

Rinse the artichokes in cold water. If necessary, trim each stem to 1 inch. Cut off the top third of the leaves from each artichoke. Remove and discard the dark green outer leaves and trim the remaining prickly tips with scissors. Rub the cut surfaces with the lemon half as you work. Pare the remaining stems down to the tender flesh. In a nonreactive pan large enough to hold the artichokes in a single layer, bring 4 cups water to a gentle boil. Add the thyme sprigs, lemon juice, salt, and artichokes, with the stems pointing up. Reduce the heat to low, cover the pan, and gently simmer the artichokes until tender and an outer leaf is easily removed, about 20 minutes. Drain and serve immediately or plunge into ice water to use later.   SERVES 6

ARTICHOKE HEARTS Allow the artichokes to cool, then pull off the leaves, remove their bristly center chokes, and trim them down to their meaty hearts. If not using immediately, toss the hearts in 1 tablespoon fresh lemon juice and 2 tablespoons olive oil.

Artichoke Pancakes

Pancakes don't have to be sweet, and they don't have to be breakfast food. At the restaurant, we've served a stack of these with salad between the layers and some cumin cream or horseradish dressing drizzled over the top. They make a wonderful first course or brunch dish. We also like to serve them with Sautéed Autumn Vegetables (page 114).

6 cooked artichoke hearts (see above), diced

¼ cup minced scallions

½ cup all-purpose flour

½ cup fine yellow cornmeal

1 teaspoon baking powder

½ teaspoon baking soda

¼ teaspoon kosher salt

¼ teaspoon finely ground black pepper

1 large egg

1 cup buttermilk

3 tablespoons olive oil

Combine the artichokes and scallions in a large bowl.

Sift the flour, cornmeal, baking powder, baking soda, salt, and pepper together and stir into the artichokes.

continued

Whisk together the egg, buttermilk, and 1 tablespoon of the olive oil and fold into the artichoke mixture.

Heat the remaining 2 tablespoons oil in a 10-inch skillet over medium-high heat. Spoon the batter into the skillet, making 3-inch cakes, and cook until small bubbles appear at the edges. Turn and cook the second side until golden. Keep warm on a heated plate while you cook the rest of the pancakes.   MAKES 8 PANCAKES

Steamed Asparagus

A field of asparagus is one of spring's most unusual sights. All you see are the beautiful green spears popping through the bare soil in neat rows, looking as if someone had stuck them there as a joke. We like to serve them with a Simple Radish Salad (page 76).

1½ pounds medium asparagus
2 tablespoons fresh lemon juice
3 tablespoons extra virgin olive oil
Kosher salt and freshly ground black pepper to taste

Slice off the tough ends of the asparagus stalks and discard them. Fill a large nonreactive pot fitted with a steamer rack with ½ inch water, place the pot over medium heat, and bring the water to a simmer. Add the asparagus, cover, and cook until just tender, 4 to 5 minutes. Transfer the asparagus to a large bowl and toss with the lemon juice and olive oil. Season with salt and pepper. Serve hot.   SERVES 4

Roasted Beets

Roasted fresh beets (instead of canned) will convert even the most devoted beet hater. We like them with dandelion green salad topped with Maytag blue cheese and spiced pecans, or with a basic green salad tossed with olive oil and balsamic vinegar. Even simpler, perhaps, is serving them as we do here.

6 medium beets

6 garlic cloves, unpeeled

2 fresh thyme sprigs, plus 2 tablespoons
*   minced fresh thyme*

5 tablespoons olive oil

Kosher salt and freshly ground black pepper to taste

Juice of ½ lemon

Preheat the oven to 400°F.

Cut the tops off the beets and trim the root ends. Toss the beets with the garlic, thyme sprigs, 2 tablespoons of the oil, and salt and pepper in a large bowl. Transfer the beets to a baking dish that holds them in a single layer, and cover it with a tight-fitting lid or aluminum foil. Roast the beets until they are tender, about 45 minutes. A knife should easily slide into the beets when they are done. Let the beets cool slightly, then remove the skin by wrapping them one at a time in a paper towel and briskly rubbing them.

Quarter the beets and place them in a large bowl. Whisk together the remaining 3 tablespoons olive oil, the lemon juice, and the minced thyme. Season with salt and pepper. Drizzle over the beets, toss to coat, and serve.

SERVES 4

Braised Broccoli Rabe

Broccoli rabe's unique bitterness provides a delicious counterpoint to the richness of roasted meat.

3 tablespoons olive oil

2 tablespoons slivered garlic

2 bunches broccoli rabe, tough stems trimmed

¼ cup water

1 tablespoon red wine vinegar or fresh lemon juice

Kosher salt and freshly ground black pepper to taste

Heat the oil in a 10-inch nonreactive skillet over medium heat and stir in the garlic. Add the broccoli rabe and cook, tossing it occasionally so that it cooks evenly, until it begins to soften and wilt. Add the water and vinegar, cover, and continue to cook until the greens soften but keep their resilient texture. Season with salt and pepper and serve immediately. **SERVES 4**

broccoli rabe Also called rapine or rape, this deliciously bitter vegetable resembles the more common broccoli only in that it has small florets at its tips. We think of it as a braising green, meaning that its leaves have a sturdy, resilient texture that holds up well to high heat.

Red Cabbage and Apples

To retain the texture of cabbage, cook it for only a short time, a method that also helps keep the apples firm.

¼ cup bacon fat (see Note)

2 tablespoons granulated sugar

1 medium yellow onion, chopped

1 small head red cabbage, shredded

1 tart green apple, such as Granny Smith, cored, peeled, and thinly sliced

2 tablespoons apple cider vinegar

½ teaspoon caraway seeds

½ teaspoon yellow mustard seeds

Kosher salt and freshly ground black pepper to taste

Melt the bacon fat in a 10-inch skillet over medium heat and add the sugar. Slowly brown the sugar, 1 to 2 minutes. Add the onions and cook until softened, 3 to 4 minutes.

Add the cabbage, apple, vinegar, caraway, and mustard seeds; gently cook, stirring frequently, until the cabbage softens, 12 to 15 minutes. You may need to add a little water while cooking to keep the cabbage moist. Season with salt and pepper and serve hot.   SERVES 4

NOTE: No, you don't have to use it, but bacon fat adds a lot of taste. The next time you make bacon for breakfast, keep the fat. Store it in a covered jar in the refrigerator, and run to the market for a red cabbage.

Grilled Summer Corn

David grew up in a small town surrounded by farms that grew "corn and corn and corn." He has no question about the best way to eat corn: You have to stand in a cornfield, just pick an ear, don't cook it, and gnaw off the kernels. When we do cook corn, we leave the husks on, then peel them back and use them as a handle while we eat. However, if it's raining out or you don't have a grill, you can steam corn on a rack over a little water on the stove, for about 30 seconds.

6 freshly picked ears sweet corn
¼ cup Basil Butter (page 16), softened
Kosher salt and freshly ground black pepper to taste

Prepare a charcoal fire.

Peel the husks of the corn back, without removing them, and carefully remove the corn silk. Butter the ears liberally with the basil butter. Season with salt and pepper. Fold the more tender leaves back over the corn to cover and protect it; remove the outer leaves. Tie the tips of each ear together with a strip of one of the outer leaves that has been removed or a piece of string.

Grill the corn over a low fire for 4 to 6 minutes, turning the ears often and being careful not to burn the husks. Peel back the husks and enjoy.   SERVES 6

Garlic Greens

We call these "garlic greens" because of the liberal
amount of fresh garlic we add to the mixture. Quick
cooking in a hot skillet preserves the flavor and nutrients
of the greens. Try serving them with roast meat and fish.

1 pound mixed braising greens, such as mustard greens,
    spinach, beet and turnip greens, kale, and/or chard
2 tablespoons olive oil
1 tablespoon minced garlic
1 tablespoon fresh lemon juice
Kosher salt and freshly ground black pepper to taste

Remove and discard the thickest stems from the greens
and tear them into manageable pieces. Rinse the greens in
several changes of water to remove any grit. Dry them in
a salad spinner.

Heat the olive oil in a nonreactive 10-inch skillet over
medium-high heat and add the garlic. Add the greens and
cook, tossing them so that they cook evenly, just until
they wilt but keep their resilient texture. Add the lemon
juice, season with salt and pepper. Drain off any excess
liquid and serve.   **SERVES 6**

Spring Mushroom and Sweet Pea Hash

Serve this early-season hash with other spring fare: roast young chicken, Roast Leg of Lamb (page 264), shad roe, or Baked Spring Flounder (page 162). Use any spring mushrooms available.

¼ cup olive oil

2½ cups peeled and diced Yukon Gold potatoes
   (see Note) (¼-inch dice)

Kosher salt and freshly ground black pepper to taste

1 cup minced yellow onions

2 teaspoons minced garlic

1 cup shelled fresh peas

1 cup halved morels or other spring mushrooms

½ cup pitted and coarsely chopped Kalamata olives

2 tablespoons unsalted butter

1 tablespoon minced fresh herbs, such as thyme, oregano,
   and/or marjoram

Juice of ½ lemon

Heat the olive oil in a large nonreactive skillet over medium-high heat. Add the potatoes and salt and pepper. Brown the potatoes on all sides, tossing occasionally.

Add the onions and garlic. Reduce the heat and cook until the onion and garlic soften. Add the peas, mushrooms, and olives and cook until tender, 3 to 4 minutes longer. Add the butter, herbs, and lemon juice and stir and cook until the butter is melted, 1 to 2 minutes longer. Season with salt and pepper. Serve hot.   SERVES 4

NOTE: This is a variety of all-purpose potato with pale brown skin and golden flesh that makes it look (and, some say, taste) as though it's full of melted butter.

Minted Snap Peas
and Young Carrots

When the farm stands hang signs announcing the arrival
of spring peas, we buy them by the bagful and start snack-
ing as we drive away. Once we get home, we snap off the
leafy crowns and cook them gently to retain the crunch.

½ pound small carrots
½ pound sugar snap peas
1 teaspoon kosher salt
1 tablespoon unsalted butter
1 tablespoon olive oil
Kosher salt and freshly ground black pepper to taste
2 tablespoons finely slivered fresh mint

Scrape the tender skin from the carrots and cut them into
¼-inch-thick slices. Snap off the crowns and pull the
strings off the peas.

Fill a 4-quart saucepan with water, add the 1 teaspoon
kosher salt, and bring the water to a boil. Fill a large bowl
with ice water. Blanch the peas and carrots separately in
the boiling water for about 2 minutes. Remove them
from the water and plunge them into the ice water. Drain.

Just before serving, heat the butter and oil in an 8-inch
nonreactive skillet. Add the carrots and peas and toss to
warm them through. Season with salt and pepper. Toss
them with the fresh mint, and serve at once.   SERVES 4

snap peas   These aren't flat pea pods, the kind you
see in Chinese dishes, but fat pods with baby peas inside.
It's sometimes hard to get really fresh spring peas, but
these edible-podded ones are widely available and have
the same delicate flavor. Eat them raw or lightly cooked.

vegetables

Roasted Mushrooms

When you cook mushrooms, which have a very high water content, they tend to weep out much of the water and with it, the flavor. We find that roasting them in a hot oven helps avoid this and concentrates their goodness.

½ *pound assorted mushrooms, such as cremini, shiitake,*
  and/or portobello
3 *fresh thyme sprigs*
¼ *cup olive oil*
2 *garlic cloves, thinly sliced*
Kosher salt and freshly ground black pepper to taste

Preheat the oven to 450°F.

Halve or quarter the mushrooms (if using shiitakes, stem them first) so that they are all about the same size. Toss the mushrooms with the remaining ingredients and spread them in a single layer on a baking sheet. Roast until browned, 12 to 15 minutes. Transfer the mushrooms to a serving dish and serve hot, or spread them on a plate in a single layer to cool if they are to be marinated.

Once you have these simply roasted mushrooms, you can refrigerate them in an airtight container just the way they are for 3 to 5 days, or you can marinate them with a little vinegar and spice. Following are a couple of ways that we treat them.   **SERVES 4**

ROASTED MUSHROOMS WITH GINGER
AND MUSTARD SEEDS After you have cooled
the roasted mushrooms, toss them in a bowl with 2 tablespoons sherry wine vinegar, 2 teaspoons minced ginger,
and 1 teaspoon crushed yellow mustard seeds. We enjoy
these mushrooms scattered over a piece of grilled salmon.

ROASTED MUSHROOMS WITH ROSEMARY
AND BALSAMIC VINEGAR After you have cooled
the roasted mushrooms, toss them in a bowl with
2 tablespoons balsamic vinegar and 2 teaspoons chopped fresh
rosemary. These are especially wonderful with a charcoal-
grilled steak.

Red Pepper Sauce

This is a quick and simple sauce that can be served with a variety of foods. Good with any grilled fish, it also makes an excellent sandwich spread and looks beautiful drizzled on cold soup.

6 red bell peppers, roasted (see below) and cut into
* ½-inch dice*
1 cup olive oil
2 tablespoons red wine vinegar
¼ cup warm water or chicken stock, preferably
* homemade (page 54)*
1 teaspoon kosher salt
¼ teaspoon cayenne pepper

Place the diced peppers in a food processor or blender and purée until smooth. With the machine running, add the olive oil and vinegar in a slow, steady stream, then slowly add the water. Season with the salt and cayenne. Strain through a fine-mesh strainer. The sauce can be kept refrigerated for up to 3 days; reheat over low heat before serving. **MAKES 3 CUPS**

to roast peppers   If you have a gas stove, roast the peppers by placing them directly on a lighted burner on your stovetop. If you have an electric stove, place the peppers on a baking sheet and place them under the preheated broiler. Either way, allow the skins to blister and turn black all over, turning the peppers so that they roast evenly. Allow the peppers to cool, then rub off the skins with a damp cloth. Remove the stems and seeds.

Radish Sauce

Our friend Eva Lebowitz showed us how to make this elegant sauce. We serve it with grilled salmon, soft-shelled crabs, or with a plate of Steamed Asparagus (page 102).

2 cups thinly sliced radishes
½ cup thinly sliced red onion
1 tablespoon minced garlic
¼ cup dry white wine
2 cups water
Kosher salt and freshly ground black pepper to taste

Combine all of the ingredients except the salt and pepper in a 2-quart saucepan and bring to a simmer. Reduce the heat to low, cover, and simmer until the radishes and onions are very soft, 8 to 10 minutes.

Transfer to a food processor or blender and purée until completely smooth. Strain the sauce through a fine-mesh strainer and season with salt and pepper.   MAKES 3 CUPS

radishes Just-picked spring radishes were the season's first reward from the family garden. We still treat ourselves to the bright red, round, slightly hot radishes pulled from the ground as soon as the crown is visible through the soil. A slathering of sweet butter and a few sprinkles of salt complement the spice of just-picked spring radishes.

Sautéed Autumn Vegetables

This recipe has countless variations. Don't bother making a shopping list: We usually go to the market and come home with the vegetables we find there. Then cook them quickly: You can muddy the flavor of even the freshest vegetables with prolonged cooking and overzealous seasoning.

1 teaspoon kosher salt

1 small butternut squash, peeled, seeded, and cut into
  ½-inch dice

1 tablespoon olive oil

1 small red onion, cut into ¼-inch dice

1 tablespoon chopped garlic

1 red bell pepper, cut into ½-inch dice

1 small zucchini, cut into ½-inch dice

1 small yellow squash, cut into ½-inch dice

1 tablespoon chopped fresh herbs, such as thyme,
  sage, and/or rosemary

Kosher salt and freshly ground black pepper to taste

Fill a 4-quart saucepan with water, add the 1 teaspoon kosher salt, and bring it to a boil. Fill a large bowl with ice water.

Blanch the butternut squash in the boiling water until it is just tender, 1 to 2 minutes. Drain and immediately plunge the squash into the ice water to cool.

Heat the olive oil in a 10-inch skillet over medium-high heat. Add the red onions and garlic and cook until the onions soften, about 4 minutes. Drain the squash, pat dry, and add it to the skillet along with the remaining vegetables. Cook until softened, about 2 minutes. Add the herbs and season with salt and pepper. Serve hot.   SERVES 4

POTATOES

Our house is in the middle of Long Island's potato country. The field across from our house is planted in potatoes, and every year we watch the cycle of growth. When the plants flower, their blossoms look like white daffodils, so you can imagine the beauty of twenty-five acres of potato blossoms in full bloom. During the harvest, we listen for the early-morning clank of the potato harvester and drink our coffee out on the front porch, watching the lumbering truck fill with tons of potatoes when it slides up to the harvester. If we wave hello, the generous farmer will usually toss us a few.

We both love potatoes.

Yukon Gold
Mashed Potatoes

We like mashed potatoes to be a little chunky and with a moderate amount of butter, cream, and salt, somewhere between those that are puréed smooth and piped out of pastry bags and those that are left lumpy and chunky. Some cooks rice the potatoes; we mash them with a spoon or an old-fashioned hand-held masher to retain the coarse texture.

3 pounds Yukon Gold potatoes, peeled and sliced
1 teaspoon kosher salt
½ cup whole milk
2 tablespoons unsalted butter
¼ cup sour cream
Kosher salt and freshly ground black pepper to taste

Place the potatoes and the 1 teaspoon kosher salt in an 8-quart pot and fill it with enough water to cover the potatoes. Bring the water to a gentle boil and cook the potatoes until they are tender. Drain the potatoes, return them to the pot, and stir over medium heat for 1 minute to dry them. Meanwhile, heat the milk and butter together in a small saucepan until the butter melts. Add the hot milk mixture to the potatoes and mash the potatoes with a potato masher until the milk is incorporated once the potatoes are smooth. Fold in the sour cream and season with salt and pepper. Serve immediately.

SERVES 6

Potato and Celery Root Mash

The addition of celery root makes these mashed potatoes take on a delicate and aromatic flavor.

1¼ pounds russet potatoes, peeled and sliced
1¼ pounds celery root, peeled and sliced
4 garlic cloves, peeled
1 teaspoon kosher salt
½ cup whole milk
4 tablespoons (½ stick) unsalted butter, softened
Kosher salt and freshly ground black pepper to taste

Place the potatoes, celery root, garlic, and the 1 teaspoon kosher salt in an 8-quart pot. Fill the pot with enough water to cover the ingredients, bring it to a gentle boil, and cook until the potatoes and celery root are tender. Drain, return the mixture to the pot, and stir over medium heat for 1 minute to dry the potatoes and celery root. Meanwhile, heat the milk and butter in a small saucepan until the butter is melted.

Add the hot milk mixture to the potatoes and mash with a potato masher until the milk is incorporated and the potatoes are smooth. Season with salt and pepper and serve immediately. **SERVES 6**

Mashed Potatoes with
Roasted Mushrooms

These potatoes are superb served with a hefty piece of prime beef, such as our Standing Rib Roast (page 244).

1 pound assorted fresh mushrooms, such as portobello,
    shiitake, and/or cremini, trimmed
¼ cup olive oil
Kosher salt and freshly ground black pepper to taste
2½ pounds russet potatoes, peeled and sliced
6 garlic cloves, peeled
1 teaspoon kosher salt
1 cup whole milk
6 tablespoons (¾ stick) unsalted butter, softened
2 tablespoons chopped fresh parsley

Preheat the oven to 350°F.

Place the mushrooms in a large baking dish, coat them with the olive oil, and season with salt and pepper. Cover the dish with aluminum foil and roast until the mushrooms are tender, about 35 minutes. Let cool, then cut them into ½-inch dice.

Place the potatoes, garlic, and the 1 teaspoon kosher salt in an 8-quart pot. Fill the pot with enough water to cover the potatoes and bring the water to a gentle boil. Cook the potatoes until they are tender. Drain, return them to the pot, and stir over medium heat for 1 minute to dry the potatoes.

Meanwhile, heat the milk and butter in a small saucepan until the butter is melted. Add the hot milk mixture to the potatoes and mash with a potato masher until the milk is incorporated and the potatoes are smooth. Fold in the roasted mushrooms and chopped parsley and season with salt and pepper. Serve immediately.   SERVES 6

ARTICHOKE MASHED POTATOES

When we want mashed potatoes that are a little elegant, we substitute 3 large sliced artichoke hearts (pages 100–101) for the roasted mushrooms and use 8 tablespoons (1 stick) of butter instead of 6.

Mashed Potatoes with Apples and Fennel

The unusual addition of sage and ground coriander complements the balance of sweet and tart in the apples in this dish. We like to serve this with Smoked Duck Breasts (page 230) and sautéed Garlic Greens (page 107).

2 pounds Yukon Gold potatoes, peeled and cut into
½-inch dice

½ cup diced fennel (½-inch dice)

1 teaspoon kosher salt

2 large tart apples, such as Gravenstein or Pippin

1 tablespoon fresh lemon juice

4 tablespoons (½ stick) unsalted butter, softened

¼ cup diced yellow onion (¼-inch dice)

½ cup chicken stock, preferably homemade (page 54)

¼ cup whole milk or heavy cream

1 teaspoon minced fresh sage

1 teaspoon minced fresh parsley

½ teaspoon toasted and ground coriander seeds

Kosher salt and freshly ground black pepper to taste

continued

Place the potatoes, fennel, and the 1 teaspoon kosher salt in an 8-quart pot and fill the pot with enough water to cover the potatoes. Bring the water to a gentle boil and cook until the potatoes and fennel are tender. Drain the potatoes and fennel in a colander, return them to the pot, and stir over medium heat for 1 minute to dry them. Turn them back out into the colander.

Meanwhile, core and peel the apples and cut them into ½-inch dice. Toss them with the lemon juice.

Melt 2 tablespoons of the butter in the same pot over medium heat. Add the potatoes and fennel, apples, and onion and gently cook for 3 minutes. Meanwhile, heat the remaining 2 tablespoons butter, the stock, and milk in a small saucepan over low heat until the butter is melted.

Add the hot stock mixture to the potato mixture. Add the sage, parsley, and coriander, and mash with a potato masher, then stir until the stock mixture is incorporated and the potatoes are smooth. Season with salt and pepper and serve immediately.   SERVES 4 TO 6

Mashed Sweet Potatoes with Orange and Shallots

At Thanksgiving, we forgo the traditional yam-and-marshmallow casserole and make mashed sweet potatoes instead. Adding orange juice and shallots brings out the potatoes' bright sweetness.

2¼ pounds sweet potatoes, peeled and sliced

1 teaspoon kosher salt

1 tablespoon olive oil

2 shallots, diced

¾ cup orange juice

½ cup whole milk

2 tablespoons unsalted butter

Kosher salt and freshly ground black pepper to taste

Place the sweet potatoes and the 1 teaspoon kosher salt in an 8-quart pot and fill it with enough water to cover the potatoes. Bring the water to a gentle boil and cook the potatoes until they are tender. Drain the potatoes, return them to the pot, and stir over medium heat for 1 minute to dry the potatoes.

Meanwhile, heat the olive oil in a small saucepan over medium heat. Add the shallots and slowly cook until they are softened and translucent. Add the orange juice, increase the heat, and boil until the liquid is reduced by half. Add the milk and butter and heat until the butter is melted.

Add the hot milk mixture to the potatoes and mash with a potato masher until the milk is incorporated and the potatoes are smooth. Season with salt and pepper. Serve immediately.   SERVES 4

Garlic Potato Cakes

Tater Tots, that staple of childhood, were a manufactured food, with no real connection to the farm or field. But we grew up on them, and sometimes we miss them. These garlic potato cakes satisfy a yen for Tots. We serve them at breakfast topped with poached eggs, at lunch with garlicky sautéed greens, and at dinner alongside prime sirloin.

2½ pounds red potatoes, scrubbed and halved

12 garlic cloves, peeled

1 teaspoon kosher salt

½ cup fine yellow cornmeal

2 tablespoons chopped fresh parsley

1 large egg

1 large egg yolk

2 tablespoons whole milk

3 tablespoons olive oil

Kosher salt and freshly ground black pepper to taste

Place the potatoes, garlic, and the 1 teaspoon kosher salt in an 8-quart pan and fill with enough water to cover the potatoes. Bring the water to a gentle boil and cook until the potatoes are just tender. Drain the potatoes, return them to the pot, and stir over medium heat for 1 minute to dry the potatoes.

Add 3 tablespoons of the cornmeal and the parsley and mash everything together with a potato masher, leaving the mixture chunky.

Whisk together the egg, egg yolk, milk, and 1 table-spoon of the oil in a small bowl. Stir the mixture into the potatoes and season with salt and pepper. Spread the potatoes out on a large plate, cover with plastic wrap, and refrigerate for at least 1 hour or up to 4 hours.

Preheat the oven to 350°F.

Form the chilled potato mixture into 16 cakes about ¾ inch thick. Put the remaining 5 tablespoons cornmeal in a shallow dish and coat the potato cakes in the cornmeal.

Heat the remaining 2 tablespoons olive oil in a 10-inch skillet over medium heat. Add the potato cakes, in batches, and brown them on both sides.

Transfer the potato cakes to a baking sheet and bake until heated through, 10 to 15 minutes.   **SERVES 8**

POTATO AND SARDINE CAKES David invented this dish as a way to use up leftover mashed potatoes the first time we served brunch at Home Restaurant. He found some excellent sardines at the market, combined the two, and made patties. The crisp-fried cakes became a base for poached eggs and Red Pepper Sauce (page 112), and the dish hasn't come off the menu since. At the restaurant, we make larger cakes and serve one to a person.

Prepare the potato cakes as directed, folding 3 whole salt-cured sardines, rinsed and chopped, into the potato mixture just before seasoning it. Cook as directed above.

Potato Pancakes

A good helping of grated sharp Cheddar adds sparkle to this versatile dish. A little bit like the grated-potato latkes that are served at Hanukkah celebrations, these are rich and crunchy enough to eat all by themselves. Use all-purpose russet, or Idaho, potatoes when you make potato pancakes. The high starch content helps hold the potato shreds together.

4 cups peeled and grated russet potatoes

1 cup grated Cheddar cheese

1 large egg

2 tablespoons all-purpose flour

2 teaspoons kosher salt

½ teaspoon freshly ground black pepper

2 tablespoons olive oil

Squeeze the excess water from the grated potatoes and place them in a large bowl. Add the grated cheese and toss with the potatoes. Whisk the egg in a small bowl until frothy, then stir it into the potato mixture. Add the flour, salt, and pepper and lightly toss the mixture; it will be loose.

Heat the olive oil in a 10-inch nonstick skillet over medium heat. Drop 3 tablespoons of the mixture into the skillet and spread it out in the skillet to make a 4-inch pancake. Shape 2 more pancakes in the skillet and cook, turning once, until brown and crispy on both sides, 6 to 8 minutes. Transfer to a plate and cover loosely to keep warm. Repeat with the remaining potato mixture. Serve hot. **MAKES TWELVE 4-INCH PANCAKES**

Potatoes Roasted
in the Grill

When you cook in foil, be sure it's heavy-duty and that you have the shiny side facing in (to prevent the foil from deflecting the heat away from the food). Despite the high heat of the coals, foil cooking is actually steaming. The food doesn't ever brown, but the concentration of the juices makes it intensely delicious.

1½ pounds small red or white new potatoes, halved
¼ cup olive oil
8 garlic cloves, unpeeled
8 fresh herb sprigs, such as thyme, rosemary,
    and/or parsley
Kosher salt and freshly ground black pepper to taste

Prepare a charcoal grill.

Toss all the ingredients together in a large bowl, coating the potatoes well with the olive oil. Place the ingredients on a large sheet of heavy-duty aluminum foil and spread the potatoes in a single layer. Fold the foil over and crimp it tightly to seal it. Place the package at the edge of the hot coals in your grill. Let it cook for 20 minutes, turn it over, and cook for about 20 minutes longer. To see if the potatoes are done, take a fork and pierce a potato directly through the foil.   SERVES 4

MOM ROUGHING IT IN A TRAILER
WHILE DAD BUILT OUR FIRST HOME, 1955

When my mother, Felicia, felt particularly doting, she would surprise the family by making scalloped potatoes for dinner. Grabbing her thickest pot holders, she'd take the heavy dish from the oven and carry it to the table, where she'd set it on a metal trivet and warn everyone not to touch. As the bubbling subsided, she'd dig in, spooning heaps of gooey, creamy potatoes onto the family's plates. I remember going back for seconds and thirds and feeling like a king. —DAVID

Mom Page's
Scalloped Potatoes

5 tablespoons unsalted butter, softened

8 medium russet potatoes, peeled and sliced ⅛ inch thick

1 large yellow onion, thinly sliced

1 cup heavy cream

2 teaspoons kosher salt

1 teaspoon freshly ground black pepper

¼ teaspoon ground nutmeg

½ cup grated hard cheese, such as Parmesan, Dry Jack
  or pecorino Romano

2 tablespoons chopped fresh herbs, such as thyme, parsley,
  and/or chives

Preheat the oven to 350°F. Grease a 12 x 9-inch ceramic or glass baking dish with 1 tablespoon of the butter.

Toss together the potatoes, onions, cream, salt, pepper, and nutmeg in a large bowl. Line the bottom of the baking dish with an even layer of potatoes and onion. Dot the surface with 1 tablespoon of the remaining butter. Repeat layering until the dish is full and pour any remaining cream over the top. Press down on the potatoes so that they are an even thickness. Dot the surface with any remaining butter and sprinkle with the cheese.

Bake uncovered until the potatoes are tender, the cream is absorbed, and the cheese is golden and crisp, about 1 hour. Sprinkle the herbs on top of the dish just before serving.   SERVES 8

Easy Summer Potato Salad

Slicing the potatoes while they're still warm and immediately tossing them with the oil and vinegar allows them to absorb the flavors of the dressing. If you make it ahead of time and refrigerate it, let it come back to room temperature before you serve it.

3 pounds small Yukon Gold or white potatoes, scrubbed
1 teaspoon kosher salt
1½ cups minced scallions (excluding the dark green tops)
1½ cups olive oil
½ cup apple cider vinegar
Kosher salt and freshly ground black pepper to taste

Place the potatoes and the 1 teaspoon kosher salt in an 8-quart pot and fill it with enough water to cover the potatoes. Bring the water to a gentle boil and cook the potatoes until tender. Drain well. While the potatoes are still warm, slice them and place in a large bowl. Add the scallions.

Whisk together the olive oil and vinegar in a small bowl. Add the dressing to the potatoes and toss together. Season with salt and pepper. Serve at room temperature.

SERVES 6

Warm Potato Salad

Serve this light and tangy potato salad warm, with grilled meats and fish.

2 pounds small red potatoes, scrubbed

1 teaspoon kosher salt

6 tablespoons extra virgin olive oil

3 tablespoons white wine vinegar

2 tablespoons chopped fresh dill

1 tablespoon whole-grain mustard

Kosher salt and freshly ground black pepper to taste

Place the potatoes and the 1 teaspoon kosher salt in an 8-quart pot and fill it with enough water to cover the potatoes. Bring the water to a gentle boil and cook the potatoes until tender. Drain the potatoes and halve or quarter them while they are still warm. Transfer to a large bowl.

Whisk together the olive oil, vinegar, dill, and mustard in a small bowl. Add the dressing to the potatoes and toss together. Season with salt and pepper. Serve warm.

SERVES 4

This potato salad, from David's sister Elizabeth, has as many eggs as it has potatoes and two full cups of mayonnaise. It's like Elizabeth, a little bit playful.

AT THE DROVER FARM, EASTER 1965:
DAVID AND ELIZABETH (LEFT), JOANNE (TOP RIGHT),
PATRICK (CENTER), AND COUSINS

ELIZABETH WITH GRANDMOTHER PAGE,
CONFIRMATION DAY, 1968

Elizabeth's Potato Salad

12 russet potatoes, scrubbed

1 teaspoon kosher salt

2 cups Homemade Mayonnaise (page 9)

¼ cup evaporated milk

2 tablespoons apple cider vinegar

3 tablespoons Dijon mustard

2 tablespoons granulated sugar

12 large eggs, hard-cooked, peeled, and sliced
  ¼ inch thick

1 large yellow onion, cut into ⅛-inch dice

3 celery ribs, cut into ⅛-inch dice

Kosher salt and freshly ground black pepper to taste

½ teaspoon mild paprika

2 tablespoons chopped fresh chives

Place the potatoes and the 1 teaspoon kosher salt in an 8-quart pot and fill it with enough water to cover the potatoes. Bring the water to a gentle boil and cook the potatoes until tender. Drain. Peel the potatoes while they are still warm and slice them ½ inch thick.

Whisk together the mayonnaise, evaporated milk, vinegar, mustard, and sugar in a small bowl.

In a large bowl, combine one third of the potatoes, eggs, onion, and celery with about one third of the mayonnaise mixture. Repeat with the remaining ingredients, combining them one third at a time until they are well mixed. Season with salt and pepper. Refrigerate for 1 hour, then garnish with the paprika and chives.

SERVES 8 TO 10

GRAINS and BEANS

GRAINS AND BEANS

It's probably our midwestern roots that make us hungry for wild rice, wheat, and barley, all year round. In summer, we often combine grains in zesty salads and offer them as a first course with something grilled over them or alongside meat or fish. In winter, we usually serve them hot, enjoying their pleasing sturdiness and earthy flavors.

Beans range in flavor from a velvety creaminess to a spritely nuttiness. White beans and navy beans impart a rich creamy flavor to dishes, successfully mingling ingredients. Beans to be used in highly seasoned chilis and spicy stews should have flavors that will complement the heat of the dish; kidney, cranberry, or Christmas beans are perfect. Pay attention to cooking times and taste the beans while they simmer to assure the proper texture.

Wild Rice, Barley, and Blackberry Salad

Supersweet, juicy ripe blackberries are delicate; they should be gently added to the salad right before it's served to avoid discoloring the grains.

1 tablespoon unsalted butter

½ cup plus 1 tablespoon olive oil

¾ cup minced leeks

¾ cup minced onions

2 cups cooked wild rice, cooled

2 cups cooked barley, cooled (see Note)

¼ cup red wine vinegar

2 tablespoons minced fresh chives

2 tablespoons chopped fresh parsley

Kosher salt and freshly ground black pepper to taste

½ pint fresh blackberries, sliced in half

Heat the butter and 1 tablespoon of the olive oil in an 8-inch skillet over medium heat. Add the leeks and onions and cook until they are softened, about 4 minutes. Transfer to a large bowl and let cool.

Add the wild rice and barley to the leek mixture. Whisk together the remaining ½ cup olive oil, the vinegar, chives, and parsley in a small bowl. Add the dressing to the grains, toss, and season with salt and pepper. Gently fold in the blackberries and serve. **SERVES 4 TO 6**

NOTE: Like brown rice, barley takes a long time to cook. For 2 cups cooked, add ½ cup uncooked barley to 2 to 2½ cups of water, along with a little salt. Bring to a boil, reduce the heat, cover, and simmer for about 45 minutes. Take the pot off the heat and drain the barley.

Three-Grain Salad with Cucumber and Tomato

One of our favorite salads—in fact, one we served at our wedding feast—this refreshing dish was inspired by Raymond Sokolov's fascinating *With the Grain*, a book about the history of grains around the world.

1 cup cooked Wehani rice, cooled (see Note)

1 cup cooked barley, cooled

1 cup cooked bulgur wheat, cooled

1 medium English cucumber, peeled, halved lengthwise, seeded, and cut into ¼-inch dice

⅔ cup seeded and diced tomatoes (¼-inch dice)

½ cup olive oil

2 tablespoons fresh lemon juice

⅓ cup chopped fresh parsley

Kosher salt and freshly ground black pepper to taste

Combine the rice, barley, bulgur wheat, cucumber, and tomatoes in a large bowl.

Whisk together the olive oil, lemon juice, and parsley in a small bowl. Add the dressing to the grains, toss, and season with salt and pepper.   SERVES 6

NOTE: You can find Wehani rice at health food and gourmet stores. More clay-colored than red in color, with a fragrance a little like popcorn, Wehani was developed in California and is aromatic, like basmati.

Eggplant and
Bulgur Wheat Salad

Because they are a little more robust than all-vegetable mixtures, grain salads are a good way to show off the bounty of the harvest season. Mashed eggplant makes this a moist dish you can spoon on top of salad greens.

4 medium eggplants

2 cups cooked bulgur wheat, cooled (see Note)

4 tablespoons chopped fresh parsley

¼ cup olive oil

2 tablespoons fresh lemon juice

½ teaspoon minced garlic

Kosher salt and freshly ground black pepper to taste

Preheat the oven to 400°F.

Poke each eggplant a few times with a fork, place them on a baking sheet, and roast until they are completely soft, 30 to 40 minutes. Cool to room temperature.

Cut the eggplants in half, scrape out the insides and discard the skins; chop the pulp fine. Combine the eggplant, bulgur, and parsley in a large bowl.

Whisk together the olive oil, lemon juice, garlic, and salt and pepper in a small bowl, add the dressing to the eggplant mixture and toss together.

NOTE: You may know bulgur as the grain in tabbouleh. It's made of wheat kernels that have been steamed, dried, and then cracked into small nuggets. This makes preparation quick and easy. All that's needed is a quick soak in boiling water to make it fluff up into tender grains: Place it in a large bowl and pour boiling water over. Cover the bowl with plastic wrap and let stand for 20 minutes.

Hasty Pudding

Some sort of ground corn pudding is made wherever corn is eaten, whether it's called cornmeal mush, polenta, or hasty pudding. It is delicious cooked in milk and sweetened with maple syrup or molasses, but more often we make hasty pudding with a simple combination of water, milk, and butter.

4 cups water
1 tablespoon unsalted butter
1 cup fine yellow cornmeal
Kosher salt and freshly ground black pepper to taste

Bring the water to a boil in a 4-quart saucepan. Reduce the heat to medium and add the butter, then slowly add the cornmeal, whisking constantly. Reduce the heat to low and continue whisking for 3 minutes. Season with salt and pepper. Remove the pan from the heat, cover, and let stand for 5 minutes before serving.   SERVES 4

cornmeal   Cornmeal can be yellow, white, or blue, depending on the variety of corn. The tastes are quite different, and different parts of the country have their own favorites. Because this is a New England dish, it calls for yellow cornmeal.

Fresh stoneground cornmeal, as opposed to the containers bought at the grocery store, can be purchased from small mills throughout America. The freshest cornmeal we've ever had was made from corn grown on the back ten acres of our farm. Our friend Butch Rowehl grows it there, sends it to a mill, and gives us small packages of it. If you are lucky enough to find fresh cornmeal, refrigerate it to preserve it.

Tomato Couscous

We've come to love the adaptability of these tiny pasta nuggets that soak up the taste of whatever liquid you cook them in. Serve this alongside Simply Roasted Chicken (page 211) and the meaty juices will add another layer of flavor.

1 cup couscous

2 tablespoons olive oil

Kosher salt and freshly ground black pepper to taste

1¼ cups tomato juice

¼ cup water

½ cup seeded and chopped tomatoes

2 tablespoons chopped fresh parsley

1 tablespoon fresh lemon juice

In a large bowl, toss the couscous with the olive oil and salt and pepper and rub it between your fingers until it is completely coated with the oil.

In a small saucepan, bring the tomato juice and water to a boil. Pour this over the couscous, stir with a fork, and cover the bowl tightly with plastic wrap. Place the bowl in a warm area and let stand for 15 to 20 minutes.

Fluff the couscous with a fork. Fold in the chopped tomatoes, parsley, and lemon juice. Serve at once.

SERVES 4

Lemon-Asparagus Rice

We serve this dish as a meatless meal or alongside grilled salmon and Roasted Beets (page 103).

1 tablespoon olive oil

½ cup diced yellow onion (½-inch dice)

1½ cups long-grained white rice

3 cups water

2 tablespoons unsalted butter

1 lemon slice (1 inch thick)

1 teaspoon minced lemon zest

1 pound fresh asparagus

Kosher salt and freshly ground black pepper to taste

Heat the olive oil in a medium saucepan, add the onion, and cook until the onion softens, about 4 minutes. Add the rice and toast the grains, stirring occasionally, until the rice begins to look opaque (bright white), about 4 minutes. Add the water, butter, lemon slice, and lemon zest, reduce the heat to low, cover, and simmer for 25 minutes.

Meanwhile, slice off the tough ends of the asparagus stalks and discard them. Cut the spears on a diagonal into 1-inch lengths. Fill a large nonreactive pot filled with a steamer rack with ½ inch water, place the pot over medium heat, and bring the water to a simmer. Add the asparagus, cover, and cook until just tender, 4 to 5 minutes.

Transfer the cooked rice to a serving bowl and toss in the asparagus. Season with salt and pepper and serve.

SERVES 2 AS A MAIN DISH OR 4 AS A SIDE DISH

Cremini Mushroom Rice

You can use this recipe as a model for any flavored rice. Creminis are the teenage version of portobellos, dark brown, slightly firmer, and more flavorful than white mushrooms. If you can't find creminis, you can use shiitake or portobellos.

3 tablespoons olive oil

1 tablespoon unsalted butter

¼ cup chopped onion

1½ cups diced cremini mushrooms (½-inch dice)

1 teaspoon fresh thyme leaves

1 cup long-grain white rice

2 cups water or Mushroom Stock (page 64)

Kosher salt and freshly ground black pepper to taste

Heat the oil and butter in a 2-quart saucepan over medium heat. Add the onion and cook until it is softened. Add the mushrooms and thyme and cook until the mushrooms are softened, about 4 minutes. Add the rice and cook, stirring, until the rice begins to look opaque (bright white), about 4 minutes. Add the water, bring to a simmer, and cover the pan. Reduce the heat and simmer for 18 to 20 minutes.

Fluff the rice with a fork and season with salt and pepper. Serve, or cover on the back of the stove until ready to serve.   **SERVES 4**

Mushroom Rice Cakes

You can make these crisp rice cakes from scratch or double the recipe for Cremini Mushroom Rice (page 142) and save the leftovers to use as a base. (You'll need 3 to 4 cups cooked rice.)

For an exotic "small bite" at parties, make the cakes smaller—the size of half dollars—and top them with sour cream.

¼ ounce dried shiitake mushrooms

1½ cups water

1 tablespoon unsalted butter

½ cup minced yellow onion

1 teaspoon fresh thyme leaves

1 fresh bay leaf

¾ cup long-grain white rice

1 large egg yolk

5 tablespoons all-purpose flour, plus more for dusting

2 tablespoons minced scallions

2 teaspoons soy sauce

Kosher salt and freshly ground black pepper to taste

3 tablespoons olive oil

Bring the dried mushrooms and the water to a boil in a small saucepan, remove from the heat, and set aside.

Melt the butter in a 2-quart saucepan over medium-low heat. Add the onion, thyme, and bay leaf and gently cook for 2 to 3 minutes. Add the rice and cook, stirring, for 1 to 2 minutes. Remove the mushrooms from the soaking liquid and set aside. Strain the mushroom soaking liquid and add it to the rice. Cover the pan, reduce the heat to low, and cook the rice for 15 to 18 minutes. Remove the bay leaf. Transfer the rice to a bowl, cover it, and set it aside to cool.

continued

Chop the reconstituted mushrooms. When the rice has cooled, stir in the mushrooms, egg yolk, flour, scallions, and soy sauce. Season with salt and pepper. Cover and refrigerate for 1 hour.

Shape the rice mixture into 4 round cakes about ½ inch thick. Dust each cake with flour.

Heat the olive oil in a large, nonstick skillet over medium heat. Place the rice cakes in the skillet and brown them on each side for 3 to 5 minutes. Serve hot.

SERVES 4

leftovers We use all our leftovers, either as they are or redefined in a new dish. If you can use a leftover in a way nobody recognizes, like these rice cakes, that's really creative. Of course, there are some things that are even better the next day. Then we take them out for lunch and it's like being able to have a second helping when you're not full anymore. The memory of the first time is part of the enjoyment of the second.

Oatmeal

Since childhood, my favorite breakfast is a warm bowl of oatmeal with brown sugar, raisins, and butter melting on top. But now I vary it according to the seasons. In the spring and summer we like fresh fruit with our oatmeal. When raspberries come into season, we heat them with a little sugar and top our oatmeal with warm berries and slivered almonds. In the summer, we have our oatmeal with peaches and blueberries drizzled with honey. In the cooler months, we like to add maple syrup, cinnamon, and ginger to the milk mixture and top our oatmeal with pecans, raisins, apples, and assorted dried fruits.

—BARBARA

2 cups whole milk
2 tablespoons unsalted butter
½ teaspoon kosher salt
1 cup old-fashioned rolled oats

Heat the milk, butter, and salt in a 2-quart saucepan until the butter melts. Add the oats, bring to a boil, and boil uncovered for 2 minutes. Remove the pan from the heat, cover, and let stand for 5 minutes. Serve warm.

SERVES 2

BEANS AND RICE

Taken together, beans and rice make the perfect protein. Nutritious and filling, this combination sustains many cultures. We love the flavor and seek it out no matter where we are living or traveling. When we lived in the richly cultured Mexican and Central American Mission District in San Francisco, we ate rice and beans a few times a week in neighborhood *taquerías*. When we moved to New York, we found a Puerto Rican lunch counter downtown that dished up hundreds of bowls a day of yellow rice, black or pinto beans, and chicken, pork, or beef stew. Most recently, we found a small South American market in Riverhead, New York, that serves hot lunches of rice and beans accompanied by traditional meat stews.

Pork Stew with Pinto Beans and Achiote Rice

We love traditional South American pork stew so much that we cook it at home. Because of its long cooking time, we start the stew in the early afternoon, which fills the house with smells that make us homesick for the hustle and bustle and good food of our old neighborhood in San Francisco.

This dish is assembled by spooning the rice into a bowl, topping the rice with some beans in their broth, and topping that with the stew. You may substitute chicken or beef for the pork in the stew. Alongside, we always serve warm flour tortillas.

FOR THE STEW

2 tablespoons olive oil

1 large yellow onion, cut into ½-inch dice

1 tablespoon minced garlic

¾ cup diced celery (½-inch dice)

¾ cup peeled and diced carrots (½-inch dice)

1 tablespoon achiote (see page 149)

3 cups water

2 pounds boneless country-style pork ribs
    (or other pork stew meat), cut into 1-inch cubes

1 tablespoon cumin seeds

1 teaspoon cayenne pepper

1 teaspoon chopped fresh oregano

ACCOMPANIMENTS

Pinto Beans (recipe follows)

Achiote Rice (recipe follows)

continued

grains and beans

Heat the olive oil in a 4-quart saucepan over medium heat. Add the onions, garlic, celery, and carrots and cook until the vegetables soften, about 4 minutes. In a small bowl, dissolve the achiote in the water. Add the pork, achiote water, cumin seeds, cayenne, and oregano to the vegetables. Reduce the heat to low and simmer covered until the pork is tender, about 2 hours.

Meanwhile, prepare the soaked pinto beans and the achiote rice. To serve, spoon the rice into 4 bowls, topping each with beans and broth and then the stew.　　SERVES 4

❖ PINTO BEANS ❖

Pinto beans are a light red-and-white-speckled bean. They are mildly nutty and wonderfully creamy in texture. Remember, the beans need to soak at least two hours or the night before preparing for use in the stew.

1 cup dried pinto beans

1 tablespoon olive oil

1 medium yellow onion, cut into ½-inch dice

1 tablespoon minced garlic

2 cups chicken stock, preferably homemade (page 54),
　　or water

1 fresh bay leaf

1 fresh thyme sprig

Kosher salt and freshly ground black pepper to taste

Place the beans in a bowl and add enough water to cover them. Soak them for at least 2 hours or overnight. Drain and rinse the beans.

Heat the olive oil in a 2-quart saucepan over medium heat. Add the onions and garlic and cook until softened, about 4 minutes. Reduce the heat to low, add the chicken stock, bay leaf, and thyme, and season with salt and pepper. Simmer covered until the beans are tender, about 1¼ hours. The beans will be brothy.   **SERVES 4**

❖ ACHIOTE RICE ❖

Achiote is a paste made from annatto seeds, garlic, oregano, and cumin. You will find it in Latin American groceries and in the international sections of some supermarkets.

1 tablespoon olive oil
½ cup diced yellow onion (½-inch dice)
2 teaspoons achiote
2 tablespoons water
1½ cups uncooked long-grain white rice
1 fresh thyme sprig
1 fresh bay leaf
3 cups water

Heat the olive oil in a saucepan over medium heat. Add the onion and cook until softened, about 4 minutes. In a small bowl, dissolve the achiote in the 2 tablespoons of water. Add the rice, thyme sprig, bay leaf, and achiote water to the onion and toast the grains, stirring occasionally, until the rice begins to look opaque (bright white), about 4 minutes. Add the 3 cups of water, reduce the heat to low, cover, and simmer for 25 minutes.

Remove the thyme sprig and bay leaf and fluff the grains with a fork before serving.   **SERVES 4**

Shrimp with Black Beans
and Lemon-Orange Rice

Shrimp stews served with rice and beans are a mainstay in much of the country, especially in the South. In Louisiana the shrimp are big meaty Gulf shrimp, while in South Carolina the shrimp are bay shrimp with an earthy flavor all their own. We like to use medium-size shrimp for the balance of taste and texture they bring to the rice and beans. Here, the rice and beans are folded together, spooned into a bowl, and then topped with the stew. Buttered warm flour tortillas are a delicious accompaniment.

ACCOMPANIMENTS

Black Beans (recipe follows)

Lemon-Orange Rice (recipe follows)

FOR THE SHRIMP

2 tablespoons olive oil

1 medium yellow onion, diced (¼-inch dice)

2 tablespoons minced shallots

1 tablespoon minced garlic

1 tablespoon minced fresh ginger

2 fresh thyme sprigs

2 fresh bay leaves

2 medium leeks, white parts only, thinly sliced

2 large tomatoes, peeled, seeded, and diced (½-inch dice)

1 teaspoon ground coriander

¾ cup dry white wine

½ cup fresh orange juice

1½ cups fish stock, preferably homemade (page 61)

1 pound medium shrimp, peeled

2 teaspoons coarsely ground dried ancho chiles

Kosher salt and freshly ground black pepper to taste

1 tablespoon chopped fresh cilantro, for garnish

Prepare the soaked black beans according to the directions on page 152. Set the beans aside, keeping them warm.

While the beans are cooking, prepare the Lemon-Orange Rice according to the directions on page 152. Set the rice aside, keeping it warm.

Meanwhile, heat the olive oil in a large saucepan over medium-high heat. Add the onions, shallots, garlic, ginger, thyme, and bay leaves and cook until softened, about 4 minutes. Add the leeks and cook until softened, about 6 minutes longer. Add the tomatoes, coriander, white wine, and orange juice and simmer for 8 minutes. Add the fish stock and simmer 2 to 3 minutes longer. Add the shrimp and chiles and cook until the shrimp are just cooked through, 3 to 4 minutes. Remove the thyme sprigs and bay leaves. Season with salt and pepper.

Fold the cooked black beans into the cooked rice. Place a portion of the bean-and-rice mixture into each of 4 large bowls. Ladle the shrimp stew over the top and garnish with cilantro. Serve immediately.   SERVES 4

❖ BLACK BEANS ❖

½ cup dried black beans

1 tablespoon olive oil

1 garlic clove, minced

¼ cup minced yellow onion

1 fresh thyme sprig

1 fresh bay leaf

Kosher salt and freshly ground black pepper to taste

Place the beans in a bowl and fill with enough water to cover the beans. Soak the beans for at least 2 hours or overnight. Drain and rinse the beans.

continued

grains and beans

Heat the olive oil in a small saucepan over medium heat. Add the garlic and onion and cook until softened, about 3 minutes. Add the thyme, bay leaf, and beans. Add enough water to the pan to just cover the beans, reduce the heat to low and simmer until the beans are tender, 45 minutes to 1 hour. About two thirds of the way through cooking the beans, season with salt and pepper. When the beans are done, drain the remaining liquid from the pan.   SERVES 4

❖ LEMON-ORANGE RICE ❖

1 tablespoon olive oil

½ cup diced yellow onion (½-inch dice)

2 cups uncooked long-grain white rice

4 cups water

2 teaspoons fresh lemon juice

½ teaspoon minced lemon zest

½ teaspoon minced orange zest

1 fresh bay leaf

1 fresh thyme sprig

Heat the olive oil in a medium saucepan over medium heat. Add the onion and cook until softened, about 4 minutes. Add the rice, stirring occasionally, and toast the rice until it begins to look opaque (bright white), about 4 minutes. Add the water, lemon juice, lemon zest, orange zest, bay leaf, and thyme sprig and reduce the heat to low. Cover and let cook until done, about 25 minutes.

Remove the bay leaf and thyme sprig.   SERVES 4

Baked Cranberry Beans

Cranberry beans are also known as Christmas beans. They are big and flat and crimson in color. Their robust nutty flavor works well with baked bean dishes, especially this one packed with the flavors of bacon, green peppers, and rosemary.

½ pound dried cranberry beans

⅓ pound slab bacon, cut into ½-inch cubes

1 cup diced celery (½-inch dice)

1 cup diced yellow onions (½-inch dice)

1 medium green bell pepper, cut into ½-inch dice

1 tablespoon minced garlic

1 cup peeled and chopped tomatoes

1 tablespoon mustard powder

2 cups chicken stock, preferably homemade (page 54),
or water

2 tablespoons tomato paste

1 tablespoon chopped fresh rosemary

1 cup Seasoned Bread Crumbs (page 27)

Place the beans in a small saucepan with 2 cups water. Bring to a gentle boil. Remove from the heat, cover, and let stand for 1 hour. Drain and rinse the beans.

Preheat the oven to 350°F.

Place the bacon in a medium saucepan over medium-high heat and cook until the bacon begins to brown, about 3 minutes. Add the celery, onions, green peppers, and garlic and cook until the vegetables soften, about 5 minutes longer. Add the tomatoes and mustard powder, cook for 3 minutes, then add the chicken stock, tomato paste, and rosemary. Reduce the heat to medium and continue to cook until the mixture begins to thicken, about 20 minutes.

Transfer the mixture to a 3-quart casserole dish, sprinkle the top with the bread crumbs, and bake for about 2 hours, until the beans bubble and the top browns.

SERVES 4

Cider Baked Beans with Chicken and Sausage

Every fall, when the first apples begin to appear at Wickham's Farm Stand, we know that apple cider will soon follow. Pressed from fresh apples and to be consumed soon thereafter, cider in its unpasteurized form is a special treat available only in the autumn months. We make this baked bean dish then, when our appetites yearn for something warm and filling. It is one of our favorite one-pot meals, accompanied by Garlic Greens (page 107).

½ pound dried white beans, such as navy beans

⅓ pound slab bacon, cut into ½-inch cubes

¾ cup chopped leeks

1 cup diced yellow onions (½-inch dice)

1 cup diced celery (½-inch dice)

1 tablespoon minced garlic

2½ cups fresh apple cider

2 tablespoons apple cider vinegar

6 cooked skinless boneless chicken thighs

2 tablespoons olive oil

4 bratwurst

Place the beans in a small saucepan with 2 cups water. Bring to a gentle boil. Remove from the heat, cover, and let stand for 1 hour. Drain and rinse the beans.

Preheat the oven to 350°F.

Place the bacon in a medium saucepan over medium-high heat and cook until the bacon begins to brown, about 3 minutes. Add the leeks and continue to cook until softened, about 4 minutes. Add the onions, celery, and garlic and cook until they soften, about 5 minutes longer. Reduce the heat to medium, add the apple cider, apple cider vinegar, and the beans and continue to cook until the mixture begins to thicken, about 20 minutes.

Meanwhile, quarter the chicken thighs. Heat the olive oil in a medium skillet and brown the chicken on all sides, about 5 minutes.

Add the chicken and sausages to the beans and transfer the mixture to a 3-quart casserole dish. Bake for about 2 hours, until the beans bubble and the top browns.

SERVES 4

Quick White Beans

After the two-hour drive from New York City to our home on Long Island, we don't have much time to prepare a meal. This is one we can put together using canned beans from the pantry. Almost anything can be added to it. Toss in cooked chicken meat, shellfish, or diced ham for the last five minutes of cooking.

1 tablespoon olive oil

1 tablespoon unsalted butter

1 cup peeled and diced carrots (¼-inch dice)

½ cup diced yellow onion (¼-inch dice)

½ cup diced celery (¼-inch dice)

2 garlic cloves, minced

1 (18-ounce) can white or cannellini beans,
   rinsed and drained (see Note)

½ cup chicken stock, preferably homemade (page 54),
   or water

1 teaspoon chopped fresh thyme leaves

Kosher salt and freshly ground black pepper to taste

Heat the olive oil and butter in a 2-quart saucepan over medium heat. Add the carrots, onion, celery, and garlic and cook until they are softened, 4 to 5 minutes. Add the beans, stock, and thyme. Season with salt and pepper. Simmer until the beans are heated through and the stock is reduced, about 15 minutes. Serve hot.   SERVES 2

NOTE: Canned white beans may not be quite as good as the ones we soak and cook ourselves, but they're a reasonable substitute and save us a great deal of time. Remember to drain and rinse them with water to remove some of the salt.

Artichoke and
White Bean Dip

This white bean dip is a little more contemporary than the kind our parents served at cocktail parties in the 1960's. But it still brings back floods of memories.

3 cups cooked white beans, such as navy beans

6 cooked artichoke hearts (see pages 100–101; see Note)

2 teaspoons minced garlic

3 tablespoons fresh lemon juice

5 tablespoons extra virgin olive oil

Kosher salt and freshly ground black pepper to taste

½ cup seeded and chopped tomatoes

2 tablespoons chopped fresh parsley

Purée the beans, artichoke hearts, garlic, and lemon juice in a food processor or blender until smooth. With the machine running, slowly add the olive oil until it is completely incorporated. Season with salt and pepper.

Transfer to a serving bowl, garnish with the chopped tomatoes and parsley, and serve.   **MAKES 6 CUPS**

N O T E : If you don't have home-cooked artichoke hearts, go ahead and use the ones in jars or cans. Drain and rinse them to get rid of the brine or salt.

SPICY PITA CHIPS The dip is delicious scooped up in these spicy chips. Cut 8 pita breads into 8 wedges each and toss the wedges with 3 tablespoons olive oil, 1 tablespoon toasted and ground cumin seeds, 1 tablespoon paprika, 1 teaspoon cayenne pepper, salt, and black pepper. Bake them on an ungreased baking sheet in a 325°F oven until crisp, 10 to 12 minutes. When cool, they can be eaten or stored airtight for up to 1 week.

FISH and SHELLFISH

FISH

Baked Spring Flounder   162

Roasted Whole Wild Black Sea Bass   163

Skillet Blackfish and Littleneck Clams   166

Fish Fry   167

Salmon Cakes   168

Baked Salt Cod Casserole with Cream and Potatoes   170

Grilled Striped Bass with Fresh Mint   172

Grilled Trout with Lemon Dressing and Griddle Cakes   173

Porgies Wrapped in Grape Leaves   175

SMOKED FISH

Hot-Smoked Trout   180

Smoked Fish Salad with Fresh Horseradish Dressing   181

Smoked Eel Salad with Fennel and Dill   182

SHELLFISH

Oysters on the Half Shell with Ice Wine Dressing   184

Oyster Stew with White Wine and Orange   185

Oyster Stew with Saffron, Leeks, and Bacon   186

Steamer Clams with Local Ale   187

Shinn Family Clams Casino   189

Clam Pie   190

Bay Scallops with Delicata Squash, Cauliflower,
and Brussels Sprouts   191

Pan-Smoked Shrimp with
Warm Horseradish Cocktail Sauce   193

Shrimp and Hominy Stew   195

Shrimp and Andouille Sausage Gumbo   196

Summer Lobster and Vegetable Salad   198

Lobster Rolls   199

Lobster Kebabs   200

Slow-Cooked Squid Stew   202

Octopus Stew with Red Wine and Rosemary   204

FISH

We both grew up on midwestern lakes and river fish like perch and catfish and pike. When we got to California, we discovered wild Pacific salmon and Dungeness crab and abalone, that whole West Coast bounty that is just as astounding in the variety of seafood as it is in fruits and vegetables. When I got my first cooking job, the chef used to cook sand dabs for lunch for us. I would sit there in the dining room, eating the tiny fish cooked with lemon butter and parsley, and think I had never tasted anything as good in my life. When we got to the East Coast, and particularly to Long Island, there was the whole Atlantic family to get to know, bluefish and porgies and the newly abundant wild striped bass. Fish is a still-wild food, more local in its way than any other food that we eat.   —DAVID

Baked Spring Flounder

When spring warms the bay near our house, the flounder that have been in semihibernation through the winter swim into shallower waters, becoming an easy catch for bay fishermen. We know the season has started when we see ospreys, or fish hawks, performing daredevil dives as they hunt for the newly awakened fish.

Handling a whole fish can be unwieldy, but it's worth it for the rich flavor of fish cooked on the bone—and for the dramatic moment when you serve it. If you can't get flounder, use fluke instead.

We serve this with Simple Radish Salad (page 76) and Steamed Asparagus (page 102).

1 flounder, about 1½ pounds, cleaned and head
*   and fins removed*
¼ cup extra virgin olive oil
2 tablespoons chopped fresh dill
Kosher salt and freshly ground black pepper to taste
½ cup dry white wine
1 lemon, cut into ⅛-inch-thick slices
Fresh dill sprigs and lemon slices for garnish

Preheat the oven to 375°F.

Dry the fish and place it on a large platter. Coat the flounder with the olive oil and chopped dill and season it with salt and pepper.

Place the white wine and lemon slices in the bottom of a baking dish large enough to hold the fish. Carefully place the fish in the baking dish. Bake until it just begins to flake when tested with a fork about 20 minutes. With a large metal spatula, remove the fish to a serving platter. Garnish the fish with the dill sprigs and lemon. Serve hot.

SERVES 2

Roasted Whole
Wild Black Sea Bass

This is a very simple, homey presentation with nothing extraordinary about it except the freshness of the fish. We often serve whole fish at Home, where our customers are divided into two camps: those who love it and those who are squeamish about the head and worried about the bones, and who, therefore, don't order it.

A 1¼-pound bass makes a great single serving. If you can't get wild black sea bass, you can use any kind of bass or snapper.

4 black sea bass, about 1¼ pounds each, cleaned
*   and fins removed*
¼ cup plus 3 tablespoons olive oil
Kosher salt and freshly ground black pepper to taste
16 small fresh herb sprigs, such as thyme, marjoram,
*   and/or tarragon*
8 lime slices

Preheat the oven to 450°F. Place a large roasting pan in the oven to preheat.

Place the fish on a work surface. Using a sharp chef's knife, score each side of each fish with two 3-inch-long Xs. Coat the fish with the ¼ cup olive oil and season them inside and out with salt and pepper. Insert the sprigs of fresh herbs and lime slices into the fish.

Coat the bottom of the hot roasting pan with the remaining 3 tablespoons olive oil. Carefully place the fish in the pan, return the pan to the oven, and roast until just cooked through, 15 to 18 minutes. Carefully remove the fish to a serving platter or individual plates and serve hot. SERVES 4

fish and shellfish

GRANDPA SHINN WITH A MARLIN, ATLANTIC CITY, 1930

Uncle Gene may have been the saltiest dog of the

sea. He took no sissy attitude from any man, woman,

child, or animal. His family, therefore, is as strong-willed

as he was, which is why Aunt Barb is called the Sergeant

and her children are as thick-skinned as a tuna. Uncle

Gene spent as much time on the rough Atlantic as on

land and had a lot of stories to tell over a triple shot of

scotch. Uncle Gene walked with his head thrust forward

as if with every step he was looking through a doorway

into a new world. He was the first to pass judgment on any subject and easily dismissed entire topics as a "bunch of malarkey." He even brushed off his aging as if it were simply a bothersome bee hovering around him. It came as no surprise when we were talking about different fish and extolling the virtues of striped bass that Uncle Gene harumphed and proclaimed striped bass to be bland and flavorless. He liked fish that actually tasted like something, like mackerel or bluefish. It was then that I realized that the American palate may be becoming spoiled by the abundance of "finer"-quality fish and as a result is no longer accustomed to the fishy taste of "inferior" fish. Personally, when we see gleaming, firm, whole mackerel in the fish store or see a fish tub overloaded with a run of blues, we look forward to the moment when we will sit down that night for a flavor-packed dinner. To us, all fish are equal, fishy or not; some of them just speak a little louder than others. —BARBARA

Skillet Blackfish and Littleneck Clams

So many blackfish live in the Long Island Sound and Peconic Bay that we can catch them with rod and reel off the beach behind our home. Blackfish feed on shellfish, particularly clams, which accounts for their buttery sweet richness. However, they can be troublesome to cook because they have tiny bones that are difficult to remove, making them one of those fish that are worth buying already filleted. If your market doesn't have blackfish, you can substitute bass, cod, or perch.

24 littleneck clams, scrubbed

1 tablespoon unsalted butter

1 tablespoon minced shallots

2 teaspoons minced garlic

4 skinless blackfish fillets, about 8 ounces each and
  1 inch thick

1½ cups dry white wine

2 tablespoons fresh lemon juice

1 tablespoon minced fresh herbs, such as parsley, chives,
  and/or lemon thyme

Kosher salt and freshly ground black pepper to taste

Rinse the clams in several changes of cold water; set aside.

Melt the butter in a 12-inch skillet over medium-low heat. Add the shallots and garlic and cook gently until they are softened, about 2 minutes. Add the blackfish fillets, clams, and white wine. Cover and simmer just until the clams open, 6 to 8 minutes. Add the lemon juice and herbs and season with the salt and pepper. Serve hot in shallow bowls.   SERVES 4

Fish Fry

In Wisconsin, where I grew up, most restaurants and bars serve fried fish, potato salad, and coleslaw on Friday nights. When I go back to see my family, we always make a point of having Friday-night fish fry together.

This recipe replicates the wonders of a Wisconsin Friday-night fish fry, especially if you serve it with Elizabeth's Potato Salad (page 131), Classic Cabbage Slaw (page 88), and tartar sauce. In Wisconsin, we used lake perch, but here on the East Coast, we use our local salt-water fish. —DAVID

1½ cups whole milk

4 firm skinless white-fleshed fish fillets, such as perch,
*   pike, bass, or cod, 6 to 8 ounces each*

1 cup all-purpose flour

⅓ cup fine yellow cornmeal

1 teaspoon paprika

1 tablespoon kosher salt

1 teaspoon freshly ground black pepper

½ cup peanut oil

Pour the milk into a large shallow bowl, lay the fish in it, and soak in the refrigerator for at least 1 hour, or overnight.

Whisk together the flour, cornmeal, paprika, salt, and pepper in a large shallow bowl. Heat the oil to smoking in a 12-inch cast-iron skillet over medium heat.

Lightly coat the fish with the seasoned flour; do not pat on extra coating. Transfer the fish to the hot oil and fry until golden, 2 to 3 minutes on each side. Serve hot.

SERVES 4

fish and shellfish

Salmon Cakes

Fish cakes, once a beloved American supper dish, have given way to the ubiquitous crab cake. That's a shame, because richly flavored salmon is great in cakes. We add only a minimal amount of bread crumbs, allowing the flavor of the fresh fish, and the vegetables, to dominate.

While we think its flavor can't match that of wild salmon, the reasonably priced, farm-raised salmon from Maine or Canada, Norway or South America, is just fine.

FOR THE SALMON

2 cups dry white wine

2 cups water

½ cup diced onion (½-inch dice)

½ cup diced celery (½-inch dice)

½ cup peeled and diced carrots (½-inch dice)

1 fresh bay leaf

1 fresh thyme sprig

8 black peppercorns

4 salmon fillets, about 8 ounces each and 1 inch thick

FOR THE CAKES

2 tablespoons unsalted butter

½ cup minced yellow onion

½ cup minced celery

¼ cup minced red bell peppers

2 large egg yolks

2 tablespoons Dijon mustard

2 tablespoons fresh lemon juice

2 tablespoons minced fresh chives

1 tablespoon Worcestershire sauce, preferably homemade (page 249)

2 teaspoons Tabasco or other hot sauce

1 teaspoon cayenne pepper

1 teaspoon kosher salt

½ cup Seasoned Bread Crumbs (page 27)

FOR THE COATING

½ cup all-purpose flour

2 large eggs, beaten

1 cup Seasoned Bread Crumbs (page 27)

3 tablespoons olive oil

Place the white wine, water, onion, celery, carrots, bay leaf, thyme, and peppercorns in a large pot over medium heat. Bring to a simmer, cover, and cook for 25 minutes.

Add the salmon, cover, and gently simmer, being careful not to let the liquid boil, until the salmon is cooked through, 6 to 8 minutes. Remove the salmon from the poaching liquid, cover, and refrigerate for about 20 minutes, until cool. Flake the fish into a bowl.

For the cakes, melt the butter in an 8-inch skillet over medium heat. Add the onion, celery, and red peppers and cook until softened, about 5 minutes. Transfer to a shallow bowl and refrigerate for about 10 minutes.

Whisk together the egg yolks, mustard, lemon juice, chives, Worcestershire, Tabasco, cayenne, and salt in a large bowl. Add the flaked salmon, the cooked vegetables, and the bread crumbs and gently stir the mixture together.

Shape the mixture into 14 cakes about 3 inches across and 1 inch thick. Place the cakes on parchment paper on a baking sheet and refrigerate for at least 30 minutes.

For the coating, dust the cakes with flour, dip them in the eggs, and then in the bread crumbs to cover.

Heat the olive oil in a 10-inch skillet over medium heat. Fry the salmon cakes in batches until golden, about 3 minutes on each side. Serve hot.

MAKES 14 SALMON CAKES; SERVES 4 TO 6

fish and shellfish

Baked Salt Cod Casserole with Cream and Potatoes

The inspiration for this was undeniably brandade, the dish of rehydrated salt cod pounded with garlic, cream, and, sometimes, potatoes. Instead of puréeing the cod, however, we make it into a creamy casserole, a bit like scalloped potatoes with cod layered into them. Allow enough time to rehydrate the salt cod in several changes of water for twenty-four hours, and you'll have fish that's firm, silken, and moist from the soaking and the cream.

We like to serve Sage Corn Bread (page 304) with this.

½ pound salt cod

FOR THE CREAM SAUCE

2 tablespoons unsalted butter

2 teaspoons minced garlic

2 tablespoons all-purpose flour

1 cup chicken stock, preferably homemade (page 54)

¾ cup heavy cream

¼ teaspoon freshly ground black pepper

½ cup all-purpose flour

1 tablespoon olive oil

2 large russet potatoes

½ cup grated hard cheese, such as Dry Jack or Parmesan

Place the salt cod in a large deep glass or ceramic bowl and add cold water to cover. Let stand for 24 hours, refrigerated, changing the water every 8 hours. Drain and pat dry.

For the sauce, melt the butter in a small heavy saucepan over low heat. Add the garlic and gently cook for 1 minute. Whisk in the flour a little at a time, being careful that no lumps form, and cook until it turns a light golden color, about 2 minutes. Pour in the chicken stock in a steady stream, whisking constantly so that it is smoothly incorporated. Stir in the cream and pepper and continue cooking and stirring until the mixture thickens, about 3 minutes. Remove from the heat.

Preheat the oven to 350°F.

Cut the salt cod fillets into ¼-inch-thick strips. Place the flour in a shallow bowl and lightly coat each piece of cod with flour.

Heat the olive oil in a 10-inch skillet over medium-high heat. Add the cod and fry for about 1 minute on each side. Transfer the cod to paper towels and let drain for about 5 minutes.

Peel the potatoes and slice into thin discs no thicker than ⅛ inch. Line the bottom of an 8-inch round baking dish or pie plate (or four 10-ounce individual casseroles) with half of the potatoes; follow with half of the salt cod (it will flake as you distribute it) and top with half of the cream sauce and half of the grated cheese. Repeat.

Cover with aluminum foil and bake the large dish for 1½ hours or the smaller dishes for 1 hour 20 minutes. Remove the foil halfway through so that the top browns. Let sit for 5 to 10 minutes before serving. Serve hot.

SERVES 4

salt cod Salting cod began as a way to store and transport fish inland without threat of spoilage. The preparation became so popular that fishermen salted the cod on shipboard, so there were times when fresh cod became scarce. Scandinavians brought their taste for salt cod to the Midwest, and although it's long been an important part of Latin and Mediterranean diets, it's yet to become widely popular in this country.

Grilled Striped Bass
with Fresh Mint

The most successful fish story we know is that of striped bass. After being fished almost to extinction during the 1980's, they were then protected by strict policies for years. Now the waters are teeming with striped bass, and we can enjoy their rich clean flavor once again.

We served this fish at our wedding celebration, held in a field of Sauvignon Blanc grapevines at Paumanok Vineyard on Long Island. The fish grilled with fresh mint was a perfect meal for a hot afternoon in a vineyard. Serve it with Three-Grain Salad with Cucumber and Tomato (page 137) and Summer Three-Bean and Radish Salad (page 76).

6 fresh mint leaves, thinly slivered
2 tablespoons extra virgin olive oil
1 tablespoon Home Spice Mix (page 26)
4 striped bass fillets with skin, about 8 ounces each
Kosher salt and freshly ground black pepper to taste

Whisk together the mint, oil, and spice mix in a medium bowl. Place the fillets in the marinade and turn to coat. Let the fish marinate in the refrigerator for 1 hour, then bring to room temperature for 15 minutes before grilling.

Prepare a charcoal grill.

Season both sides of the fish with salt and pepper. Place the fish skin side down and grill over a medium-high fire for 5 to 7 minutes. Turn the fish over to the flesh side and grill for 4 to 6 minutes longer. Serve hot.   SERVES 4

Grilled Trout with Lemon Dressing and Griddle Cakes

Trout has such a delicate flavor that we like to prepare it simply, just letting the grill put a light char on the skin (see Note). We serve this trout with griddle cakes and Garlic Greens (page 107), often followed by Frozen Lemon Icebox Cake with Strawberry Sauce (page 374).

The lemony dressing, which can also be made without the bacon, should always be served piping hot. We like it with grilled fish cooked on the bone. Once you get the hang of it, it's easy to separate the flesh from the skeleton at the table. Also try the dressing with baked halibut or with porgies.

4 rainbow trout, cleaned
¼ cup extra virgin olive oil
Kosher salt and freshly ground black pepper to taste

FOR THE DRESSING (MAKES 1 CUP)
¼ cup minced bacon
2 tablespoons olive oil
2 tablespoons minced celery
2 tablespoons minced yellow onion
2 tablespoons peeled and minced carrots
2 teaspoons minced garlic
1 teaspoon minced lemon zest
1½ tablespoons fresh lemon juice
2 tablespoons chopped fresh parsley
Kosher salt and freshly ground black pepper to taste

Bacon-Oregano Griddle Cakes (recipe follows)

continued

fish and shellfish

Place the trout in a large shallow dish. Drizzle with the olive oil and gently turn to coat. Season with the salt and pepper.

Prepare a charcoal grill.

For the dressing, cook the bacon in an 8-inch skillet over medium heat until it crisps; pour off the fat and discard it. Reduce the heat to low, add the olive oil, celery, onion, carrot, and garlic, and cook gently for 6 to 8 minutes.

Meanwhile, grill the trout over hot coals for 3 to 4 minutes on each side.

Remove the dressing from the heat and add the lemon zest, lemon juice, and parsley. Season with salt and pepper. Serve the trout with the hot dressing.　　SERVES 4

NOTE: When we want a grilled flavor but don't want to light our grill, we use a cast-iron skillet with raised ridges on the bottom. The ridges act as a grill grate and give the fish a pleasing char.

❖ BACON-OREGANO GRIDDLE CAKES ❖

We make these rich, savory pancakes silver-dollar size and serve them nestled up to the trout.

2 extra-thick slices slab bacon, cut in ½-inch cubes

1 cup sifted all-purpose flour

2 teaspoons baking powder

½ tablespoon granulated sugar

1½ tablespoons chopped fresh oregano or

　　1½ teaspoons dried oregano

½ teaspoon kosher salt

1 large egg, lightly beaten

¾ cup whole milk

2 tablespoons unsalted butter, melted

Heat a 10-inch skillet over medium-high heat. Add the bacon and fry until it is crispy. Remove the bacon from the skillet, keeping the bacon fat in the skillet.

Stir the flour, baking powder, sugar, oregano, and salt together in a bowl. Whisk together the egg, milk, and melted butter in a medium bowl, then stir into the flour mixture until a smooth batter is formed. Fold in the cooked bacon.

Heat the skillet containing the bacon fat over medium heat. Spoon the batter into the skillet, making silver-dollar-size cakes, and cook until small bubbles appear at the edges. Turn and cook the second side until golden. Keep warm on a heated plate while you cook the rest of the pancakes.　　**MAKES 12 PANCAKES, 3 PER SERVING**

Porgies Wrapped in Grape Leaves

Porgies are small silver fish that swim around the rocks in Long Island Sound and Peconic Bay. Very small in the spring, they grow bigger all summer, finally becoming fat as geese by Christmas. It is important that porgies be extremely fresh, for their flesh becomes mushy even by the day after they are caught. You can substitute butterfish or sand dabs, or other small white-fleshed lean fish.

Although this takes some time to put together, most of the work can be done well before guests arrive. When it's time to eat, all you have to do is put the fish on the grill. If you haven't brined your own grape leaves, use the commercial ones that can be found in any well-stocked grocery store. We like to serve this with Overnight Tomato–Balsamic Dressing (page 20).

continued

1 cup extra virgin olive oil

6 garlic cloves, chopped

6 lemon slices

6 small fresh thyme sprigs

6 small fresh oregano sprigs

6 small fresh savory sprigs

2 teaspoons red pepper flakes

Kosher salt and freshly ground black pepper to taste

6 whole porgies or other small finfish, not more than
    1 pound each, cleaned and fins removed

12 large Preserved Grape Leaves (page 357)

Olive oil, for brushing

Combine the olive oil, garlic, lemon, herbs, and red pepper flakes in a large bowl. Season with salt and pepper. Add the fish and gently toss with the marinade, making sure they are evenly coated.

Lay 1 of the grape leaves on a work surface. Place 1 of the porgies on it with its head pointing toward the stem. Place 1 lemon slice and 1 sprig of each of the herbs on top of the fish. Place a second grape leaf on top of the fish. Using butcher's twine, tie the grape leaves around the fish in 3 places. Repeat with the remaining fish. Let marinate in the refrigerator for 30 minutes, then bring them to room temperature before grilling.

Prepare a charcoal grill.

Brush the wrapped fish with olive oil, season with salt and pepper, and grill them over a medium-high fire for 4 to 5 minutes on each side. The grape leaves will get slightly charred. Remove to a serving platter. Cut off the twine and serve.   SERVES 6

SMOKED FISH

Coming of age in the Great Lakes region meant a steady diet of smoked fish. Many a meal consisted of a couple of smoked chubs, bread, mustard, pickles, and cold beer. Every good meat and fish market had a well-stocked display of freshwater fish colored gold from the smoke: Whiting, trout, sturgeon, and chubs were both popular and cheap.

It's another story in the Northeast, where smoked fish is considered a culinary delicacy, and it can be cheaper to buy prime beef than smoked whiting. In New York City, delicatessens have ostentatious displays of fish, some of them simply smoked, others cured and then smoked, and still others that are cured, spiced, and smoked. Here's where we can't resist indulging in smoked salmon, sable, mackerel, and lake fish, despite the premium price.

ONE OF THE 45 DINNERS COOKED IN THE WILD
ON OUR CROSS-COUNTRY CAMPING TRIP, 1990

June in Bighorn

June in Bighorn It was June, and in Bighorn National Forest all the mountain passes were open, so we drove high up to the Black Mountain Pass and camped for the night. The next morning, we emerged from the tent to an inch of snow. This incredibly wild national forest was just beginning to be trailblazed and we drove down to one of the new trailheads. We embarked on a hike that was to leave its mark on our memory. As we found ourselves in an expansive meadow still soft with the runoff of melted snow and spring rains, we noticed deep narrow streams lacing their way through the soft loam. As we measured their depth with sticks, it turned out that these streams were about three feet deep and only about one foot wide. The ice-cold water was running through the crevasses with such rapidity and force that we could hardly hold our arms steady against the current. All of a sudden a gray shadow ran through the water with lightning speed. If we had blinked we would have missed it. Then it happened again. And again. As we jumped over this labyrinth of streams making our way to the other side of the meadow, we must have witnessed hundreds of brook trout coursing through the meadow on their way to a rendezvous unknown to us. We would have given anything for a fishing pole and a map to the secret lake that these trout were destined for.

Hot-Smoked Trout

First brining trout and then smoking it gives the skin a sweet flavor and the flesh a subtle smokiness. When it's done, the fish will have a silky, moist texture and should release easily from the bone.

4 cups water

1½ cups molasses

1½ cups (packed) brown sugar

1 cup kosher salt

Peel of 1 orange, removed in large strips

¼ teaspoon coriander seeds

¼ teaspoon black peppercorns

1 fresh bay leaf

6 rainbow or brook trout, 12 to 14 ounces each, cleaned

Combine the water, molasses, sugar, salt, orange peel, coriander, peppercorns, and bay leaf in a 2-quart saucepan and bring to a boil over medium heat. Reduce the heat and simmer uncovered for 10 minutes. Remove the pan from the heat and set it aside to cool, about 30 minutes.

Place the trout in a large shallow bowl, pour the cooled brine over it, cover, and refrigerate for 48 hours.

To smoke the fish, prepare a hot smoker with applewood chips (see page 231).

Remove the trout from the brine. Rinse them and pat dry. Smoke the trout over the lightest smoke and heat possible until fully cooked, 1½ to 2 hours. Cool the trout on a wire rack. The trout will keep refrigerated up to 1 week.   SERVES 6

Smoked Fish Salad with Fresh Horseradish Dressing

Think of this as a sophisticated variation on tuna salad. We make it for cocktail parties, surrounding it with toast points. Guests looking for something to nibble can spread the creamy salad on the thin, crisp toasts.

4 cups flaked smoked fish, such as whiting or trout

3 tablespoons grated fresh horseradish

2 tablespoons Roasted Garlic Purée (page 5)

1 tablespoon minced shallots

1 tablespoon tarragon vinegar

1 tablespoon fresh lemon juice

2 teaspoons Dijon mustard

1 teaspoon honey

½ teaspoon granulated sugar

1 cup olive oil

Kosher salt and freshly ground black pepper to taste

Place the fish in a large bowl. Purée the horseradish, garlic purée, shallots, vinegar, lemon juice, mustard, honey, and sugar in a food processor or blender. With the machine running, slowly add the olive oil and process until it is incorporated.

Add the dressing to the fish and mix together. Season with salt and pepper. Cover and refrigerate. Serve chilled.

MAKES ENOUGH FOR 50 SMALL TOASTS; SERVES 10

fish and shellfish

Smoked Eel Salad with
Fennel and Dill

Cooked eel is so good: sweet and firm, like monkfish, but better. Smoked eel is especially good, as the rich silky flesh can withstand a good amount of smoke. To get big chunks of meat, buy the largest eel you can find. If you cannot find smoked eel, smoked trout or whiting can be substituted. Serve this salad alongside fresh spinach or arugula dressed with olive oil and fresh lemon juice.

¾ *cup minced celery*

¾ *cup minced fennel*

¼ *cup minced red onion*

2 cups flaked smoked eel

½ *cup Homemade Mayonnaise (page 9)*

2 tablespoons minced fresh dill

1 tablespoon Dijon mustard

2 teaspoons fresh lemon juice

Kosher salt and freshly ground black pepper to taste

Combine the celery, fennel, red onion, and eel in a large bowl.

Stir together the mayonnaise, dill, mustard, and lemon juice in a small bowl. Add the dressing to the eel mixture and stir together. Season with salt and pepper.

SERVES 6

SHELLFISH

One reason we're glad we're not in the Midwest anymore is that now we can eat oysters whenever we want. David had them first in New Orleans, when he walked into an oyster bar advertising a happy hour of freshly shucked oysters for ten cents apiece. He ate six dozen, and only his youth saved him from a terrible stomachache. We ate them together in Apalachicola, Florida, where the oysters are known for their creamy flavor. We bought five dozen of them; by midnight there were oyster shells filling every container in our hotel room, including the bathroom sink. Now that we're in New York City, we go to the Oyster Bar in Grand Central Station every few months for a fix of Grand Central Oyster Stew. And perhaps, best of all, on Long Island we sometimes go out with Charlie Manwaring from the Southold Fish Market when he harvests his oysters; eating one when it's been out of the bay for only a minute is exquisite. —BARBARA

Oysters on the Half Shell
with Ice Wine Dressing

Fresh oysters on the half shell call for a bracing squeeze of lemon or the traditional black pepper, shallot, and vinegar dressing. When we want something different, we make an ice wine dressing, whose sweetness marries well with the briny oysters. If you can't find an ice wine, try another sweet wine, such as muscat or sauternes.

FOR THE DRESSING

½ cup ice wine (see Note)

¾ cup champagne vinegar

1 tablespoon cracked black peppercorns

2 tablespoons minced shallots

1 tablespoon minced fresh thyme

½ teaspoon kosher salt

24 to 36 oysters, scrubbed

For the dressing, whisk all the ingredients together in a small bowl.

Slip an oyster knife into the hinge of each shell and twist. Leave the oysters in their cupped bottom shells. Serve with the dressing. **SERVES 4 TO 6**

NOTE: Ice wines are made in cooler viticultural regions, such as Long Island, upstate New York, Canada, and northern Germany. When the climate allows, the grapes are left literally to freeze on the vines. The grapes are pressed while they're still frozen, and as they begin to thaw, they release their fruity nectar, leaving the frozen water behind in the press. The juice is then made into a deliciously unctious sweet wine.

Oyster Stew with
White Wine and Orange

The crunch of fennel and celery sets off the richness of
oysters and cream in this creamy stew.

2 tablespoons unsalted butter

¼ cup minced yellow onion

¼ cup minced celery

¼ cup minced fennel

1 teaspoon minced garlic

1½ cups dry white wine

2 teaspoons minced orange zest

1 cup fresh orange juice

3 cups heavy cream

36 oysters, shucked (reserve their liquor) (see Note)

Kosher salt and freshly ground black pepper to taste

2 teaspoons minced fresh tarragon

Melt the butter in a 4-quart saucepan over medium-low
heat. Add the onion, celery, fennel, and garlic and cook
until the vegetables are softened, about 4 minutes Add the
white wine, orange zest, and orange juice, and simmer
until the liquid is reduced by two thirds, 10 to 12 minutes.
Add the heavy cream and bring it to a gentle boil. Reduce
the heat to low and simmer for 10 to 12 minutes longer.

Add the oysters and their liquor and gently cook until
they are just heated through and their edges begin to
curl, about 2 minutes. Do not boil. Season with salt and
pepper. Garnish with the tarragon and serve hot.

SERVES 4 TO 6

N O T E : Opening oysters is work, a job you just have to get
through. You slip an oyster knife into the hinge and twist,
trying to get leverage so you can cut and free the muscle.

fish and shellfish

Oyster Stew with Saffron, Leeks, and Bacon

If we have the patience to wait for this smoky stew, we make Oyster Crackers (page 310) first to float on top.

1 cup dry white wine

2 tablespoons minced shallots

8 saffron threads

2 slices bacon, cut into ¼-inch dice

1 leek, thinly sliced

2½ cups heavy cream

2 tablespoons unsalted butter

24 oysters, shucked (reserve their liquor)
   (see Note, page 185)

Kosher salt and freshly ground black pepper to taste

Dash of paprika

Combine the wine, shallots, and saffron in a 4-quart saucepan over medium-low heat and simmer gently until the liquid is reduced by half.

Meanwhile, cook the bacon in an 8-inch skillet until it is crispy, then pour off all but 1 tablespoon of the fat. Add the leeks to the bacon and gently cook until softened.

Add the bacon mixture to the reduced wine. Add the cream, butter, and the liquor from the oysters and simmer for 12 to 15 minutes. Add the oysters and simmer until they just begin to curl, about 2 minutes. Season with salt and pepper and garnish with paprika. Serve hot.

SERVES 4

saffron   You get a lot of aromatic flavor and golden color when you steep just a few of the red threads in liquid, then add it to rice, fisherman's stew, or this oyster stew.

Steamer Clams with Local Ale

When we got married, our rehearsal dinner—or, rather, rehearsal barbecue and brouhaha—started with big buckets of steamers. We kept the party going with an endless supply, accompanied by melted butter and cold beer. We can still feast our way through dozens on a summer night. This recipe is best prepared in two batches, dividing the ingredients in half for each batch.

8 tablespoons (1 stick) unsalted butter

¼ cup minced garlic

2 (12-ounce) bottles good local ale

4 pounds steamer clams, scrubbed

¼ cup fresh lemon juice

½ cup chopped fresh parsley

Freshly ground black pepper to taste

In a 14-inch skillet with a tight-fitting lid, melt the butter over medium heat. Add the garlic and cook it gently for 2 to 3 minutes. Add the ale and heat it to a simmer. Add the clams, cover, and cook for 3 to 4 minutes, shaking the skillet often so that the clams are evenly cooked.

When the clams are open, add the lemon juice, parsley, and pepper. Serve the clams and broth in deep bowls or buckets, with mugs of cold ale, melted butter for dipping, and a platter of thinly sliced homemade salami (page 277).   SERVES 4

eating steamers To avoid ending up with gritty sand in your mouth, when the bowl of hot steamers is set on the table, grasp a clam by the dark neck and remove it from its shell. Dip it back into the hot clam juice to act as a final rinse, then into drawn butter, and pop it into your mouth, pulling away and discarding the black sheath.

MY OLDER SIBLINGS LEE AND KATHY, AND COUSIN B.J.,
MARGATE BEACH, SUMMER 1959

Every July, my family would get together at

the Jersey Shore and make clams casino. The men bought

the clams and did the shucking, the children chopped the

vegetables, and the women worked the broilers. Aunt Kay

would bring her sausage grinder from Mississippi and

clamp it to the edge of the kitchen table, where it was

used to grind the green peppers and onions. Meanwhile,

my father and Uncle Bruce would shuck clams. There

was a lot of swearing as the clams fought, muscle to mus-

cle, with the men.

As the first batch of sweet cooked clams came out of

the broiler bubbling with bacon fat, everyone grabbed for

one. Loads kept going under the broiler as the adults

moved on to cards and the kids got to take over. At the

end of the night, the kitchen was a disaster, but everyone

was happy. —BARBARA

Shinn Family Clams Casino

24 littleneck clams, scrubbed
2 tablespoons unsalted butter
¼ cup diced red bell peppers (¼-inch dice)
¼ cup diced green bell peppers (¼-inch dice)
¼ cup diced yellow onion (¼-inch dice)
Kosher salt and freshly ground black pepper to taste
3 thick slices bacon

Shuck the clams, keeping them in their bottom shells but being sure to loosen each from its shell. Arrange the clams in a single layer on a broiler pan and refrigerate.

Preheat the broiler.

Melt the butter in a small skillet over medium-low heat. Add the peppers and onion and gently cook until they are softened, about 5 minutes. Season with salt and pepper and remove from the heat.

Cut the bacon into 1-inch pieces. Spread each clam with a small amount of the onion mixture and top with a piece of bacon. Season with pepper. Broil until the bacon is browned and the clams are warm. Serve hot.

SERVES 4 AS AN APPETIZER OR 2 AS A MAIN DISH

fish and shellfish

Clam Pie

We make clam pie with whatever vegetables are in the farm stands that day. This one uses autumn eggplant and red bell peppers.

Buttery Pie Dough (page 395), made without the sugar
24 large chowder clams (quahogs), scrubbed
3 tablespoons olive oil
3 tablespoons minced garlic
4 cups peeled and diced eggplant (¼-inch dice)
2 cups diced red bell peppers (¼-inch dice)
1 cup diced yellow onions (¼-inch dice)
2 tablespoons fresh lemon juice
2 tablespoons all-purpose flour
1 cup heavy cream
1¾ cups shredded Monterey Jack cheese
2 tablespoons chopped fresh herbs, such as parsley
  or oregano
Kosher salt and freshly ground black pepper to taste
½ cup Seasoned Bread Crumbs (page 27)

Line an 8-inch pie plate with the dough. Trim and flute the edge. Refrigerate.

Preheat the oven to 350°F.

Fill a 14-inch skillet with 1 inch water, place the clams in it, cover, and steam over medium heat until they just open, 7 to 10 minutes. Transfer the clams to a bowl. Remove them from the shells and mince the meats.

Heat the olive oil and garlic in a 10-inch skillet over medium heat. Add the eggplant, red peppers, and onions and gently cook until the vegetables are softened, about 5 minutes. Add the lemon juice and cook for 2 minutes longer. Add the flour, stir to evenly coat the vegetables, and cook for 2 minutes longer. Add the cream and continue cooking until thickened, about 2 minutes longer. Add the clams, shredded cheese, and herbs. Season with salt and pepper.

Spoon the filling into the pie shell and top with the bread crumbs. Bake until the bread crumbs are browned and the cream is bubbling, about 40 minutes. Serve hot.

SERVES 4 TO 6

NOTE: This recipe can also be baked in 4 individual ramekins lined with the pastry dough; reduce the baking time to about 30 minutes.

chowder clams Sometimes our fish market has big quahogs, or chowder clams, that are about three inches across and very meaty. When these are steamed, they can be tough and have to be minced to make them palatable, which is probably the genesis of clam pie.

Bay Scallops with Delicata Squash, Cauliflower, and Brussels Sprouts

Bay scallops are smaller than sea scallops and are known for their sweetness. We love them in this dish tossed with the sweet delicata squash and one of our favorite vegetables, brussels sprouts. Any fresh scallop works well in this recipe, but try to find bay scallops if you want a real treat.

If you are unfamiliar with delicata, it has a moist orange flesh that may remind you of sweet potatoes. If you can't find it, use acorn or another sweet squash.

continued

fish and shellfish

2 delicata or acorn squash, about 1 pound each

Kosher salt and freshly ground black pepper to taste

4 tablespoons (½ stick) unsalted butter

1 tablespoon kosher salt

1 small head cauliflower, cut into small florets
   (about 2 cups)

2 cups small brussels sprouts, trimmed

1 leek, cut into ¼-inch dice

¼ cup olive oil

1 teaspoon minced serrano chile

1½ pounds bay scallops, tough side muscle removed

½ cup dry white wine

Juice of 1 lemon

2 tablespoons minced fresh mint

Preheat the oven to 350°F.

Halve the squash lengthwise and scoop out the seeds. Separate the seeds from the strings and season them with a little salt. Spread them on a baking sheet and toast them in the oven, stirring occasionally, for about 15 minutes. Remove them from the oven and set them aside.

Place the squash cut side up in a large baking dish. Dot with 2 tablespoons of the butter and season with salt and pepper. Bake until just tender, about 35 minutes.

While the squash is baking, bring a large pot of water to a boil and add the 1 tablespoon kosher salt. Blanch the cauliflower and brussels sprouts separately for about 2 minutes each. Immediately cool them under cold running water and set aside to drain.

Heat the remaining 2 tablespoons butter in a 10-inch skillet over medium heat. Add the leeks, and gently cook until they are softened, about 3 minutes. Add the olive oil, chile, cauliflower, and brussels sprouts and gently stir the vegetables until they are just heated through, about 5 minutes.

Add the scallops and gently combine them with the vegetables. Add the white wine and simmer until the scallops are just cooked through, about 3 minutes. Add the lemon juice and mint and season with salt and pepper.

Serve the scallops and vegetables spooned into the warm squash halves and garnish with the toasted squash seeds.

SERVES 4

Pan-Smoked Shrimp with Warm Horseradish Cocktail Sauce

There's no such thing as bad cocktail sauce, and we think our version is superlative. In the winter we serve it with these pan-smoked shrimp. The aroma from the toasted spices alone makes it a hit.

1 pound medium shrimp, peeled but tails left on

4 tablespoons Home Spice Mix (page 26)

1 teaspoon cayenne pepper

Kosher salt and freshly ground black pepper to taste

3 tablespoons olive oil

FOR THE COCKTAIL SAUCE

1 cup Famous Tomato Ketchup (page 11)

2 tablespoons prepared horseradish

1 tablespoon fresh lemon juice

1 teaspoon Tabasco sauce

2 tablespoons chopped fresh parsley

continued

fish and shellfish

Toss the shrimp with the spice mix, cayenne, salt, and black pepper in a large bowl.

Heat the olive oil in a 10-inch skillet over medium-high heat. Add as many shrimp as will fit in a single layer and cook until they turn pink and the spices are toasted and smoky, 1 to 2 minutes on each side. Transfer to a serving platter and repeat with the remaining shrimp. Meanwhile, combine the ketchup, horseradish, lemon juice, and Tabasco in a small saucepan over low heat and simmer until warm, 2 to 3 minutes. Transfer to a small bowl.

Sprinkle the shrimp with the parsley, and serve warm with the warm cocktail sauce.   SERVES 6

to cook shrimp Shrimp is sold by the number (count) of shrimp it takes to make a pound, counting down from jumbo 8s and 10s to tiny 60s. Medium shrimp are somewhere in the range of 16 to 20 per pound.

For shrimp cocktail, we cook the shrimp in a very light aromatic broth of water and white wine with lemon, some bay leaves, thyme, and black peppercorns. After it simmers for about 15 minutes, we add the shrimp in their shells and simmer them for about 6 minutes. Once they're firm and pink, we drain them, ice them down, and put them in the fridge until we are ready to use them. Then we serve them with our horseradish cocktail sauce, also chilled.

Shrimp and Hominy Stew

We both love the flavor of hominy. We grew up on corn that had big starchy kernels, not like today's supersweet hybrids, and hominy has that same starchy rich quality.

Hominy is a kind of dried white corn that's been soaked so the hulls burst off and the inner kernels puff up. High in iron and other nutrients, it's a real American food that played a major part of the Algonquin Indian diet and, when it was adopted by the early settlers, became important to their survival. Buy it dried or canned in the Latin section of supermarkets; if it's dried, you'll have to soak the kernels in water overnight to soften them for cooking.

1 tablespoon unsalted butter

1 tablespoon olive oil

½ cup diced yellow onion (¼-inch dice)

½ cup diced celery (¼-inch dice)

2 teaspoons minced garlic

½ cup stemmed and sliced fresh shiitake mushrooms

¼ cup diced red bell peppers (¼-inch dice)

½ cup dry white wine

4 cups fish stock, preferably homemade (page 61)

4 cups water

1 cup cooked hominy

1 pound rock shrimp or medium shrimp, peeled

1 teaspoon minced lemon zest

½ teaspoon cayenne pepper

Kosher salt and freshly ground black pepper to taste

2 tablespoons chopped fresh parsley

continued

Heat the butter and olive oil in a 4-quart saucepan over medium heat. Add the onion, celery, and garlic and gently cook until the vegetables are softened, about 5 minutes. Add the mushrooms and red peppers and cook for 2 to 3 minutes longer. Add the wine and reduce by half. Add the stock, water, and hominy; simmer uncovered for 15 minutes.

Add the shrimp, lemon zest, and cayenne; simmer uncovered until the shrimp are just cooked through, 3 to 5 minutes. Season with salt and pepper and garnish with the parsley. Serve hot.   **SERVES 6 TO 8**

Shrimp and Andouille Sausage Gumbo

It's so strange how foods go in and out of style. Gumbo isn't chic at all today, but it was all the rage in the 1980's, when people were lining up to see Paul Prudhomme at his restaurant K Paul's in New Orleans and making him one of the first American celebrity chefs. Gumbo is really good food and truly American, so we should consider it a classic.

2½ quarts chicken stock, preferably homemade (page 54)
6 cups clam juice
½ cup peanut oil
½ cup all-purpose flour
1½ cups diced celery (¼-inch dice)
1½ cups diced yellow onions (¼-inch dice)
¾ cup diced red bell peppers (¼-inch dice)
¾ cup diced yellow bell peppers (¼-inch dice)

1 tablespoon minced garlic

2 pounds large shrimp, peeled

1 pound okra, sliced ½ inch thick

1 pound smoked andouille sausage, sliced ¼ inch thick

2 tablespoons sassafras or filé powder

1 teaspoon cayenne pepper

Bring the chicken stock and clam juice to a simmer in a 4-quart saucepan.

Meanwhile, heat the oil in a large soup pot over medium heat. Gradually add the flour, whisking vigorously, and cook, whisking constantly, until the flour turns a dark rich brown, 1 to 3 minutes. Add the celery, onions, red and yellow peppers, and garlic and cook until softened.

Slowly ladle the simmering stock into the vegetable mixture, stirring gently after each addition, and bring to a simmer. Stir in the shrimp, okra, andouille, sassafras, and cayenne and simmer for 10 to 12 minutes. Serve hot.

SERVES 8 TO 10

Summer Lobster
and Vegetable Salad

This salad is dressed lightly in only a tiny bit of olive oil, mustard, lemon, and herbs, allowing the lobster and summer vegetables to remain sweet and vibrant.

3 tablespoons olive oil

½ cup minced white onion

1 garlic clove, minced

1 cup diced yellow squash (¼-inch dice)

1 ear sweet corn, kernels cut from the cob

2 teaspoons kosher salt

½ cup shelled fresh peas

1 medium tomato

¾ pound cooked lobster (from 1½-pound lobster;
   see page 200) cut into ½-inch pieces

1 tablespoon Dijon mustard

1 tablespoon fresh lemon juice

1 tablespoon chopped fresh dill

¼ teaspoon cayenne pepper

Kosher salt and freshly ground black pepper to taste

Heat 2 tablespoons of the olive oil in an 8-inch skillet over medium heat. Add the onion and garlic and cook until they are softened, about 1 minute. Add the squash and corn and cook for 1 minute longer. Transfer to a large bowl and let cool.

Fill a large pot with water, add the 2 teaspoons kosher salt, and bring it to a boil. Fill a large bowl with ice water.

Blanch the peas in the boiling water for 1 to 2 minutes, remove them from the water, and plunge them into the ice water. Let them cool in the ice water for about 5 minutes, then drain.

Meanwhile, cut a small X in the bottom of the tomato and cut out the core from the top. Place the tomato in the boiling water for about 1 minute, remove it from the water, and plunge it into the ice water. Let cool. Slip the skin off the tomato, cut it in half, and scoop out the seeds. Cut the tomato flesh into ½-inch dice.

Add the lobster, tomato, and peas to the corn mixture and toss together. Whisk together the remaining 1 tablespoon olive oil, the mustard, lemon juice, dill, and cayenne in a small bowl. Add just enough of the dressing to coat the salad, toss, and season with the salt and pepper. Cover and refrigerate. Serve slightly chilled.   SERVES 4

Lobster Rolls

The mayonnaisey lobster salad should be piled so high in each roll that you can hardly get the first bite in your mouth.

1½ pounds cooked lobster from two 1½- to 2-pound
   lobsters (page 200), cut into ½-inch pieces
3 tablespoons olive oil
2 tablespoons unsalted butter
4 ribs celery, minced
1 medium white onion, minced
1 tablespoon minced jalapeño chile
2 garlic cloves, minced
½ bunch scallions, excluding the dark green tops, minced
1 cup Basil Mayonnaise (page 10)
Kosher salt and freshly ground black pepper to taste
4 hero sandwich rolls, each 8 inches long

continued

fish and shellfish

Place the lobster in a large bowl. Heat the olive oil and butter in a 10-inch skillet over medium-low heat. Add the celery, onion, chile, and garlic and gently cook until the vegetables are softened, about 5 minutes. Let cool.

Add the onion mixture to the lobster along with the scallions, and toss together. Stir in the basil mayonnaise. Season with salt and pepper. Refrigerate for at least 30 minutes.

Split each roll lengthwise in half and pull out some of the bread from each half, forming a shallow cradle. Fill the bottom halves of the rolls with the lobster salad, top with the remaining halves, and serve.   **SERVES 4**

to cook lobster In our kitchen, lobsters are steamed, not boiled, which we think makes them too watery. We make a broth similar to the one we use for shrimp (see page 194) in a tall stockpot. Then we put in a rack, add the lobsters, cover tightly, and cook them for anywhere from 10 to 30 minutes, depending on how many lobsters are in there. We like to sprinkle a lot of Old Bay Seasoning into the water and over the lobsters.

Lobster Kebabs

We can think of few things more tantalizing than slipping hot pieces of lobster off the skewers onto our plates and dipping them in fresh Basil Mayonnaise. We sometimes serve these with Warm Horseradish Cocktail Sauce.

4 lobsters, 1 to 1¼ pounds each
2 tablespoons Old Bay Seasoning
6 tablespoons extra virgin olive oil
8 large fresh basil leaves, thinly slivered

Juice of 2 lemons

Kosher salt and freshly ground black pepper to taste

Basil Mayonnaise (page 10) or Warm Horseradish
   Cocktail Sauce (page 193)

Place a steaming rack in the bottom of a lobster pot. Fill a large bowl or basin with ice water. Fill the lobster pot with 2 inches of water, add the Old Bay Seasoning, and bring to a boil. Reduce the heat to a simmer, place the lobsters in the pot, cover, and steam for 7 to 8 minutes; the lobsters will turn bright red but will be slightly undercooked. Immediately plunge the lobsters into the ice water for 5 minutes to stop them from continuing to cook.

Shell the cooled lobsters, being careful to leave the claw meat whole and intact. Cut the tails lengthwise in half.

Prepare a charcoal grill.

Whisk together the olive oil, basil, and lemon juice in a large bowl. Season with salt and pepper. Add the lobster meat and toss gently in the marinade, coating it well. Starting with the smaller end of each halved lobster tail, slide the meat onto 8 skewers. It is best to skewer the meat lengthwise so that it remains firmly in place. Thread the meat from one knuckle and then from one claw onto each skewer.

Grill the skewers over hot coals until the lobster is just warmed through, about 2 to 3 minutes on each side. Serve with the mayonnaise or cocktail sauce.

SERVES 8 AS AN APPETIZER

fish and shellfish

Slow-Cooked Squid Stew

Once rarely found in American markets, squid has become a popular source of low-fat protein. If you've only eaten calamari breaded and deep-fried in shore seafood restaurants, you'll be surprised by how tender and succulent it can be.

The cook's adage is that you have to cook squid for either about two minutes or forty minutes. Do it quickly on the grill or sauté pan, and it's firm, fresh, and vibrant; overcook it even slightly, and you can't chew it. But if you stew the squid slowly, it will relax and become a beautiful seafood dish.

3 tablespoons olive oil

½ cup diced yellow onion (¼-inch dice)

½ cup diced celery (¼-inch dice)

½ cup diced fennel (¼-inch dice)

1½ tablespoons chopped garlic

1 tablespoon minced serrano or jalapeño chiles

1 fresh bay leaf

2 teaspoons grated orange zest

1 teaspoon toasted and ground coriander seeds

1 tablespoon minced anchovy

¾ cup fresh orange juice

¾ cup dry white wine

1½ pounds cleaned squid, fresh if possible, cut into
    1½-inch pieces
1 cup diced pepperoni or other hot dry sausage
    (¼-inch dice)
6 cups peeled, seeded, and chopped fresh tomatoes
1½ cups clam juice or fish stock, preferably homemade
    (page 61)
½ cup long-grain white rice, rinsed
Kosher salt and freshly ground black pepper to taste
3 tablespoons chopped fresh mint

Heat the olive oil in a large soup pot over medium-low heat. Add the onion, celery, fennel, garlic, and chiles and cook until the vegetables are softened, 5 to 7 minutes. Add the bay leaf, orange zest, coriander, and anchovy and cook for 2 to 3 minutes longer. Add the orange juice and wine and boil until reduced by half, about 10 minutes.

Add the squid, pepperoni, tomatoes, and clam juice and simmer uncovered for 15 minutes. Add the rice and simmer uncovered until the rice is cooked and the squid is tender, about 20 minutes longer. Season with salt and pepper. Ladle into bowls and garnish with the mint.

SERVES 4 TO 6

Octopus Stew with
Red Wine and Rosemary

Tasting like squid but much meatier, octopus can be delicious. We like to stew the sweet meat in red wine and our roasted tomato sauce, making a robust meal.

1 large fresh or frozen octopus, about 3 pounds,
    thawed if frozen

2 tablespoons extra virgin olive oil

2 cups diced yellow onions (¼-inch dice)

2 cups diced fennel (¼-inch dice)

1 tablespoon minced garlic

2 cups dry red wine

2 cups Roasted Tomato Sauce (page 20)

2 tablespoons coarsely chopped fresh rosemary

1 teaspoon red pepper flakes

1 wine cork (see Note)

Kosher salt and freshly ground black pepper to taste

1 tablespoon chopped fresh parsley

Grated zest of 1 lemon

Bring 1 gallon of water to a simmer in a large stockpot and lower the octopus into it. Cover and simmer the octopus for 45 minutes. Remove the octopus from the hot water and let it cool on a clean work surface, about 15 minutes.

Peel off the dark purple outer membrane from the tentacles and discard it. Clean the head. Cut the meat into 2-inch pieces and set aside.

Heat the olive oil in a large heavy pot over medium-low heat. Add the onions, fennel, and garlic and cook, until the vegetables are softened, about 5 minutes. Add the octopus, wine, tomato sauce, rosemary, red pepper flakes, and the cork. Cover and gently simmer until the octopus is tender to the bite, 1½ to 2 hours. During this time you may have to add a little water; the consistency of the sauce should be that of a slightly thickened broth. Season to taste with salt and pepper.

Ladle into bowls and garnish with the parsley and lemon zest.   **SERVES 4 TO 6**

NOTE: The cork is said to tenderize the octopus.

BIRDS

CHICKEN

Simply Roasted Chicken 211

Mom Page's Skillet-Fried Chicken with
Our Green Olive Gravy 213

Oven-Fried Chicken 215

Chicken in a Pot 216

Chicken, Tomato, and Butter Bean Stew 217

Creamy Chicken and Ham Casserole
with Artichokes 219

Pesto Grilled Chicken 220

TURKEY

Roast Turkey 222

Turkey Meatloaf 227

QUAIL AND DUCK

Grilled Quail with Orange, Ginger,
and Marjoram 229

Smoked Duck Breasts 230

Potted Duck 232

Grilled Duck Breasts with Lavender,
Honey, and Merlot Glaze 235

Grilled Duck Breast Salad
with Apricot Mustard 236

CHICKEN

When we were planning Home Restaurant, the first main dish we knew we had to have was roast chicken. It's still the number one seller there (except on those occasional nights when spiced pork chops win out). Chicken is what people think of when they think of home cooking.

We care a lot about the quality of the chicken we serve, probably in large part because of David's memory of his grandmother's farm-raised chickens. When Grandmother Drover hung out her laundry, her chickens would scurry around underfoot, hoping she'd toss some grain to them. They seemed more like pets, even though next to the clothesline was the tree stump on which they would meet their end: a lesson in life on the farm.

When Grandma cooked her first store-bought chicken, she was suspicious of the Styrofoam and plastic wrapping it came in, but she wanted to show she could be as modern as the next cook. Once the bird was in the oven, however, she began stomping around, saying it smelled wrong and must be unhealthy to eat. She flat-out refused to eat that chicken, and David certainly wasn't going to eat it if she didn't.

Years later, when he encountered free-range chickens in California that tasted just like Grandma Drover's birds, he knew that Grandma Drover was indeed a wise woman.

Simply Roasted Chicken

We roast our chickens at a high temperature to give them crackling-crisp skin and deep flavor. We have found that placing the bird on a roasting rack allows the heat to surround it and brown it evenly.

1 chicken, about 3½ pounds
½ lemon, cut in half
Kosher salt and freshly ground black pepper to taste
1 fresh thyme sprig
1 fresh rosemary sprig
10 large fresh basil leaves

Preheat the oven to 450°F.

Rub the inside of the bird with the cut lemon. Season inside and out with salt and pepper. Drop the herbs into the cavity of the bird and tie the bony ends of the legs together, covering the opening of the cavity. Twist the wing tips behind the thick part of the wings.

Place the bird on a roasting rack on a baking sheet. Roast until the skin is golden and crackling crisp, 35 to 40 minutes. Reduce the oven temperature to 350°F and roast the bird for 25 to 30 minutes longer. Test the doneness of the bird by piercing the thickest part of the thigh with a thin-bladed knife. The juices should run clear. Transfer the bird to a cutting board and let rest for 10 to 15 minutes before carving.   **SERVES 2 TO 3**

My mother would come home after

work and cook chicken for seven hungry mouths. As

each batch came out of the cast-iron skillet, it was set to

keep warm in the oven. When the three chickens were

done, everyone dashed to the table and grabbed for the

juiciest pieces. If it happened today, I'd make sure Mom

got first pick.

Skillet frying takes so much concentration and time—

25 minutes of close attention from start to finish—that

we can't do it in the restaurant. So we make it at home,

with a piquant olive-salty gravy that's our addition. But

we think Mom would approve.   —DAVID

Mom Page's
Skillet-Fried Chicken with
Our Green Olive Gravy

1 chicken, about 3½ pounds

3 cups buttermilk

FOR THE GRAVY (MAKES 2 CUPS)

1 tablespoon unsalted butter

½ cup minced yellow onion

2 tablespoons balsamic vinegar

1½ cups chicken stock, preferably homemade (page 54)

¾ cup heavy cream

2 tablespoons minced green olives

1 tablespoon Roasted Garlic Purée (page 5)

Kosher salt and freshly ground black pepper to taste

FOR THE COATING

1 cup all-purpose flour

½ cup fine yellow cornmeal

1 tablespoon kosher salt

1½ teaspoons freshly ground black pepper

1½ teaspoons mild paprika

1½ teaspoons ground yellow mustard seeds

½ cup vegetable oil

Cut the chicken into 8 pieces: 2 breasts, 2 thighs, 2 drumsticks, and 2 wings. Place the chicken in a deep bowl and pour the buttermilk over it. Cover and let stand at room temperature for 30 minutes.

Preheat the oven to 200°F.

Meanwhile, for the gravy, melt the butter in an eight-inch nonreactive skillet over medium heat. Add the onion and gently cook until softened, about 4 minutes. Add the vinegar and cook for 1 minute. Add the chicken stock and simmer until it is reduced by half, about 8 minutes. Add the cream, olives, and garlic purée; continue to simmer until the gravy is thick enough to coat the back of a spoon, 10 to 12 minutes. Season with salt and pepper. Remove from the heat and set aside.

For the coating, whisk together the flour, cornmeal, salt, pepper, paprika, and mustard in a wide shallow bowl. Coat the pieces of chicken thoroughly with the flour mixture, then arrange them on a platter in a single layer. Let stand for 15 minutes.

Heat the oil in a 10-inch cast-iron skillet over medium heat. Gently place the chicken pieces in the hot oil, being careful not to crowd the skillet. (We usually fry about half of the pieces at a time.) Fry the chicken on all sides until it is golden brown, about 25 minutes. Transfer the chicken to a baking sheet or platter and keep warm in the oven until ready to serve.

Just before serving, reheat the gravy over low heat, stirring occasionally. Serve the chicken with the gravy.

SERVES 2 TO 3

Oven-Fried Chicken

In the late 1960's, oven-fried chicken took the country by storm in the form of Shake-'n-Bake. Freed from the messiness of frying oil and batter-covered counters, Shake-'n-Bake moms gave smiling testimonials on TV as they shook their poultry in brown paper bags. We don't use a paper bag in our method, but the herbed bread crumbs and oven baking take us back to that era.

1 chicken, about 3½ pounds

3 cups buttermilk

1½ cups Seasoned Bread Crumbs (page 27)

½ cup grated Dry Jack or Parmesan cheese

1 tablespoon fresh thyme leaves

1 tablespoon finely chopped fresh rosemary

Kosher salt and freshly ground black pepper to taste

Cut the chicken into 8 pieces: 2 breasts, 2 thighs, 2 drumsticks, and 2 wings. Place the chicken in a deep bowl and pour the buttermilk over it. Let stand at room temperature for 30 minutes.

Whisk together the bread crumbs, cheese, thyme, rosemary, salt, and pepper in a wide shallow bowl. Evenly coat the chicken with the bread crumb mixture and place the pieces on a baking sheet. Let stand for 15 minutes.

Meanwhile, preheat the oven to 375°F.

Bake the chicken until the juices run clear when the thigh is pierced with a thin knife, 35 to 40 minutes. Serve hot. **SERVES 2**

Chicken in a Pot

The first time David prepared this dish at home was a blustery early spring day when it had been raining for eleven days straight and the forecast predicted more of the same. I, who had hoped to spend the weekend planting my garden, was confined to the house and feeling grumpy. The comfort of this one-pot dish saved the day, and we now make it whenever we're in need of a mood lifter. We also like to add ingredients as they strike our fancy, such as chicken sausages and green cabbage. Serve it in roomy soup bowls along with Hasty Pudding (page 139) and freshly grated hard dry cheese, such as Dry Jack, Asiago, or Parmesan. —BARBARA

1 chicken, about 3½ pounds

2 tablespoons unsalted butter

2 tablespoons olive oil

2 cups diced yellow onions (½-inch dice)

6 garlic cloves, peeled and minced

3½ cups diced celery (¼-inch dice)

3½ cups peeled and diced carrots (¼-inch dice)

2 fresh bay leaves

2 fresh thyme sprigs

1 cup chicken stock, preferably homemade (page 54)

½ cup dry white wine

3 cups Stewed Tomatoes (page 362) or 1 (28-ounce) can

Kosher salt and freshly ground black pepper to taste

2 tablespoons minced fresh herbs, such as parsley, thyme, and/or chives

Preheat the oven to 300°F.

Cut the chicken into 8 pieces: 2 legs, 2 thighs, 2 breasts, and 2 wings.

Melt the butter with the olive oil in a large Dutch oven over medium heat. Add the onions and garlic and cook until they are softened, about 4 minutes. Add the celery, carrots, bay leaves, and thyme sprigs and cook for 4 to 5 minutes. Add the chicken, stock, wine, and tomatoes and season with salt and pepper.

Cover the Dutch oven and place it in the oven for 1½ hours. The chicken should be falling-off-the-bone tender and there should be a good amount of broth. Remove the bay leaves and thyme sprigs and garnish with the fresh herbs. Serve hot.   SERVES 4

Chicken, Tomato, and Butter Bean Stew

Butter beans are wide flat beans with a creamy, buttery texture. Their large size gives this stew a character we associate with simple home cooking; you can, however, use any fresh white shell bean, such as Great Northern, navy, or cannellini. You could think of this as a variation on the theme of chicken in the pot. It's another one of those infinitely comforting dishes that tastes best when it's eaten from a bowl.

continued

1 chicken, about 3½ pounds

3 tablespoons olive oil

3 cups thinly sliced yellow onions

6 garlic cloves, thinly sliced

2 fresh bay leaves

2 fresh thyme sprigs

3 cups seeded and chopped fresh tomatoes

2 cups water

Kosher salt and freshly ground black pepper to taste

2 cups fresh butter beans

1 cup grated Asiago or Parmesan cheese

3 tablespoons chopped fresh herbs, such as thyme, chives,
  basil, and/or parsley

Cut the chicken into 8 pieces: 2 legs, 2 thighs, 2 breasts, and 2 wings.

Heat the olive oil in a 5-quart soup pot over medium heat. Add the onions and garlic and gently cook until they are softened. Add the bay leaves and thyme, then add the chicken pieces and brown them for 2 to 3 minutes on each side. Reduce the heat to low, add the tomatoes and water, and season with salt and pepper. Cover and simmer for 1 hour.

Add the butter beans and simmer for 30 minutes longer. Remove the bay leaves and thyme sprigs. Divide the chicken among 4 large bowls and ladle the stew over the chicken. Garnish with the grated cheese and the fresh herbs. SERVES 4

Creamy Chicken
and Ham Casserole
with Artichokes

Economy was probably the driving force behind the creation of one-dish meals like this one, since leftovers extended with noodles add up to a practically cost-free dinner. We take it to the table in the casserole and spoon it out onto dinner plates or bowls.

2 tablespoons olive oil

2 tablespoons unsalted butter

1½ cups minced yellow onions

1½ cups minced celery

1 tablespoon minced garlic

⅛ teaspoon ground nutmeg

1 fresh bay leaf

2 tablespoons all-purpose flour

1 cup diced ham (¼-inch dice)

½ cup dry white wine

2 cups whole milk

4 cups shredded cooked chicken

4 cooked large artichoke hearts (see pages 100–101),
*   quartered*

½ cup sour cream

¾ cup grated Parmesan cheese

1 pound pasta, such as rotelle, penne, or rigatoni,
*   cooked and drained*

½ cup Seasoned Bread Crumbs (page 27)

Preheat the oven to 350°F. Lightly butter a 12 x 9 x 2-inch baking dish.

Heat the olive oil and butter in a 6-quart pot over low heat. Add the onions, celery, garlic, nutmeg, and bay leaf and cook until the onions are softened. Add the flour and cook for 2 to 3 minutes. Add the ham and cook for 2 to 3 minutes. Stir in the wine and simmer for 3 minutes, then stir in the milk and simmer, stirring, until the mixture is thickened, 3 to 5 minutes. Add the chicken, artichokes, and sour cream and simmer for 3 minutes. Add the cheese and cooked pasta and mix thoroughly.

Transfer the mixture to the baking dish and top with the bread crumbs. Bake until the sauce is bubbling, about 30 minutes.   SERVES 6

Pesto Grilled Chicken

During the summer, when basil grows faster than the weeds, we use it in every manner imaginable. This herbal "barbecue sauce," a.k.a. pesto, becomes charred and aromatic when it's cooked over a hot fire. Corn on the cob and tomato halves blistered on the grill are perfect accompaniments to this dish.

FOR THE PESTO (MAKES 2 CUPS)
4 cups (tightly packed) fresh basil leaves
2 garlic cloves, minced
¾ cup olive oil
½ cup grated pecorino Romano, Parmesan, or
    Dry Jack cheese
½ cup walnuts or pine nuts
Kosher salt and freshly ground black pepper to taste

1 chicken, about 3½ pounds
Kosher salt and freshly ground black pepper to taste

For the pesto, place the basil and garlic in a food processor or blender and process to a purée. With the machine running, slowly add the olive oil, processing until it is incorporated. Add the cheese and nuts and process to a purée. Season with salt and pepper.

Prepare a charcoal grill.

Meanwhile, cut the chicken into 8 pieces: 2 breasts, 2 thighs, 2 drumsticks, and 2 wings. In a large bowl, toss the chicken pieces with the pesto until evenly coated. Season with salt and pepper. Let marinate at room temperature for 20 minutes.

Grill the chicken over a medium-hot fire, turning occasionally, until the skin is crispy and slightly charred and the juices run clear when the thigh is pierced with a knife, 20 to 25 minutes.   SERVES 2

TURKEY

Roast Turkey

This is the turkey we now make every Thanksgiving. Over the years, we've tried out lots of different methods of roasting the bird, but we think this one, which is cooked at a steady temperature and has lots of herbs and spices rubbed into the surface, is the best yet.

1 fresh turkey, 12 to 14 pounds, neck and giblets removed

1 orange, halved

Kosher salt and freshly ground black pepper

1 onion, halved

1 bulb garlic, halved

2 ribs celery

3 fresh thyme sprigs

2 fresh sage sprigs

2 tablespoons unsalted butter, softened

1 tablespoon dried tarragon

1 tablespoon dried marjoram

1 tablespoon crushed coriander seeds

2 teaspoons kosher salt

6 thick slices bacon

OPTIONAL ACCOMPANIMENTS

Country Stuffing with Ham (recipe follows)

Bourbon-Cranberry Sauce (recipe follows)

Mushroom Gravy (recipe follows)

Preheat the oven to 350°F.

Rub the cavity of the turkey with the orange halves, then season it liberally with salt and pepper. Fill the cavity of the turkey with the orange halves, onion, garlic, celery, thyme, and sage. Rub the turkey all over with the butter.

In a small bowl, combine the tarragon, marjoram, coriander, the 2 teaspoons kosher salt, and 1 teaspoon pepper and rub the mixture all over the turkey.

Place the turkey on a rack in a roasting pan and lay the bacon over the breasts. Place the pan in the oven with the legs of the turkey pointing toward the back of the oven, and roast for 3 to 3½ hours, removing the bacon after 2 hours and turning the pan around every 40 to 50 minutes. The turkey is done when the juices run clear when a knife is inserted into the thickest area of the thigh or a meat thermometer inserted into the thickest part of the thigh reaches 180°F. If the breast becomes too brown, cover it with aluminum foil.

Remove the turkey from the oven and let rest, loosely covered with foil, for 15 to 25 minutes before carving.

Serve with the stuffing, cranberry sauce, and gravy if desired.　　　　　　　　　　　**SERVES 8 TO 10**

❖ COUNTRY STUFFING WITH HAM ❖

Without stuffing, the Thanksgiving meal would be incomplete: no overstuffed bellies and no excuse for ostentatious consumption of gravy. We call this "country" stuffing because of the country ham and apples. If you prefer corn bread stuffing, go ahead and use that instead of bread. Our Sage Corn Bread (page 304) will be a good start; you'll need to make a double recipe of it. We like this with Mushroom Gravy (page 226).

continued

3 tablespoons unsalted butter

2 cups chopped yellow onions

2 cups chopped celery

2 tablespoons minced garlic

1 fresh bay leaf, crushed

3 tart green apples, cored, peeled, and cut into
½-inch dice

½ pound Smithfield ham, cut into ¼-inch dice

3 cups chicken stock, preferably homemade (page 54)

2 large eggs

½ cup heavy cream

2 tablespoons minced fresh sage

3 tablespoons chopped fresh parsley

8 cups cubed crusty bread, toasted (about 1-inch cubes)

Kosher salt and freshly ground black pepper to taste

Preheat the oven to 350°F. Butter a large baking dish.

Melt the butter in a 4-quart saucepan over medium heat. Add the onions, celery, garlic, and bay leaf and gently cook until the vegetables are softened and translucent. Add the apples and ham and cook for 1 minute. Remove from the heat.

Whisk together the chicken stock, eggs, cream, sage, and parsley in a large bowl. Add the bread and gently toss to coat it evenly. Add the sautéed vegetables and toss to combine. Season with salt and pepper.

Transfer the stuffing to the baking dish. Cover and bake for 35 to 40 minutes. Remove the cover and bake uncovered for 15 to 20 minutes longer.   SERVES 8

❖ BOURBON-CRANBERRY SAUCE ❖

Most people, we find, politely avoid Thanksgiving's super-sweet and bitter cranberry sauce. But not this one. It's nicely tart, it's not overly sweet, and the bourbon provides a satisfying mellowness and zing.

¼ cup dry white wine

¼ cup water

¼ cup granulated sugar

2 tablespoons bourbon

1 tablespoon molasses

1 (12-ounce) bag fresh cranberries, rinsed and drained

Grated zest and juice of 1 lime

Grated zest and juice of 1 orange

Place the wine, water, sugar, bourbon, and molasses in a 4-quart saucepan and cook over medium heat, stirring occasionally, until the sugar dissolves. Add the cranberries and citrus zest and juice, then simmer until all the cranberries pop, about 15 minutes. Cool for at least 1 hour before serving.   MAKES 3 CUPS

GRANDPA SHINN (IN APRON) AND LONGTIME FRIEND, MR. CHRISTENSEN, A THANKSGIVING DINNER, 1946

birds

*This gravy is rich and earthy, with a strong mushroom flavor.
Don't wait for Thanksgiving to serve it: Use it with Simply
Roasted Chicken (page 211) or Turkey Meatloaf (page 227).*

3 tablespoons unsalted butter

½ cup minced onion

2 teaspoons minced garlic

½ cup stemmed and diced fresh shiitake mushrooms

½ cup diced fresh portobello mushrooms

6 tablespoons all-purpose flour

½ fresh bay leaf

2 fresh thyme sprigs

¼ cup dry red wine

2 teaspoons sherry wine vinegar

6 cups chicken stock, preferably homemade (page 54)

1 cup heavy cream

2 tablespoons dry sherry

2 tablespoons minced fresh chives

2 tablespoons chopped fresh parsley

Kosher salt and freshly ground black pepper to taste

Melt 1 tablespoon of the butter in a 3-quart saucepan over
medium-low heat. Add the onion and garlic and cook
until softened, about 4 minutes. Add the mushrooms and
cook for 3 to 5 minutes. Sprinkle the flour over the mushrooms and cook for 2 minutes. Add the bay leaf and thyme
and deglaze the pan with the red wine and sherry vinegar.

Add the chicken stock and simmer until the gravy is
reduced by one third. Add the cream and reduce until
thick enough to coat the back of a spoon. Reduce the heat
to low and whisk in the remaining 2 tablespoons butter
and the sherry. Add the chives and parsley and season
with salt and pepper. Serve hot.   **MAKES 4 CUPS**

Turkey Meatloaf

Rich, moist, and well-seasoned, this meatloaf is best made with freshly ground turkey breast, ensuring that you're getting quality turkey meat. Order it from your butcher a few days before you'll need it so you can be sure he will have it. If you wish, you can substitute turkey bacon for the regular bacon.

2½ cups diced bacon (¼-inch dice) (about ½ pound)

2½ cups diced onions (⅛-inch dice)

2 tablespoons minced garlic

3½ pounds ground turkey

1½ cups plus 2 tablespoons Seasoned Bread Crumbs
  (page 27)

1 cup Famous Tomato Ketchup (page 11)

½ cup whole-grain mustard

¼ cup Tabasco sauce

¼ cup minced scallions

¼ cup minced fresh herbs, such as parsley, thyme, chives,
  and/or sage

2 tablespoons Home Spice Mix (page 26)

2 large eggs, beaten

Preheat the oven to 350°F. Grease an 18 x 12-inch baking sheet.

Heat a 10-inch cast-iron skillet over medium heat. Add the bacon and cook until it has rendered most of its fat, about 2 minutes. Carefully drain off the fat from the pan. Add the onions and garlic and cook until they are softened and translucent, about 4 minutes. Transfer the bacon, onions, and garlic to a large bowl and let cool.

Add the ground turkey, 1½ cups of the bread crumbs, ½ cup of the ketchup, the mustard, hot sauce, scallions, herbs, spice mix, and eggs to the bacon mixture; mix well.

continued

birds

Form the mixture into an oblong loaf about 15 inches long and 4 inches high on the prepared baking sheet, making sure to pack the mixture tightly to avoid air pockets. Spread the remaining ¼ cup ketchup on top of the loaf and sprinkle with the remaining 2 tablespoons bread crumbs.

Cover tightly with aluminum foil and bake for 1 hour. Uncover and continue baking for 30 minutes longer, or until cooked through.   SERVES 6

JOSEPHINE DROVER, SISTER-IN-LAW ELEANOR,
AND BEST FRIEND DOROTHY,
HUNTING ON THE DROVER FARM, 1965

QUAIL AND DUCK

Grilled Quail with Orange, Ginger, and Marjoram

Like most Americans, we have the same Thanksgiving menu every year. We call ours a "little bird, big bird" party because after a first course of Potted Duck (page 232), olives, a selection of American-made cheeses, and a plate of David's home-cured salami (page 277), we serve these tiny quail before we go on to the turkey. Although small, quail has a big flavor; it's all dark meat.

8 quail

2 tablespoons olive oil

1 tablespoon chopped fresh marjoram

2 teaspoons honey

1 teaspoon minced ginger

1 teaspoon minced garlic

1 teaspoon crushed juniper berries

1 fresh bay leaf, crushed

Grated zest and juice of 1 orange

Kosher salt and freshly ground black pepper

Using poultry shears, cut out the backbone from each quail. Carefully remove the breastbone and wishbone. Open them out so that they lie flat.

Whisk together all of the remaining ingredients except the salt and pepper in a wide shallow bowl. Add the quail and turn them to coat. Cover the bowl with plastic wrap and let stand at room temperature for 1 hour or as long as overnight in the refrigerator. (If refrigerated, allow quail to come to room temperature.)

continued

birds

Season the quail on both sides with salt and pepper. Lightly oil a large cast-iron grill pan and place over medium-high heat. When the pan is hot, add 4 of the quail and cook 3 to 4 minutes on each side, turning once, until medium-rare to medium. Transfer to a platter and set aside in a warm place. Repeat with the remaining 4 quail. Allow the quail to rest for 5 to 7 minutes, then serve warm or at room temperature. **SERVES 8**

Smoked Duck Breasts

No longer needed as the preserving agent it once was, smoking is now used for the wonderful flavor it imparts.

4 boneless, skinless duck breasts, about 6 ounces each

FOR THE CURE

1½ cups kosher salt

½ cup granulated sugar

Grated zest of 1 orange

1 fresh bay leaf, crushed

4 fresh thyme sprigs

1 tablespoon cracked black peppercorns

2 tablespoons coriander seeds

FOR THE GLAZE

¾ cup orange juice

½ cup pure maple syrup

2 tablespoons honey

2 tablespoons (packed) dark brown sugar

2 teaspoons kosher salt

1 teaspoon ground ginger

1 teaspoon ground coriander seeds

Place the duck breasts in a wide shallow bowl. Combine the ingredients for the cure in a small bowl and pour over the duck, turning the duck to coat it with the cure. Cover the bowl with plastic wrap and refrigerate for 24 hours.

For the glaze, stir together all the ingredients in a 2-quart saucepan over low heat and cook until it is reduced to a thick syrup, 20 to 25 minutes. Remove from the heat and let cool for about 30 minutes. Transfer the glaze to a medium bowl.

Prepare a hot smoker with cherry wood chips.

Remove the duck from the refrigerator and wipe it clean of the curing mix. Toss the duck breasts with the glaze until they are well coated. Smoke the duck breasts until they are medium-rare. Remove the duck from the smoker and let cool.

To serve, thinly slice the breasts crosswise and place them atop a crisp salad.   SERVES 4

to smoke your own meats If you have a covered kettle grill, you can make your own hot-smoked meats. Soak 1 cup wood chips in water for 1 hour. Wrap the chips in a sheet of aluminum foil and pierce several holes in the top. Build a fire in the grill. Once it is hot, lay the foil package over the coals with the pierced side up. Place the grate on the grill and lay the meat or fish on the grate. Cover the grill, open the vents slightly to maintain the desired temperature, and cook until done. Meat or fish usually cooked quickly are smoked at a higher temperature for a short time. Those usually brined, or cured, and cooked longer are smoked at a lower temperature for a longer period. Experiment.

Potted Duck

David's grandmother cured meat and game in the barrels that his grandfather used to age bootleg whiskey. That gave them a special something that we haven't been able to match. Nonetheless, we're proud of this duck spread that we serve with salami and pickles as part of our Thanksgiving bird-tasting menu.

FOR THE CURE

¾ cup kosher salt

2 tablespoons granulated sugar

¾ teaspoon crushed juniper berries

½ teaspoon crushed black peppercorns

⅛ teaspoon ground allspice

⅛ teaspoon minced fresh thyme

1 fresh bay leaf, crushed

FOR COOKING THE DUCK

4 pounds duck fat (see Note)

12 garlic cloves

for potting the duck

2 tablespoons unsalted butter, softened

2 tablespoons extra virgin olive oil

2 teaspoons fresh thyme leaves

1 teaspoon grated lemon zest

1 teaspoon grated orange zest

1 teaspoon minced garlic

1 teaspoon minced ginger

1 teaspoon toasted and ground coriander seeds

½ teaspoon cayenne pepper

Kosher salt to taste

Cut the duck into 8 pieces: 2 breasts, 2 thighs, 2 drumsticks, and 2 wings. Trim the excess fat from the pieces and set the fat aside for later use. Place the duck in a wide shallow bowl.

Stir together the ingredients for the cure in a small bowl and pour the mixture over the duck, turning to coat completely. Cover the bowl with plastic wrap and refrigerate for 24 hours.

Place the duck fat in a heavy ovenproof 8-quart pot over low heat and render the fat, about 1 hour.

Meanwhile, preheat the oven to 225°F. Remove the duck from the refrigerator, wipe the curing mix off the pieces, and dry them with a towel.

Add the garlic and the duck parts to the fat, transfer to the oven, and bake until the duck is cooked through, 1½ to 2 hours. Remove the duck from the fat and let cool to room temperature, about 30 minutes. Strain the fat through a fine-mesh strainer and reserve 2 tablespoons of it.

At this point, the fat can be poured over the duck pieces and the pieces stored in the refrigerator for another use. Otherwise, strip the duck meat from the bone and shred it into small pieces.

Place all of the remaining ingredients except the duck in the bowl of a heavy-duty mixer and beat them together using the paddle attachment. Gradually incorporate the duck. Transfer to a container, cover, and refrigerate for at least 1 hour. The potted duck can be stored in the refrigerator for up to 2 weeks.　　**MAKES 6 CUPS**

NOTE: Large quantities of duck fat such as that called for here are available from D'Artagnan, which ships nationwide. Visit its Web site at www.ippi.com/dartagnan or call 1-800-DARTAGN.

LEE SHINN, 1957

The barbecue Heat is the essence of barbecue. Use

any hardwood charcoal that is available. Avoid briquettes,

composed of materials that impart unwanted flavors to

grilled foods. A fire made from hardwood charcoal heats

longer and more evenly than one made from briquettes.

For these reasons, do not use pine, fir, or cedar wood.

Have your grate searing hot when you place food on it

or the food will stick. A "hot fire" is one that you can hold

your hand over for no more than 2 to 3 seconds. Let it

burn for about 5 minutes and then knock it down, so that

only hot embers, not flames, are in the grill.

Grilled Duck Breasts with Lavender, Honey, and Merlot Glaze

This is a pretty fancy recipe, but we love the caramelization the hot grill gives to the marinated meat. We serve it with Wild Rice, Barley, and Blackberry Salad (page 136).

FOR THE DUCK

6 boneless, skinless duck breasts, about 6 ounces each

¼ cup olive oil

1 tablespoon honey

1 tablespoon minced shallots

2 teaspoons minced fresh lavender

1 teaspoon cracked black peppercorns

1 teaspoon cracked yellow mustard seeds

1 teaspoon cracked coriander seeds

FOR THE GLAZE

1¾ cups merlot wine

½ cup honey

2 tablespoons minced shallots

2 teaspoons minced fresh lavender

Kosher salt and freshly ground black pepper to taste

Place the duck breasts in a wide shallow bowl. Whisk together the olive oil, honey, shallots, lavender, peppercorns, mustard seeds, and coriander in a small bowl. Pour the marinade over the duck breasts and gently turn them to coat. Cover the bowl with plastic wrap and let marinate at room temperature for 1 hour or in the refrigerator overnight.

continued

Meanwhile, for the glaze, simmer the wine, honey, shallots, and lavender in a 2-quart nonreactive saucepan over low heat until the liquid is reduced by two thirds. The glaze will be quite thick. Season with salt and pepper. Strain through a fine-mesh strainer and let cool.

Prepare a charcoal grill.

Grill the duck breasts over medium-hot coals for 3 to 5 minutes on each side. Transfer the duck to a cutting board, cover with foil, and rest for 5 minutes. Slice the duck across the grain into ⅛-inch-thick slices and serve, drizzled with the glaze. **SERVES 6**

merlot When we eat duck, which is quite often, we drink merlot. It's a matter of place, since both are Long Island products. Merlot is the predominant red wine grape in local vineyards, including Shinn Vineyard, our own twenty-two acre, newly planted vineyard. This glaze also works well with many lamb dishes, especially roast leg of lamb.

Grilled Duck Breast Salad with Apricot Mustard

We buy duck breasts from a farm on the North Fork. We like to use them in barbecue season, when we sometimes take advantage of the fact that the fire is already lit for steaks or fish and start the meal with a grilled salad.

3 boneless, skinless duck breasts, about 6 ounces each

3 tablespoons olive oil

1 tablespoon minced shallots

1 tablespoon fresh thyme leaves

Kosher salt and freshly ground black pepper to taste

¼ pound young salad greens

¼ cup Mustard-Thyme Dressing (page 83)

2 tablespoons Apricot Mustard (page 10)

Place the duck breasts in a wide shallow bowl. Whisk together the olive oil, shallots, and thyme in a small bowl and season with salt and pepper. Pour the marinade over the duck breasts and gently turn them to coat. Cover the bowl with plastic wrap and let marinate at room temperature for 1 hour or in the refrigerator overnight.

Prepare a charcoal grill.

Grill the duck over medium-hot coals for 3 to 5 minutes on each side for medium-rare. Transfer the duck to a cutting board, cover with foil, and let rest for 5 minutes. Slice the duck across the grain into ⅛-inch-thick slices.

Toss the salad greens with the dressing and divide the salad among 6 plates. Arrange the still-warm slices of duck on the salad. Drizzle the duck with the apricot mustard, and serve. SERVES 6

long island duckling Long Island was once the home to several duck farms, making Long Island duckling, a white-feathered descendant of Peking duck, popular among regional chefs. There are only two farms on the island now, but "Long Island ducklings" are also raised in other states, so they're readily available.

MEAT

MEAT

Roast meats were a fixture of our childhoods. We remember roast beef, big hams, legs of lamb, and pot roast simmered in beer and tomato paste. People say that we're eating less meat these days, and while some might think it's for health reasons, we think it's because the meat that's being raised now has little fat and less taste. We have a hard time with the lean and leaner thing: It's really depressing to sit down in front of a steak and find it has no flavor at all, that it tastes like cardboard. Eat meat less often if you want, but when you do eat it, cuts that are well marbled with streaks of flavorful fat will taste really good.

BEEF

We might have had to serve beef even if we didn't love it, because Home has had a long, long relationship with the tiny Florence Meat Market around the corner, which is famous for its Newport steak. This cut, invented by Jack Ubaldi, who opened Florence in 1936, was a favorite of New York's former mayor Ed Koch and is on our menu. A delicious triangular piece of meat cut from the sirloin butt, prime Newport can be difficult to obtain. Although we don't include a recipe here, if you can find it, you can prepare Newport as you would T-bone, hanger, or flank steak.

Beef Stew with Red Wine

We once had a verbal contest with a French chef. He said, "Pâté," and we countered, "Meatloaf." He said, "Pot au feu," and we said, "New England boiled dinner." He snorted, "boeuf bourguignonne"; we retorted, "Beef stew with red wine."

You can buy stew meat at the supermarket, but you'll find there's a lot of gristle and waste you'll have to trim off. We like to buy a chuck roast and cut it into 2-inch cubes ourselves.

1 cup all-purpose flour

2¾ pounds beef chuck, cut into 2-inch cubes

Kosher salt and freshly ground black pepper to taste

3 ounces fatback or salt pork, cut into ⅛-inch dice

5 ribs celery, 2 cut into ⅛-inch dice, 3 cut into
   2-inch lengths

4 medium carrots, peeled, 1 cut into ⅛-inch dice,
   3 cut into 2-inch lengths

1 medium onion, cut into ⅛-inch dice

10 garlic cloves, peeled

2 fresh bay leaves

1 (750-milliliter) bottle dry red wine

2 tablespoons tomato paste

Kosher salt and freshly ground black pepper to taste

6 small white potatoes, quartered

Chopped fresh parsley, for garnish

Place the flour in a wide shallow bowl. Season the beef with salt and pepper, then lightly coat the pieces with the flour.

Cook the pork fat in a large heavy pot over medium heat until it renders its fat. Brown the beef on all sides in the rendered fat, about 5 minutes. Remove the beef and set aside.

Add the diced celery and carrot, the onion, and garlic to the pot and slowly cook until softened, about 4 minutes. Add the bay leaves, red wine, and tomato paste and stir to dissolve the tomato paste. Add the beef chunks, season with salt and pepper, cover the pot, and simmer over low heat until the meat is fork-tender, 2½ to 3 hours.

Add the potatoes and the remaining carrots and celery and continue to simmer until they are just cooked, 25 to 30 minutes longer. Serve in wide bowls and garnish with fresh parsley.   SERVES 4

Standing Rib Roast

This makes a munificent meal served with freshly grated horseradish, Mom Page's Scalloped Potatoes (page 127), and Braised Broccoli Rabe (page 104).

1 (4-rib) standing rib roast, 6 to 8 pounds
Kosher salt and freshly ground black pepper to taste
3 tablespoons olive oil
4 tablespoons coarsely chopped fresh herbs, such as
    rosemary, thyme, or chives

Preheat the oven to 275°F.

Liberally sprinkle the roast with salt and pepper. Rub the meat with the olive oil and sprinkle on the herbs to coat. Place it rib side down on a roasting rack in a roasting pan. Roast for about 1½ hours to an internal temperature of 115°F for rare, 120°F for medium-rare, 130°F for medium, or 145°F for well done.

When the roast is done, transfer it to a cutting board, cover with aluminum foil, and let rest for 20 minutes before carving.   SERVES 4

carving the roast Roasting meat with the bone in enhances its flavor and succulence, but it can make carving tricky. Ask the butcher to remove the rib bones and then tie them back in place. Just cut the twine and remove them before you carve; the caveman in the group can gnaw at the bones.

A primer on Roasting

There are three popular roasting methods. One employs high heat—up to 500°F—from beginning to end: a 16-pound turkey takes only 2 hours. However, it's best for small cuts of meat, small birds, fish, and vegetables.

The second method uses high heat for the initial searing and then a much lower temperature to finish. It's effective for medium-size roasts and poultry.

A third uses long cooking times at low heat, as low as 275°F. We like this method for standing rib roasts, where we want melting tenderness. This method allows some margin for error, a comfort for less-experienced cooks.

My mother taught me how to make pot roast when I was a young boy. She made it once a week, and it was clear that she enjoyed the fact that once it was assembled in midafternoon, she could forget about it for several hours and go about her day. This recipe isn't exactly the same as hers, but whenever we make it, we think of her and the warmth and comfort of her kitchen. If you can't get boneless short ribs, have the butcher suggest another cut; we've successfully substituted brisket and round steak. —DAVID

Mom Page's Pot Roast
of Beef Short Ribs

½ cup all-purpose flour

2 pounds boneless beef short ribs, cut into 3-inch pieces

Kosher salt and freshly ground pepper to taste

¼ cup diced salt pork (½-inch dice)

4 garlic cloves, peeled

1 fresh thyme sprig

2 fresh bay leaves

2 tablespoons malt vinegar

1 cup chicken stock, preferably homemade (page 54)

1 cup dark beer

3 large wedges green cabbage

3 small parsnips, peeled and quartered

2 small russet potatoes, quartered

2 medium carrots, peeled and quartered

2 ribs celery, cut into 3-inch lengths

1 medium yellow onion, quartered

1 medium turnip, peeled and cut into 6 pieces

1 teaspoon yellow mustard seeds

2 tablespoons chopped fresh dill

Preheat the oven to 300°F. Place the flour in a wide shallow bowl. Season the short ribs with salt and pepper and lightly coat them with the flour.

Heat a Dutch oven over medium heat for 1 minute. Add the salt pork and render, 4 to 5 minutes. Add the short ribs and brown on both sides, 4 to 5 minutes. Add the garlic, thyme, and bay leaves, then deglaze with vinegar, stock, and beer.

Add the vegetables along with the mustard seeds and season with salt and pepper. Cover and bake for about 2 hours; the meat should be fork-tender. Serve in large bowls, garnished with the chopped dill. SERVES 4

Grilled Hanger Steak with Our Own Worcestershire Sauce

Hanger steak is a long narrow piece of beef that "hangs" from the hind end of the short loin. Rich and succulent, it has an intense beef flavor and is best cooked rare or medium-rare. If you can't find hanger steaks—not all butchers carry them—skirt or flank steak makes a fine substitute for this dish.

The sauce is quick and simple to prepare, once you've assembled the ingredients. It will keep, tightly covered, in the refrigerator for several months.

6 hanger steaks, 6 to 8 ounces each

¼ cup olive oil

3 tablespoons soy sauce

2 tablespoons minced fresh herbs, such as parsley, rosemary, and/or tarragon

1 tablespoon minced garlic

1 teaspoon cracked yellow mustard seeds

1 teaspoon cracked black peppercorns

½ teaspoon red pepper flakes

Homemade Worcestershire Sauce (recipe follows)

Place the hanger steaks in a large shallow bowl. Whisk together the olive oil, soy sauce, herbs, garlic, mustard seeds, peppercorns, and pepper flakes in a small bowl. Pour the marinade over the steaks and turn to coat. Cover the bowl with plastic wrap and let marinate at room temperature for 1 hour or in the refrigerator overnight.

Prepare a charcoal grill.

Grill the steaks over hot coals for 4 to 6 minutes on each side for medium-rare. Transfer the steaks to a cutting board, cover with foil, and let rest for 5 minutes before slicing. Serve with the sauce.   SERVES 6

HOMEMADE
❖ WORCESTERSHIRE SAUCE ❖

2 cups apple cider vinegar

¼ cup molasses

¼ cup dark corn syrup

1 tablespoon soy sauce

⅓ cup minced shallots

2 tablespoons minced fresh tarragon

1 anchovy, minced

1½ teaspoons minced garlic

1½ teaspoons tamarind paste

½ teaspoon freshly ground black pepper

¼ teaspoon red pepper flakes

Combine all the ingredients in a 4-quart saucepan over medium heat and bring to a boil. Reduce the heat and simmer the sauce uncovered for 20 minutes. Let cool.

Purée the sauce in a food processor or blender, then strain it through a fine-mesh strainer.   MAKES 3 CUPS

MY TWO BROTHERS AND COUSIN AT
THE KIDS' TABLE (THAT'S ME ON THE LEFT), 1964

Once my older siblings had moved out, my father decided he could afford to have steak every Saturday night. He always made T-bones on the grill, setting mine to the side so it would be rare. I'd douse it with Thousand Island dressing and mash copious amounts of butter into a huge Idaho potato.

One of the most popular and recognizable steak cuts in America, the T-bone consists of a strip steak and a small piece of tenderloin connected by a T-shaped bone.

—BARBARA

Dad Shinn's
Grilled T-Bone Steak with Red Onions and Basil

1 T-bone steak, preferably prime, about 1½ pounds
   and 2 inches thick
2 medium red onions, cut crosswise into
   ½-inch-thick slices
3 tablespoons olive oil
2 cloves garlic, thinly sliced
6 large fresh basil leaves, chopped
2 tablespoons balsamic vinegar
Kosher salt and freshly ground black pepper to taste

Place the steak and red onion slices in a large shallow bowl. Whisk together the olive oil, garlic, basil, and vinegar in a small bowl. Coat the steak and onions with the marinade, keeping the onion slices intact. Cover with plastic wrap and let marinate at room temperature for 20 minutes or up to 2 hours, or in the refrigerator overnight.

Prepare a charcoal grill.

Season the steak and onions with salt and pepper. Grill the steak for 5 to 6 minutes on each side for rare, 8 to 10 minutes on each side for medium-rare. Meanwhile, carefully grill the onions until charred, about 2 minutes on each side. Transfer the steak to a cutting board, cover with foil, and let rest for 5 to 6 minutes before slicing. Serve the steak with the onions.   SERVES 2

Grilled Marinated
Flank Steak

The original London broil, flank steak is a thin, flat, nearly fat-free cut of meat that comes from the underside of the cow. With its excellent flavor and chewy—some say tough—texture, it makes a fine meal that will not be tough as long as it's quickly cooked and sliced thin across the grain. We like to marinate flank steak with a thick rub of spices and herbs, which adds a wonderful layer of flavor, and serve it with Roasted Mushrooms (page 110) and Roasted Beets (page 103).

1 flank steak, about 1½ pounds, trimmed

3 tablespoons dry white wine

1½ tablespoons olive oil

2 tablespoons mild paprika

1 tablespoon cracked black peppercorns

1 tablespoon minced garlic

1 tablespoon minced shallots

1 tablespoon minced ginger

1 tablespoon minced serrano or jalapeño chiles

2 teaspoons minced scallions

1½ teaspoons minced fresh thyme

1½ teaspoons minced fresh marjoram

Kosher salt and freshly ground black pepper to taste

Place the flank steak in a large shallow bowl. Whisk together the wine, olive oil, paprika, peppercorns, garlic, shallots, ginger, chiles, scallions, and herbs in a small bowl. Rub the paste all over the flank steak. Cover with plastic wrap and let marinate in the refrigerator for at least 4 hours or up to 24 hours.

Prepare a charcoal grill.

Lightly oil the grill rack. Season both sides of the marinated steak with salt and pepper. Grill it over hot coals for about 5 minutes each side for medium-rare. Transfer the steak to a cutting board, cover with foil, and let rest for 5 minutes. Thinly slice the steak across the grain.

SERVES 4

PORK

Really good pork is hard to find these days, and again we're talking about absence of fat. There's some movement among growers to raise fatter hogs, but it's a tiny percentage, which is why you're seeing lots of recipes for brining, as cooks try to get some flavor back into the meat they are preparing.

Lately we've gotten good pork from Faicco's Pork Store, right in our neighborhood. Greenwich Village feels more and more like the small towns we grew up in, where we knew everyone and they all knew us.

Pork Tenderloin with Home Barbecue Sauce

Pork tenderloins used to come attached to bone-in loin roasts, but in recent years, they've been sold alone, and have become popular for their small size and waste-free lean meat. They're cooked whole in this recipe, but other times we cut them into cubes for kebabs or strips for stir-fries, or slice and pound them flat to stand in for more-expensive veal cutlets. When we're in the mood for barbecue but it's midwinter, we simply use a skillet on the stovetop.

3 tablespoons olive oil

4 pork tenderloins, about 6 ounces each

¾ cup chicken stock, preferably homemade (page 54)

4 fresh rosemary sprigs

1 cup Home Barbecue Sauce (page 13)

Kosher salt and freshly ground black pepper to taste

Heat the olive oil in a 10-inch cast-iron skillet over medium heat. Place the tenderloins in the skillet and sear them on all sides for 2 to 3 minutes. Add the chicken stock and rosemary and simmer uncovered for 4 to 6 minutes. Stir in the barbecue sauce and salt and pepper and simmer for 4 to 6 minutes longer.

Slice the tenderloins into 1-inch-thick slices and serve with the warm sauce.   SERVES 4

Spiced Pork Chops

A customer at Home once quipped that if you looked up the word "indulgence" in the dictionary, the definition would be "Home's spiced pork chops." The fact that we serve these chops with Artichoke Mashed Potatoes (page 119) makes them doubly indulgent.

The most tender and succulent pork chops are center-cut rib and loin chops. Because they have a portion of tenderloin, you can think of them as the pig's version of T-bone or porterhouse steak.

continued

4 double-thick pork chops, 12 to 14 ounces each,
  1½ inches thick
½ cup Home Spice Mix (page 26)
Kosher salt and freshly ground black pepper to taste
¼ cup olive oil

Preheat the oven to 400°F.

Place the pork chops in a wide shallow bowl and generously coat them on all sides with the spice mix. Season them with salt and pepper.

Heat the olive oil in a 10-inch cast-iron ovenproof or stainless-steel skillet over medium heat. Add the pork chops and brown on both sides until the spices turn golden brown, about 1 minute per side. Carefully pour off the oil in the skillet.

Place the skillet in the oven and bake the chops until cooked through, 25 to 30 minutes. Every 8 to 10 minutes, remove the skillet from the oven, carefully pour off the accumulated fat, and turn the chops over. When the chops are cooked, transfer them to a large plate and let stand for 5 to 10 minutes before serving.   SERVES 4

Pulled Pork Shoulder

We love pork shoulder. During one of our drives through the South, we happened upon a Sunday-morning all-you-can-eat buffet that offered fried chicken, ham, collard greens, yams, biscuits, and most important, a huge side of pork. As other guests helped themselves to piles of fried chicken, we dug into the pork and pulled. The meat was fall-off-the-bone tender. We spent a good part of the morning there, going back for seconds and thirds. It wasn't long before we were having pork pulls at home.

Because of the girth of half a pig, we cook the more manageable shoulder instead. We set the whole shoulder in the center of the table and invite friends over to pull along with us.

1 cup apple cider vinegar

3 tablespoons minced shallots

2 tablespoons crushed yellow mustard seeds

2 tablespoons freshly ground black pepper

2 tablespoons cayenne pepper

2 tablespoons minced fresh sage

1 tablespoon minced garlic

1 bone-in pork shoulder, 4 to 5 pounds

Preheat the oven to 300°F.

Whisk together the vinegar, shallots, mustard seeds, black pepper, cayenne, sage, and garlic. Rub the mixture into the pork, coating it evenly with the mixture.

Place the pork in a large roasting pan and cover with a tight-fitting lid or aluminum foil. Cook until the meat is very tender, about 6 hours.   **SERVES 4 TO 6**

Roasted Fresh Ham

Fresh hams are legs of pork that haven't been brined, cured, or smoked. Although they're not often found in the market today, they make excellent roasts, and they are a good value too. For a hearty late-autumn meal, serve this roast with Red Cabbage and Apples (page 105) and Quick White Beans (page 156).

continued

1 small bone-in fresh ham, 8 to 12 pounds

½ cup olive oil

3 tablespoons apple cider vinegar

2 tablespoons minced garlic

2 tablespoons minced fresh sage leaves

2 tablespoons mild paprika

2 tablespoons ground yellow mustard seeds

Kosher salt and freshly ground black pepper to taste

Preheat the oven to 325°F.

Place the ham on a work surface. Carefully slide a thin knife under the skin and remove it in one piece. Whisk together the olive oil, vinegar, garlic, sage, paprika, and mustard seeds in a small bowl. Season the ham with salt and pepper, then rub it evenly with the paste. Replace the skin and tie it securely to the ham using butcher's twine. With a sharp knife, score the skin with diagonal cuts.

Place the ham on a roasting rack in a roasting pan and roast for 30 minutes per pound. Transfer the roast to a cutting board, cover it with aluminum foil, and let rest for 20 minutes before carving.

Remove the twine. As you carve the meat, the crisp crackling skin will fall away and can be served along with the slices of ham.　　**SERVES 8 TO 10**

Pork Roast with Sweet Onions, Cabbage, and Lime

The vegetables stew along with the meat, in this perfect autumn dish. When we carve the roast, we like thick slices, about 1½ inches, and we serve the stewed cabbage alongside. It is also delicious with Hasty Pudding (page 139).

3 tablespoons olive oil

2 tablespoons unsalted butter

3 large garlic cloves, thinly sliced

1 large Vidalia onion, thinly sliced

5 small leeks, chopped

Kosher salt and freshly ground black pepper to taste

5 large stuffing mushrooms, quartered

1 small savoy cabbage, cored and sliced into
    1-inch squares

3 medium tomatoes, peeled, seeded,
    and coarsely chopped

3 tablespoons chopped fresh oregano

1 boneless pork roast, 3 pounds, tied

Juice of 2 limes

2 tablespoons chopped fresh chives

Preheat the oven to 425°F.

Heat 2 tablespoons of the olive oil and the butter in a large ovenproof skillet over medium-low heat. Add the garlic, onion slices, and leeks, season with salt and pepper, and cook until they begin to soften, about 3 minutes. Add the mushrooms and allow them to brown. Add the cabbage and cook about 5 minutes longer. Add the tomatoes and 1 tablespoon of the oregano. Cover the skillet and cook for 20 minutes.

Meanwhile, heat the remaining olive oil in a medium skillet over medium-high heat. Season the pork with salt and pepper and place it in the hot skillet. Brown evenly on all sides, turning the pork every 3 minutes.

Transfer the roast to the skillet of vegetables, add the lime juice, cover, and place in the oven. Cook until the roast is cooked through, about 40 minutes. Allow the roast to rest for 7 to 8 minutes before carving. Serve it with the vegetables and garnish it with the remaining oregano and the chives.   SERVES 4

GRANDMOTHER McCALL, SUMMER 1950.
WE HAVE HER CAST-IRON SKILLET NOW.

In my memory, Grandmother McCall was always in the kitchen. For forty years, she rented an upstairs apartment in Margate City, New Jersey, where, in a kitchen that was about eight feet wide, she managed to cook meals that ordinary cooks couldn't do in deluxe kitchens three times as big.

When my sister Lee married, "Mema" passed on her recipe for spaghetti and meatballs. Since then we've all made it, its classic combination of beef, pork, and veal imparting richness to the simple tomato sauce. —BARBARA

Grandmother McCall's Tomato Sauce with Meatballs and Sausages

FOR THE SAUCE

8 pounds fresh tomatoes

12 ounces tomato paste

2 tablespoons salt

1 tablespoon sugar

1½ teaspoons freshly ground black pepper

1½ teaspoons dried oregano

1½ teaspoons Worcestershire sauce

½ teaspoon red pepper flakes

⅛ teaspoon ground allspice

Pinch of ground cloves

1 fresh bay leaf

FOR THE MEATBALLS

½ pound ground beef

2 ounces ground pork

2 ounces ground veal

¼ cup dried bread crumbs

1 large egg, beaten

2 tablespoons finely chopped onion

1 tablespoon chopped fresh parsley

1 tablespoon grated hard cheese, such as pecorino Romano
or Parmesan

1½ teaspoons minced garlic

1½ teaspoons kosher salt

¼ teaspoon freshly ground black pepper

continued

2 ounces salt pork, cut into 1-inch dice

1 tablespoon olive oil

1 large onion, cut into ½-inch dice

½ teaspoon minced garlic

½ pound sweet Italian sausage links (about 6 sausages)

For the sauce, core the tomatoes. If you have a food processor, quarter the tomatoes and purée them. If not, finely chop the tomatoes. Push the tomatoes, in batches, through a strainer to remove the seeds and skins.

Combine the strained tomatoes in a large pan with the rest of the ingredients for the sauce. Bring to a boil. Reduce the heat and gently cook uncovered for 2 hours.

For the meatballs, combine the beef, pork, and veal in a large bowl. In a small bowl, moisten the bread crumbs with the egg. Add the mixture to the meat along with the remaining ingredients. Combine well, being careful not to overwork the meat. Shape the mixture into 2-inch meatballs.

In a large skillet, brown the salt pork in the olive oil over medium-high heat. Add the onions and garlic and cook for 1 minute. Add the sausages and cook until they are browned on all sides. Remove the onions and sausages, and set aside. Carefully place the meatballs in the skillet and brown on all sides. Remove and set aside until you are ready to add them to the sauce.

Cut the cooled sausages in half. Add the sausages, meatballs, and onions to the sauce and continue to cook for 1 hour more. Serve over cooked spaghetti. SERVES 8

LAMB

Why don't Americans eat more lamb? David's mother told him she has cooked leg of lamb just once in her life, and he has a niece who's never tasted lamb, not even chops. We serve lamb in stews, as steaks cut from the leg, and, now and then, as a big stuffed shoulder of lamb or even butterflied on the grill.

Roast Rack of Lamb with Honey and Mint

The rack is the whole rib section of the lamb, before it's cut apart into individual chops. A rack usually weighs around one and a half to two pounds, has seven or eight chops, and feeds two to three people. Because racks of lamb are small, timing is crucial. Be sure to allow this meat to sit at room temperature for fifteen minutes before it goes in the oven.

1 (8-rib) rack of lamb, trimmed, about 1½ pounds
¼ cup extra virgin olive oil
2 tablespoons balsamic vinegar
2 teaspoons honey
2 teaspoons minced fresh mint
1 teaspoon cracked black peppercorns
Kosher salt to taste

continued

Place the lamb in a wide deep bowl. Whisk together the oil, vinegar, honey, mint, and peppercorns in a small bowl. Pour the marinade over the lamb and let marinate in the refrigerator for 4 hours. Let the lamb sit at room temperature for 15 minutes before roasting.

Preheat the oven to 375°F.

Season the lamb with salt. Place it in a roasting pan or a large cast-iron skillet and roast it in the upper third of the oven for 30 to 35 minutes for medium-rare. Remove the lamb from the oven, cover with aluminum foil, and let rest for 10 to 12 minutes before carving.   SERVES 2

Roast Leg of Lamb with Red Wine Sauce

You can serve the lamb without sauce, but why deny yourself something so good? Ask the butcher to save the shank bone and to cut it into 4-inch lengths for the sauce.

FOR THE SAUCE (MAKES 2 CUPS)

Reserved lamb shank bone, cut into 4-inch lengths

1 tablespoon olive oil

1 medium carrot, peeled and cut into ½-inch dice

1 small onion, cut into ½-inch dice

2 ribs celery, cut into 2-inch lengths

4 garlic cloves, peeled

1 tablespoon tomato paste

2 cups dry red wine

2 cups water

2 fresh thyme sprigs

1 fresh bay leaf

Kosher salt and freshly ground black pepper to taste

1 leg of lamb, about 8 pounds, hip and shank bone
removed (shank bone reserved) and trimmed of
excess fat
2 tablespoons extra virgin olive oil
3 garlic cloves, thinly sliced
2 tablespoons minced fresh herbs, such as thyme,
rosemary, and/or parsley
Kosher salt and freshly ground black pepper to taste

Preheat the oven to 400°F.

For the sauce, toss the lamb bones with the olive oil in a large cast-iron skillet and roast them until they are golden, about 20 minutes.

Remove the skillet from the oven and pour off any fat in the pan. Add the vegetables, garlic, and tomato paste and gently toss the bones and vegetables until they are coated with the tomato paste. Roast until the vegetables are golden, about 15 minutes. (Leave the oven on.)

Transfer the bones and vegetables to a large pot and add the red wine, water, thyme, and bay leaf. Gently simmer uncovered over low heat for 1½ hours, until slightly thicker than a broth; skim often. Remove the bones and discard. Season the sauce with salt and pepper; strain through a fine-mesh strainer.

Meanwhile, place the lamb in a wide shallow bowl. Whisk together the olive oil, garlic, and herbs. Coat the lamb with this mixture and season with salt and pepper. Place the lamb on a roasting rack in a roasting pan. Roast for 12 to 15 minutes per pound for medium-rare.

Transfer the lamb to a cutting board, cover it with foil, and let rest for 20 minutes before carving.

Just before serving, reheat the sauce over low heat. Carve the lamb and serve with the sauce.   SERVES 8

Grilled Butterflied
Leg of Lamb

Butterflied leg of lamb has had the bone removed and the meat spread open and flattened. This makes it perfect for the grill—and a Fourth of July barbecue. Serve it along with Firecracker Relish (page 358) and all the classic accompaniments: The Simplest Tomato Salad (page 78), Classic Cabbage Slaw (page 88), Elizabeth's Potato Salad (page 131), and Strawberry Shortcake (page 378).

¼ cup extra virgin olive oil

¼ cup Home Spice Mix (page 26)

4 garlic cloves, minced

¾ teaspoon red pepper flakes

Grated zest of 1 lemon

2 tablespoons minced fresh mint

1 boneless leg of lamb, about 5 pounds, butterflied

Kosher salt and freshly ground black pepper to taste

Whisk the olive oil, spice mix, garlic, red pepper flakes, lemon zest, and mint and mix together in a small bowl. Spread the mixture all over the lamb. Place the lamb in a large shallow bowl, cover with plastic wrap, and let marinate at room temperature for 2½ hours or in the refrigerator overnight.

Prepare a charcoal grill.

Season the lamb with salt and pepper. Grill the lamb over medium-hot coals with the cover of your grill in place. It will take 15 to 20 minutes on each side for medium-rare, or 18 to 24 minutes on each side for medium. Transfer the lamb to a cutting board and let rest for 8 to 10 minutes before slicing.   **SERVES 8**

OUR FRIEND PAUL (FAR LEFT),
BUILDING HIS HOUSE IN PESCADERO, CALIFORNIA, 1992

Town Barbecues In our travels, we've happened

upon countless town barbecues. In the South, we've

pulled pork; in the West, we've tackled tangy brisket; and

on Nantucket Island, we've eaten dozens of grilled oys-

ters. We're still trying to get tickets to the always-sold-out

Cutchogue Firemen's Barbecue, where the Ladies'

Auxiliary feeds more than five thousand people.

Berlin, Wisconsin, where David grew up, had men-

only Thursday-Night Steak Fries, where the men selected

their own steaks and grilled them. Another night, the

whole family was invited to a Brat Fry, where bratwursts

were boiled in beer and then grilled.

Lamb Shanks

I first learned how to cook lamb shanks in California in the early 1980's in a southwestern-style restaurant. There, lamb shanks were glazed in a dried chile sauce, garnished with citrus zest, chopped herbs, and garlic, and served with a spicy rice. By the time I got to New York, every restaurant seemed to have its own version of lamb shanks. I often make this recipe when I'm in the mood for a hearty meal and serve it with Cremini Mushroom Rice (page 142).　　　　—DAVID

1 cup all-purpose flour

4 lamb shanks, about 1½ pounds each, trimmed

Kosher salt and freshly ground black pepper to taste

2 tablespoons olive oil

1 cup diced carrots (½-inch dice)

1 cup diced celery (½-inch dice)

1 cup diced yellow onions (½-inch dice)

1 cup chopped leeks

2½ cups dry red wine

1 garlic bulb, halved

1 teaspoon toasted cumin seeds

1 teaspoon toasted fennel seeds

1 teaspoon yellow mustard seeds

1 teaspoon whole black peppercorns

2 fresh thyme sprigs

1 fresh bay leaf

Preheat the oven to 300°F.

Place the flour in a wide shallow bowl. Season the lamb with salt and pepper, then lightly coat the lamb shanks with the flour.

Heat the olive oil in a large cast-iron or heavy-bottomed skillet over medium-high heat. Add the lamb and brown on all sides, about 5 minutes. Transfer the lamb to a large baking dish or roasting pan.

Add the carrots, celery, onions, and leeks to the skillet and cook until softened, about 4 minutes. Add the vegetable mixture to the lamb and add the remaining ingredients to the baking dish as well.

Cover the dish and cook until the meat is fork-tender, 2½ to 3 hours.

Transfer the shanks to a serving platter. Place a strainer over a pot and strain the vegetables from the cooking liquid. Discard the vegetables. Heat the liquid over medium heat until it is reduced by half, 12 to 15 minutes. Season the liquid with salt and pepper, ladle it over the lamb shanks, and serve.   SERVES 4

SAUSAGES

There's an endless variety of sausages in the world, but they're all basically ground meat and fat with seasonings added. When we make sausages, we usually have the butcher grind the meat for us. We simply season it, form it into patties, and cook the patties in a skillet with a little olive oil. If your mixer has a sausage attachment, you can grind the meat, season it, and even case the links yourself. To taste your mixture for seasoning, cook a bit in a hot frying pan, then taste it and adjust the seasoning.

Breakfast Sausage with Sage

We love the breakfast sausage from Faicco's Pork Store on Bleecker Street, a neighborhood institution for over fifty years. This recipe is as close to Faicco's as we can get.

*1 pound pork shoulder or pork butt, freshly ground
  (medium grind)*
1 tablespoon minced fresh sage
2 teaspoons minced garlic
Kosher salt and freshly ground black pepper to taste
2 tablespoons olive oil

Place the pork, sage, and garlic in a large bowl and stir until they are uniformly combined. Season with salt and pepper. Shape the mixture into 4 or 5 patties, each about 3 inches across and 1 inch thick.

Heat the oil in a 10-inch cast-iron or nonstick skillet over medium heat. Add the sausage patties and cook until they are browned on both sides and completely cooked through, 5 to 6 minutes on each side.

MAKES FOUR TO FIVE 4-OUNCE PATTIES

Sweet Pork Sausage

These are delicious served with sweet peppers and onions that have been quickly cooked with a little olive oil, garlic, parsley, and salt and pepper.

2 teaspoons fennel seeds
1 pound ground pork shoulder or pork butt, freshly ground
   (medium grind)
2 teaspoons minced garlic
Kosher salt and freshly ground black pepper to taste
2 tablespoons olive oil

Heat a 10-inch cast-iron or nonstick skillet over medium heat, place the fennel seeds in it, and toast the seeds until they pop and begin to brown, about 3 minutes.

Place the fennel seeds, pork, and garlic in a large bowl and stir until they are uniformly combined. Season with salt and pepper. Shape the mixture into 4 or 5 patties, each about 3 inches across and 1 inch thick.

Heat the olive oil in the skillet over medium heat. Add the sausage patties and cook until they are browned on both sides and completely cooked through, 5 to 6 minutes on each side. **MAKES FOUR TO FIVE 4-OUNCE PATTIES**

meat

sweet and hot sausages Italian sweet sausage isn't really sweet at all: It's called that to distinguish it from hot sausage, which usually contains cayenne pepper or red pepper flakes. But sweet sausage is often spiced with fennel seeds, which gives it a faint anise flavor that some people find sweet.

Hot Pork Sausage

You can control the amount of heat in your hot sausages by adding more or less cayenne pepper. They're awfully good sautéed in a black cast-iron skillet with sliced potatoes and bell peppers. And they make remarkably good sandwiches on crusty Italian rolls.

1 pound pork shoulder or pork butt, freshly ground
  (medium grind)
1 tablespoon mild paprika
1 teaspoon cayenne pepper
2 teaspoons minced garlic
Kosher salt and freshly ground black pepper to taste
2 tablespoons olive oil

Place the pork, paprika, cayenne, and garlic in a large bowl and stir until they are uniformly combined. Season with salt and pepper. Shape the mixture into 4 or 5 patties, about 3 inches across and 1 inch thick.

Heat the olive oil in a 10-inch cast-iron or nonstick skillet over medium heat. Add the sausage patties and cook until they are browned on both sides and completely cooked through, 5 to 6 minutes on each side.

MAKES FOUR TO FIVE 4-OUNCE PATTIES

Chicken Sausage with Lemon and Parsley

We started making chicken sausages after we tasted them in California. These are delicious served with Pineapple Ambrosia Relish (page 81).

1 pound boneless, skinless chicken, freshly ground
   (coarse grind) (see Note)
2 tablespoons minced fresh parsley
2 teaspoons minced fresh chives
1 tablespoon minced lemon zest
2 teaspoons minced garlic
2 teaspoons toasted and ground coriander seeds
Kosher salt and freshly ground black pepper to taste
2 tablespoons olive oil

Place the chicken, parsley, chives, lemon zest, garlic, and coriander in a large bowl and stir until they are uniformly combined. Season with salt and pepper. Shape the mixture into 4 or 5 patties, each about 3 inches across and 1 inch thick.

Heat the olive oil in a 10-inch cast-iron or nonstick skillet over medium heat. Add the sausage patties and cook until they are browned on both sides and completely cooked through, 5 to 6 minutes on each side.

MAKES FOUR TO FIVE 4-OUNCE PATTIES

NOTE: Ground chicken varies in fat content depending on the proportions of white and dark meat and whether any skin is included. Most supermarket ground chicken has only about 12 grams of fat per 4 ounces, which means that it can be dry if it's overcooked. But, of course, you must cook it until there's no pink showing, to avoid the risk of salmonella. We like to use meat from free-range chickens because it has a higher fat content, making juicier sausages. There is also less danger of salmonella.

meat

Lamb Sausage with
Mint and Mustard

Americans were introduced to lamb sausage through merguez, the spicy links that originated in Morocco. Ask the butcher to grind the lamb for you: It's best to use shoulder or leg meat, since it's more flavorful and has a little more fat than other cuts. We serve this sausage with Mint Pesto (page 24) or a fruit chutney. It also makes a surprisingly delicious topping for pizza.

1 pound boneless lamb shoulder or leg, freshly ground
(coarse grind)
1 tablespoon minced fresh parsley
1 tablespoon minced fresh mint leaves
2 teaspoons Dijon mustard
2 teaspoons minced garlic
1 teaspoon ground yellow mustard seeds
Kosher salt and freshly ground black pepper to taste
2 tablespoons olive oil

Place the lamb, parsley, mint, mustard, garlic, and ground mustard in a large bowl and stir until they are uniformly combined. Season with salt and pepper. Shape the mixture into 4 or 5 patties, each 3 inches across and 1 inch thick.

Heat the olive oil in a 10-inch cast-iron or nonstick skillet over medium heat. Add the sausage patties and cook until they are browned on both sides and cooked through, 3 to 4 minutes on each side.

MAKES FOUR TO FIVE 4-OUNCE PATTIES

Bratwurst and Kielbasa

Our midwestern childhoods were filled with sausages: bratwurst and kielbasas nestled in buns and smothered in spicy mustard. Big mild summer sausages that we'd slice up and snack on. At Wisconsin brat fests like the one in Sheboygan, the town park is transformed into a huge cook-out and the motto is "a beer and a brat."

Kielbasa recently came back into our lives when we walked into a Polish Town butcher shop in Riverhead, New York, and saw dozens of different sausages hanging from the ceiling. When we pointed to one, the woman behind the counter said, "Kielbasa." When we pointed to another, she also said, "Kielbasa." This went on for a while, until we decided it was probably a good idea to buy a kielbasa that day.

Bratwurst and Onions in Beer

Bratwurst is a pork and veal sausage from Germany that's seasoned with nutmeg, and sometimes, coriander and ginger. It's usually bought fresh. This is David's version of a traditional Wisconsin bratwurst dish. After the onions are cooked, we simmer the "brats" in the beer and onions for 8 to 10 minutes before we grill them. They then go on buttered and grilled potato rolls, slathered with Polish-style mustard and covered with the simmered onions. We like to serve these with Elizabeth's Potato Salad (page 131).

3 cups thinly sliced yellow onions

1 (12-ounce) bottle amber beer

3 tablespoons apple cider vinegar

1 teaspoon kosher salt

1 teaspoon yellow mustard seeds

½ teaspoon celery seeds

1 fresh bay leaf

A few grinds of black pepper

6 uncooked bratwurst

2 tablespoons softened butter

6 potato rolls

Prepare a charcoal grill.

Combine all of the ingredients except the bratwurst in a 4-quart saucepan, bring to a simmer, and simmer gently over medium-low heat for 20 minutes.

Add the bratwurst and simmer gently until cooked through, 8 to 10 minutes.

Place the bratwurst on the grill and cook over medium-high heat until charred. Butter the rolls and toast on the grill just before serving.   SERVES 6

Salami or Pepperoni
with Ginger

We like to slice this dry-cured sausage thin and serve it with an assortment of domestic cheeses as a Thanksgiving appetizer, but we also cut it on a diagonal into thicker pieces, cook them on the griddle, and have them with scrambled eggs for breakfast.

To dry-cure sausage, you need a relatively dry place that can be kept consistently between 55 and 60 degrees and is not drafty (to ensure that your sausage dries evenly). You will need to suspend a long one-inch-thick dowel from the ceiling so that your sausages can hang freely from it. You also will need an old-fashioned meat grinder with a sausage stuffing attachment, or an electric mixer equipped with a grinding attachment and a sausage stuffing horn. (Please read the instructions that come with your equipment first.) In order to successfully dry-cure sausage, you will need to add saltpeter, or potassium nitrate, a preservative that has been used in sausage making for years. Excessive amounts can be dangerous to your health, but the level of potassium nitrate in our recipes is quite low and not considered to be dangerous. Potassium nitrate helps to keep the sausages rosy pink and also protects them against botulism. It is obtainable through suppliers of sausage-making equipment.

continued

10 pounds boneless pork shoulder or pork butt,
   cut into 1-inch cubes
3 tablespoons kosher salt
1 teaspoon saltpeter (potassium nitrate)

FOR THE SALAMI

½ cup minced ginger
½ cup minced garlic
3 tablespoons yellow mustard seeds
3 tablespoons coarsely ground black pepper
½ cup light corn syrup

FOR THE PEPPERONI ADD

2 tablespoons mild paprika
1 tablespoon red pepper flakes

12 to 15 feet medium sausage casing, thoroughly rinsed

Place the pork, salt, and saltpeter in a large deep bowl and stir until they are well combined. Transfer the mixture to a large plastic container and cover the surface of the meat tightly with plastic wrap. Cover the container with a tight-fitting lid and refrigerate for 1 week.

Remove the cured meat from the refrigerator and add all the remaining ingredients, except the casing, and thoroughly combine. Cover and refrigerate for 1 hour. Also refrigerate all of your sausage-making equipment for 1 hour.

Grind the sausage through the coarse blade of your meat grinder into a large bowl. Case the sausages into 10- to 12-inch lengths (following the manufacturer's instructions). The sausages should be tightly packed, but you need to be careful not to burst the casings. Tie the sausages at each end.

At this point, the sausages are ready for drying: Simply tie the sausages to a large suspended dowel. They should not touch each other. The sausages should be dry and hard in 14 days. They will keep for several weeks longer in the refrigerator if you cover them with olive oil. To serve, wipe the oil from them and let warm at room temperature for 1 hour before slicing.   MAKES 10 TO 12 SAUSAGES

FRIEND ART SCHRADER AND GRANDPA DROVER
GRINDING MEAT FOR SAUSAGE, 1968

CHEESE

CHEESE

The frenzy of Saturday night in a restaurant kitchen is like fighting in a war and having to be extremely nice about it. One night, I stopped to say hello to some regular customers and was introduced to their brother. As we exchanged hellos, I was transfixed by a trace of the long-forgotten scent of milk, hay, sweaty cows, and manure. The smell of a Wisconsin dairy farm is never lost to those of us who spent our childhoods around them. This brother, a dairy farmer, had never been to New York and told me he had not had a day off from milking the cows for seventeen years, when he and his wife were on their honeymoon. I stopped complaining about the restaurant business and thought how lucky I was to be able to show some midwestern hospitality in New York.

Not every meal has to be a big deal. Sometimes we want to eat just one thing for supper, and we don't want to make a fuss over it. Here are some of the recipes we think of as simple dishes and snacks that tide us over. Not surprisingly, when I was growing up in Wisconsin, it was taken for granted that you'd never be without a meal if you had cheese in your kitchen. —DAVID

Cornmeal and Goat Cheese Pudding

This is the dressed-up version of cornmeal mush, a rich and fluffy side dish that has the fine tang of goat cheese melted into it.

1¾ cups whole milk
½ cup fine yellow cornmeal
1 tablespoon unsalted butter
1 teaspoon kosher salt
¼ pound fresh goat cheese
Freshly ground black pepper
2 teaspoons minced fresh rosemary

Bring the milk to a simmer in a 2-quart saucepan over low heat. Add the cornmeal in a thin stream, whisking constantly to avoid lumps. Stir in the butter and salt and cook, stirring constantly until thickened, about 5 minutes. Remove from the heat, add the goat cheese, and stir until it is completely incorporated. Sprinkle with a few grinds of black pepper and the rosemary. Serve hot.

SERVES 2

Cheese Grits

Even Yankees get tired of the same old bacon and eggs. When we want to serve something different for brunch, we make a bowl of warm cheese grits topped with Lamb Sausage with Mint and Mustard (page 274), or we spoon grits onto the plate instead of hash browns with scrambled eggs and Breakfast Sausage with Sage (page 270).

This recipe can be doubled and the leftover poured into a greased pie pan, left to stiffen, sliced, and then pan-fried the next day.

2½ cups water

1 tablespoon olive oil

1 teaspoon kosher salt

½ cup stone-ground grits (see Note)

¼ cup grated aged hard cheese, such as Dry Jack or
Vermont Cheddar

Bring the water, oil, and salt to a boil in a 4-quart saucepan. Add the grits, whisking constantly so that no lumps form. Reduce the heat, cover, and simmer for 8 minutes, stirring occasionally. Stir in the cheese and serve hot. **SERVES 2**

NOTE: When we say "grits," we mean hominy grits, a coarsely ground corn that Southerners (and others) eat as a breakfast comfort food with butter and sweet syrup. Customers say, "Oh, it's like polenta," and we tell them, "No, polenta is like grits."

DAD AT OSHKOSH SPEEDWAY, 1951

Every other Thursday night was bridge club. Mom and her friends would get together and enjoy a break from their nightly routines of feeding hungry mouths and monitoring homework. We weren't too upset, however, because we knew that for dinner Dad would make macaroni and cheese, baked in a cast-iron skillet with sliced tomatoes and bread crumbs on top.

Then he'd take us out to the country in his car and drive really fast. Being an ex-stock-car driver, Dad missed racing. I guess macaroni-and-cheese night held a lot of memories for us all. —DAVID

Dad Page's
Macaroni and Cheese

4 tablespoons (½ stick) unsalted butter

1 large yellow onion, cut into ⅛-inch dice

1 tablespoon minced garlic

3 tablespoons all-purpose flour

4 cups whole milk

1 teaspoon mild paprika

½ teaspoon ground nutmeg

2 teaspoons kosher salt

1 teaspoon freshly ground black pepper

¾ cup grated extra-sharp Cheddar cheese

¾ cup grated Wisconsin Asiago cheese

¾ cup grated Dry Jack cheese

1 pound elbow macaroni, cooked and drained

2 plum tomatoes, sliced

½ cup Seasoned Bread Crumbs (page 27)

1 tablespoon chopped fresh parsley

1 tablespoon chopped fresh thyme

1 tablespoon chopped fresh chives

Preheat the oven to 400°F.

Melt the butter in a large pot over medium heat. Add the onions and garlic and cook until they are softened, about 2 minutes. Whisk in the flour and cook, stirring constantly, until the mixture turns light brown, about 3 minutes. Gradually whisk in the milk. Add the paprika, nutmeg, salt and pepper. Reduce the heat to low and cook, stirring, until the sauce is thickened, about 5 minutes. Add the cheeses and stir until they are melted. Add the macaroni and stir until the noodles are thoroughly coated. Remove from the heat.

continued

Butter two 6-inch cast-iron skillets or one 12-inch skillet. Transfer the macaroni mixture into the skillets. Top with the sliced tomatoes. Sprinkle the bread crumbs on top.

Bake until the cheese is bubbling and golden brown, about 30 minutes. Garnish with the chopped herbs.

SERVES 2 TO 4

Buttered Noodles with Wisconsin Asiago

Growing up in the Midwest, we had buttered noodles with our pot roast and elbow macaroni in our soup, but the word "pasta" was never heard in our homes. Now, after having eaten acres and acres of pasta with every kind of sauce, we've come back to enjoy the flat wide egg noodles we grew up with. This recipe is also delicious with the addition of fresh herbs and Overnight Tomatoes (page 19).

1 tablespoon extra virgin olive oil
1 pound shell noodles or bow ties
4 tablespoons (½ stick) unsalted butter, softened
¾ cup grated Wisconsin Asiago cheese
Kosher salt and freshly ground black pepper to taste

Bring 4 quarts of salted water to a boil in a large pot. Add the olive oil and pasta, stir once, and cook until the noodles still have a slight bite to them but are tender, 10 to 12 minutes. Drain well and transfer to a large bowl.

Add the remaining ingredients and toss until the butter is melted. Serve hot.　　SERVES 2

Blue Cheese Fondue
with Rosemary Toasts

I came up with this dish for the opening party of Home Restaurant. That day I was in a panic because of the hundreds of details left to deal with before the first guests arrived. It was while I was standing at the top of a ladder snaking speaker wire through a wall that I remembered my mother's fondue parties. I came down from the ladder, hurried over to Murray's Cheese Shop on the corner of Bleecker Street, and put together this quirky take on fondue.

If you like garlic bread, you'll love the rosemary toasts we serve with the fondue, or alongside hearty winter soups. They're a good way to rescue bread that's not actually stale but not quite fresh either.　　　　—DAVID

¼ pound blue cheese, crumbled

¼ pound cream cheese, cut into small pieces

3 tablespoons dry white wine

3 tablespoons buttermilk

⅛ teaspoon ground nutmeg

2 teaspoons chopped fresh rosemary

2 tablespoons extra virgin olive oil

Rosemary Toasts (recipe follows)

Combine the cheeses, wine, buttermilk, and nutmeg in a 2-quart saucepan over low heat. Whisk until smooth.

Spoon the fondue into a small serving dish, sprinkle with the rosemary, and drizzle with the oil. Serve with the rosemary toasts.　　　　**SERVES 2 TO 4**

continued

ROSEMARY TOASTS

2 tablespoons extra virgin olive oil

1 garlic clove, minced

8 (½-inch-thick) slices crusty bread

½ teaspoon chopped fresh rosemary

Preheat the oven to 325°F.

Stir the olive oil and garlic together in a small bowl. Lightly brush both sides of the bread with the garlic oil, then sprinkle with the rosemary. Bake on a baking sheet, turning once, until golden, about 15 minutes. Serve at room temperature. **MAKES 8 TOASTS**

Goat Cheese Truffles

I have strong opinions on the proper time to eat cheese. So what if the French eat it at the end of the meal? I grew up having cheese before the meal and dessert after it, that's how I think it should be. Sophisticated New Yorkers devour these tangy bites when I serve them with predinner cocktails. I call them truffles to describe their shape and show that they're something special.

We like these served on top of a Red Pepper Sauce (page 112), garnished with a few salad greens. —DAVID

1 cup fresh goat cheese curd (see Note)
1 cup minced fresh herbs, such as chives, parsley,
 and/or thyme
1 teaspoon freshly ground black pepper

Roll the cheese curd into 24 equal-size balls (or truffles). Combine the herbs with the pepper and roll the truffles in the herb mixture. Serve, or store in the refrigerator until ready to use. If the truffles have been chilled, let stand at room temperature for 15 minutes before serving them. **MAKES 24 TRUFFLES**

N O T E : You can get fresh goat cheese in specialty shops these days, but if you can't, grated sharp Cheddar, regular goat cheese, creamy blue cheese, or even cream cheese are all good in this recipe.

Eggplant Roll-ups

We like to serve these as snacks when we have friends over for wine and conversation. They are a breadless variation of a marinated vegetable sandwich we make, and while they are a little work, they are not at all hard to do.

1 large eggplant

2 to 3 scallions, trimmed

6 tablespoons olive oil

Kosher salt and freshly ground black pepper to taste

1½ cups goat cheese

10 Kalamata olives, pitted

6 large fresh basil leaves

1 cup diced tomatoes (½-inch thick)

Cut the eggplant crosswise into ¼-inch discs. Brush both sides of the eggplant slices and the scallions with 3 tablespoons of the olive oil and season with salt and pepper.

Heat a 10-inch cast-iron skillet over medium-high heat. When it is hot, add the remaining 3 tablespoons olive oil. Add the eggplant, in batches, and cook until just tender, about 4 minutes on each side. Transfer the eggplant to a clean work surface. Place the whole scallions in the skillet and cook until tender, about 4 minutes. Transfer the scallions to a cutting board and chop them.

Purée the goat cheese, olives, and basil in a food processor. Transfer this mixture to a large bowl and fold in the tomatoes and scallions. Season to taste with salt and pepper.

Spread 1 tablespoon of the goat cheese mixture on each slice of grilled eggplant disk. Roll them up and set them seam side down on a platter. These can be stored in the refrigerator for up to 6 hours; let stand at room temperature for 20 minutes before serving. **MAKES 20 ROLL-UPS**

SANDWICHES

We love the sandwiches at Whitehouse Subs in Atlantic City. They're piled high with Genoa salami, ham, capocollo, cotechino, provolone, lettuce, tomato, onion, Italian dressing, and hot red pepper relish. The real secret, however, is the soft Italian bread that envelops the meat.

A close second is at Katz's Deli in New York City. Here, it's all about the meat, because these sandwiches consist only of meat, mustard, and two thin slices of caraway rye bread. Pastrami, corned beef, and brisket aren't made better even in heaven, and there's a house special sandwich of brisket and coleslaw slathered in Russian dressing.

We've eaten oyster po' boys at the Acme Oyster Bar in New Orleans, where the first bite sends hot oyster liquor running down your arm, leaving you no choice but to lick from elbow to wrist. The pulled pork sandwiches in the Carolinas have caused us to visit one establishment for lunch and leave with a large to-go order for dinner.

cheese

But our most recent discovery is a sandwich made in our own backyard, on Bleecker Street at Faicco's Pork Store. When you walk into this old-fashioned butcher shop, the counter guys ask, "WhatcanIgetcha?" They take thick slices of roasted pork loin coated with herbs, slather it with spicy mustard, and add tomatoes, lettuce, and a few peperoncini, the pickled hot peppers that would wake a grizzly bear in December.

From time to time we have served our own variations on these classics. However, we do not include them here, preferring instead to offer three grilled cheese sandwiches that are entirely ours—and remind us of home.

Grilled Blue Cheese and Apple Sandwiches

This is our favorite grilled cheese sandwich, but we think you'll like all three presented here.

8 tablespoons (1 stick) unsalted butter, softened
12 slices walnut bread or other dark dense bread,
  such as rye or pumpernickel
1½ cups crumbled blue cheese
2 Gravenstein apples, unpeeled, cored and thinly sliced

Lightly butter one side of each slice of bread.

Melt 2 teaspoons of the remaining butter in a 10-inch nonstick skillet over medium-low heat. Place 2 slices of bread, buttered side down, in the skillet, top each slice with about ¼ cup of blue cheese and several slices of apple, and place another slice of bread on top, buttered side up. Cook until the sandwiches are golden brown on the bottom, then carefully flip the sandwiches over and brown the other side. Transfer the sandwiches to a serving platter. Repeat the process with the remaining ingredients. Slice the sandwiches in half on the diagonal and serve.

SERVES 6

Grilled Dry Jack Sandwiches with Smoked Chicken and Caramelized Onions

Dry Jack cheese is Monterey Jack cheese that has been aged so that it becomes a hard grating cheese, similar to Parmesan. If you don't have rosemary bread, sprinkle a few rosemary leaves into each sandwich if you like.

10 tablespoons (1¼ sticks) unsalted butter, softened

3 cups thinly sliced yellow onions

2 teaspoons granulated sugar

12 slices rosemary bread

¾ cup grated Dry Jack cheese

¾ cup shredded smoked chicken

Melt 2 tablespoons of the butter in a 10-inch skillet over medium heat. Add the onions and sugar and cook until the onions are golden, about 8 minutes. Transfer the onions to a shallow bowl and allow to cool.

Lightly butter one side of each slice of bread.

Melt 2 teaspoons of the remaining butter in a 10-inch nonstick skillet over medium-low heat. Place 2 slices of bread buttered side down in the skillet, top each slice with about 2 tablespoons each of cheese, chicken, and caramelized onions, and place another slice of bread on top buttered side up. Cook until sandwiches are golden brown on the bottom, then carefully flip the sandwiches over and brown the other side. Transfer the sandwiches to a serving platter. Repeat the process with the remaining ingredients. Slice the sandwiches in half on the diagonal and serve.   SERVES 6

Grilled Wisconsin Asiago Sandwiches with Ham and Overnight Tomatoes

We like to use flavorful country ham from Smithfield County, Virginia, in this sandwich.

8 tablespoons (1 stick) unsalted butter, softened

12 slices sourdough bread

¾ cup grated Wisconsin Asiago cheese

6 paper-thin slices Smithfield ham

1 cup diced Overnight Tomatoes (page 19)

1 cup (loosely packed) flat-leaf parsley leaves

Lightly butter one side of each slice of bread.

Melt 2 teaspoons of the remaining butter in a 10-inch nonstick skillet over medium-low heat. Place 2 slices of the bread buttered side down in the skillet, top each slice with about 2 tablespoons of cheese, a slice of ham, some tomatoes, and some parsley, and place another slice of bread on top buttered side up. Cook until the sandwiches are golden brown on the bottom, then carefully flip the sandwiches over and brown the other side. Transfer the sandwiches to a serving platter. Repeat the process with the remaining ingredients. Slice the sandwiches in half on the diagonal and serve.   SERVES 6

BREADS and MUFFINS

BREADS

We don't pretend to be master bread bakers, so this isn't a compendium on bread. On the other hand, we are master bread eaters: We're good at that. We've included a lot of quick breads in this chapter, because we tend to entertain spontaneously, and there's always enough time to make biscuits or corn bread while the rest of the meal is cooking. Lately we've been doing a lot of flatbreads, too, especially since we learned to use a pizza stone.

Bread is a humble food, and one that's not at all hard to make. That's lucky, because we've found that people feel happily taken care of when they sit down to a meal where there's homemade bread on the table.

Herb Bread

We have a big herb garden in the country, and whoever's in charge of making this bread for dinner goes out and picks the herbs. We've used thyme, oregano, marjoram, and chives, and the only secret is to use plenty of them. That's because this is a really basic bread that takes on added flavor nicely.

1 teaspoon active dry yeast

¼ cup warm water

2 cups bread flour

1 tablespoon kosher salt

¼ cup minced fresh herbs, such as thyme, oregano,
    and/or marjoram

5 tablespoons olive oil

⅓ cup room-temperature water

In a small bowl, dissolve the yeast in the warm water and let stand in a warm place for about 5 minutes.

Sift the flour and salt together into a large bowl. Add the herbs and stir so that they are evenly dispersed. Form a well in the center of the flour mixture and add the yeast mixture, ¼ cup of the olive oil, and the room-temperature water. Stir until the dough comes together. Turn it out onto a floured surface and knead until the dough becomes silky, about 10 minutes. Shape into a ball.

Oil a deep bowl with the remaining 1 tablespoon oil, place the dough in it, and turn it to coat with the oil. Cover the bowl with plastic wrap and let rise in a warm place until it is doubled in bulk, about 4 hours.

Punch down the dough and gently shape it into an oval loaf on a baking sheet pan, or a floured pizza peel if you are baking on a pizza stone. Cover with plastic wrap and let rise until doubled in size, about 2 hours.

Thirty minutes before the bread is ready to be baked, preheat the oven to 450°F. If you have a pizza stone, place it in the oven to heat at the same time.

Bake the bread for about 1 hour, until the loaf sounds hollow when tapped. For a crispy brown crust, spritz the loaf and oven floor lightly with water every 15 minutes.

MAKES 1 LOAF

y e a s t It may look inert, but yeast is a living organism that turns its food into carbon dioxide (in bread) and alcohol (in wine). You can buy envelopes of powdery dry yeast in the supermarket dairy case. When you rehydrate it by sprinkling it on body-temperature water, the yeast becomes active and goes to work on the carbohydrates in flour.

Garden Zucchini Bread

No doubt zucchini bread began as a way to use up the green squash that overruns everyone's backyard garden. Because our recipe isn't supersweet—not like a carrot cake—we like to serve it alongside soups and salads at lunchtime.

3 cups all-purpose flour

1 teaspoon baking soda

¼ teaspoon baking powder

1 teaspoon ground cinnamon

1 teaspoon kosher salt

3 large eggs

2 cups granulated sugar

1 cup vegetable oil

1 teaspoon vanilla extract

2 cups grated zucchini

½ cup finely chopped yellow onion

continued

Preheat the oven to 350°F. Butter and flour two 8 x 4-inch loaf pans.

Combine the flour, baking soda, baking powder, cinnamon, and salt in a large bowl.

In a separate bowl, whisk together the eggs, sugar, vegetable oil, and vanilla extract. Slowly pour the egg mixture into the flour mixture, stirring just until the ingredients are combined. Fold in the zucchini and onion. Spoon the batter evenly into the prepared loaf pans.

Bake for 1 hour, or until a toothpick inserted into the center of a loaf comes out clean. Cool the loaves in the pans on a wire rack for about 10 minutes, then remove the loaves from the pans and let them cool on the wire rack. Don't attempt to slice the bread until it is completely cool.   MAKES 2 LOAVES

Sage Corn Bread

This foolproof recipe makes a sturdy loaf to snack on, or to slice and cover with sautéed wild mushrooms, or to toast and use as a garnish for chowder or croutons for salads. It's also a traditional base for Thanksgiving stuffing (see page 223).

¾ cup yellow cornmeal

1 cup all-purpose flour

1 tablespoon sugar

1 tablespoon baking powder

½ teaspoon kosher salt

1 tablespoon minced fresh sage (see Note)

1 cup whole milk

1 large egg

2 tablespoons unsalted butter, melted and still warm

1 tablespoon unsalted butter, softened

Preheat the oven to 425°F. Grease an 8 x 4-inch loaf pan.

Sift together the cornmeal, flour, sugar, and baking powder into a large bowl. Stir in the salt and sage until evenly distributed.

In a small bowl, whisk together the milk, egg, and melted butter. Pour the milk mixture into the cornmeal mixture and stir just until combined.

Pour the batter into the greased loaf pan. Bake for 15 minutes. Spread the top of the bread with the softened butter and bake for about 10 minutes longer. The loaf is done when the top is lightly browned and firm to the touch at the center. Let cool in the pan on a wire rack for 20 minutes, then transfer the loaf to the rack to cool completely.   **MAKES 1 LOAF**

N O T E : Sage's long oval leaves are fuzzy and gray-green; its taste is pungent and slightly musty. (Think poultry seasoning and sausages.) The best way to store the fresh herb is in a plastic bag in the fridge; dried sage makes a second-best but acceptable alternative.

Pizza Dough

We often make pizza when we have friends over in the country. Everyone gets to roll or throw a crust—some of the shapes are pretty original—and to pick the toppings each wants. One very picky eater even gets to eat his crust plain, which is fine as long as the rest of us don't have to have it that way.

1½ teaspoons active dry yeast

¼ cup warm water

2 cups all-purpose flour

3 tablespoons chopped fresh herbs

¼ teaspoon kosher salt

⅓ cup room-temperature water

2 tablespoons olive oil

In a small bowl, dissolve the yeast in the warm water and let stand in a warm place for 5 minutes, or until a froth forms on the surface.

Sift the flour into a large bowl. Add the herbs and salt and stir until they are evenly distributed. Form a well in the center of the flour and add the yeast mixture, room-temperature water, and oil. Stir until the dough comes together, adding more water or flour if the dough seems either too dry or too wet. The dough will start out relaxed and wet but will firm up as it is kneaded. Turn the dough out onto a floured work surface and knead for 5 minutes.

Place the dough in an oiled bowl, turn to coat it evenly, drizzle it with olive oil, and cover the bowl with plastic wrap. Let rise in a warm place until doubled, about 3 hours. For extra elasticity, you can make the dough 12 hours in advance and refrigerate it, letting it rise very slowly. Let it warm at room temperature for 1 hour before you use it.

Thirty minutes before the dough is ready to bake, pre-heat the oven to 450°F. If you have a pizza stone, place it in the oven to heat at the same time.

Punch down the dough and form it into a ball. Cover it with plastic wrap and let it rest for 10 minutes.

Shape the dough into a flat disc and stretch it into a 12-inch circle. Place it on a floured pizza peel or greased baking sheet and top with your chosen pizza toppings. Slide it onto the preheated pizza stone or put the pan on an oven rack. Bake until the crust is golden brown, 10 to 15 minutes. MAKES ONE 12-INCH PIZZA CRUST

pizza toppings We think the most successful pizzas are topped with just a few ingredients, but those should be special. Here are just a few of our favorite toppings:

Potted Duck (page 232), sliced new potatoes, blue cheese, fresh thyme

Lamb Sausage with Mint and Mustard (page 274), goat cheese, artichoke hearts, fresh mint, and parsley

Fresh tomatoes, *Sunflower Seed Pesto (page 23),* shaved raclette or Emmentaler cheese

Homemade pepperoni (page 277), sharp Cheddar cheese, Sungold or yellow cherry tomatoes

Seeded Flatbread

Quicker and much easier to make than you'd expect, these flatbreads are very dramatic to produce since once you roll them out and put them in the pan, they puff up and take on a life of their own. They're fun to make when friends come over and you all want to get into the kitchen and cook dinner together. We serve this unleavened bread with Tomato-Cucumber Salad (page 79).

⅔ cup fine bulgur

¼ cup minced onion

2 teaspoons kosher salt

1 cup boiling water

2½ cups all-purpose flour,
  plus more if needed

1 teaspoon toasted and crushed cumin seeds

1 teaspoon toasted and crushed fennel seeds

1 teaspoon toasted and crushed sesame seeds

2 tablespoons extra virgin olive oil

1½ cups peanut oil, for frying

Combine the bulgur, onion, and salt in a small bowl. Pour the boiling water over the mixture, cover, and let stand for 10 to 15 minutes.

Combine 1 cup of the flour and all the toasted seeds in a large bowl. Stir in the softened bulgur mixture, along with the olive oil. Stir for 1 minute, or until the dough comes together. Turn the dough out onto a floured work surface and knead, adding the remaining flour, for 8 to 10 minutes. Add additional flour if needed.

Cut the dough into 8 equal pieces and shape it into balls. Roll each ball into a ¼-inch-thick circle or press it out with a tortilla press.

Heat the peanut oil in a heavy skillet to 375°F. Fry the breads one at a time, turning them once, until they are puffy and crisp, about 2 minutes on each side. Transfer them to paper towels, then to a platter, and keep warm in a 250°F oven until you are ready to serve them.

MAKES 8 BREADS

flatbreads Flatbreads are made in almost every culture: matzoh, Scandinavian rye biscuits, Armenian lavash, Indian chapattis, Latin tortillas, all-American pancakes. This recipe was inspired by one in *Flatbreads & Flavors,* by Jeffrey Alford and Naomi Duguid.

Butter Crackers

Once you've rolled the dough to the thinnest degree possible, the hard part of making these crackers is over.

1 cup all-purpose flour
½ teaspoon baking soda
3 tablespoons unsalted butter, chilled
½ teaspoon kosher salt, plus more for sprinkling
3 tablespoons cold water

Preheat the oven to 425°F. If you have a pizza stone, place it in the oven to heat at the same time.

Sift the flour and baking soda together into a large bowl. Add the butter and salt and cut in the butter with a pastry blender until the mixture resembles fine meal. Add the water 1 tablespoon at a time, until the dough comes together.

Shape the dough into a ball, then flatten it. Roll out the dough on a lightly floured surface as thin as possible.

continued

breads and muffins

The thinner the dough, the more delicate the cracker. Before the very last roll of the pin, sprinkle the dough lightly with kosher salt, then roll over it so the salt is pressed into the dough. Using a pizza cutter or sharp knife, cut the dough into 2-inch squares, then poke holes in them with the tines of a fork.

Bake on baking sheets, or the preheated pizza stone, until the crackers are golden, 4 to 5 minutes. Transfer to a rack to cool; as they cool, the crackers will crisp.

When the crackers are completely cool, store them in an airtight container. If they lose their crispness, reheat them in the oven.   **MAKES 30 CRACKERS**

p i z z a   s t o n e   We learned to use a pizza stone from Amy Scherber, owner of Amy's Bread, in New York City. She taught us that flatbreads, like crackers and pizza, are best baked on the floor of the oven, where the radiant heat creates a good bottom crust. If you can't do that, get quarry tiles or a commercial pizza stone, which act like the oven floor when they're laid on the lowest rack. Failing that, turn a heavy baking sheet upside down and let it preheat before you put the crackers directly onto it.

Oyster Crackers

Don't turn the page—these are tricky but worth the effort. Don't your fish stews and chowders deserve it?

We've always assumed these small puffed circles were named for the fact that they were eaten with oyster stew. Maybe they are supposed to look like tiny oyster shells that can be opened up. If you know, do tell us.

1 teaspoon active dry yeast

¼ cup warm water

1 cup all-purpose flour

½ teaspoon baking soda

¼ teaspoon kosher salt, plus more for sprinkling

1 tablespoon water

In a small bowl, dissolve the yeast in the warm water and let stand in a warm place for 5 minutes until the surface is frothy.

Sift the flour and baking soda together into a large bowl. Add the salt. Form a well in the center of the flour mixture, add the yeast mixture and the water, and stir until the dough comes together. Turn the dough out onto a floured work surface and knead until it begins to stiffen, about 2 minutes.

Shape the dough into a ball. Place it in an oiled bowl and cover the bowl with plastic wrap. Let the dough rise in a warm place for 2 hours.

Thirty minutes before baking, preheat the oven to 425°F. If you have a pizza stone, place it in the oven to heat at the same time.

Punch down the dough and roll it out on a floured work surface as thin as possible. Before the last roll of the pin, sprinkle the dough lightly with kosher salt, then roll over it so the salt is pressed into the dough. With a pizza cutter or a sharp knife, cut the dough into triangles no bigger than 2 inches wide.

Bake the crackers on the preheated pizza stone or on baking sheets until they puff in the center and just begin to brown, 4 to 5 minutes. Transfer to a rack to cool, then store in an airtight container for up to 1 week.

MAKES 36 CRACKERS

Graham Crackers

People don't think of making their own graham crackers, but if you've eaten only those from a box, try these and you'll realize what homemade is all about. Put them in a big mason jar and they'll keep almost forever. If they do get soggy, put them back into the oven and they'll crisp right up. We serve them dipped in chocolate with a fruit dessert or a glass of milk: classic milk and cookies.

1¼ cups cake flour

1¼ cups bread flour

½ cup whole wheat flour

½ cup (firmly packed) light brown sugar

1 teaspoon baking powder

¼ teaspoon kosher salt

6 tablespoons (¾ stick) unsalted butter, softened

½ cup honey

½ teaspoon vanilla extract

½ cup water

Preheat the oven to 325°F.

Combine the flours, brown sugar, baking powder, and salt in the bowl of an electric mixer fitted with a dough hook. With the mixer on medium, gradually add the butter, honey, vanilla, and water, mixing just until combined.

On a floured surface, roll out the dough into a ⅛-inch-thick rectangle. Using a pizza cutter or a sharp knife, cut the dough into 1 x 2-inch rectangles. Arrange the crackers 2 inches apart on ungreased baking sheets and prick with a fork.

Bake until the edges are lightly browned, 6 to 8 minutes. Cool the crackers on the baking sheets on wire racks. Graham crackers can be stored in an airtight container at room temperature. **MAKES 36 CRACKERS**

Cheddar Biscuits

We can't imagine any meal that wouldn't be improved by the addition of these rich, savory biscuits. Cheddar, a medium-firm, sharp-tasting cheese, originated in England, but some of the world's best Cheddar is now made on this continent, in Canada and in Oregon and in Vermont. If your Cheddar is orange instead of white, it was probably tinted with annatto, a spice typically used in Latin American dishes.

3 cups all-purpose flour

1 tablespoon granulated sugar

1 tablespoon baking powder

¾ teaspoon kosher salt

½ pound (2 sticks) unsalted butter, chilled,
   cut into ½-inch pieces

1½ cups coarsely shredded sharp Cheddar cheese

1 cup cold buttermilk

Preheat the oven to 375°F.

Combine the flour, sugar, baking powder, and salt in a medium bowl. Add the butter and rub it in with your fingertips until the mixture resembles coarse meal. Toss in the grated Cheddar. Gradually stir in the buttermilk, mixing only until a dough is formed.

Divide the dough into 8 to 10 pieces and roughly shape each piece into a ball. Place the biscuits 2 inches apart on an ungreased baking sheet

Bake until golden, about 30 minutes. Transfer to a wire rack to cool. **MAKES 8 TO 10 BISCUITS**

MUFFINS

We never had muffins when we were kids, but when we went to California, they were suddenly everywhere. We eventually figured out that it was the times, not that muffins were something specific to California.

Lemon-Almond Muffins

Light in flavor and texture, these are a great accompaniment to simple scrambled eggs and are special spread with one of our flavored butters (pages 17 to 18).

6 tablespoons (¾ stick) unsalted butter

½ cup pure maple syrup

2 cups all-purpose flour

½ cup granulated sugar

2 cups old-fashioned rolled oats

½ teaspoon kosher salt

2 teaspoons baking powder

1 cup slivered almonds

Grated zest of 3 lemons

2 large eggs, at room temperature

2 cups buttermilk, at room temperature

Preheat the oven to 350°F. Butter 18 muffin cups or line with paper liners.

Heat the butter and maple syrup in a saucepan over low heat until the butter is melted. Let cool for about 5 minutes.

Combine the flour, sugar, oats, salt, baking powder,

almonds, and lemon zest in a large bowl. Whisk the eggs in a medium bowl, then whisk in the buttermilk. Whisk in the butter mixture. Add the wet ingredients to the dry ingredients and stir until the ingredients are well blended.

Spoon the batter into the buttered muffin cups, filling them three-quarters full. Bake until a toothpick inserted in the center of a muffin comes out clean, 25 to 30 minutes. Cool the muffins in the pan on a rack for 5 minutes, then remove them from the pan and cool on the rack.

MAKES 18 MUFFINS

Blueberry Muffins

Anyone need an introduction to blueberry muffins?

2 cups all-purpose flour

½ cup granulated sugar

1 tablespoon baking powder

½ teaspoon kosher salt

2 eggs

¾ cup whole milk

⅓ cup (5⅓ tablespoons) unsalted butter, melted

1 teaspoon grated lemon zest

1 cup fresh blueberries

2 tablespoons superfine sugar

Preheat the oven to 350°F. Butter 12 muffin cups or line with paper liners.

Sift the flour, granulated sugar, and baking powder into a large bowl. Add the salt.

In a medium bowl, whisk together the eggs, milk, butter, and lemon zest. Add the egg mixture to the flour mixture, stirring just until the batter is combined.

continued

breads and muffins

315

In a small bowl, toss the blueberries with the superfine sugar, then stir them into the batter. Spoon the batter into the muffin cups, filling them three-quarters full.

Bake until a toothpick inserted into the center of a muffin comes out clean, 25 to 30 minutes. Cool the muffins in the pan on a rack for 5 minutes, then remove them from the pan and cool on the rack.

MAKES 12 MUFFINS

Carrot-Nut Muffins

We think these are several notches above ordinary carrot muffins. Just remember that when you combine the wet and dry ingredients, do so only until you can't see the flour anymore; overmixing makes muffins too dense, and these are quite dense enough.

2 cups all-purpose flour

2 teaspoons baking soda

1 teaspoon ground cinnamon

½ teaspoon ground ginger

¼ teaspoon ground cloves

¼ teaspoon kosher salt

1¼ cups granulated sugar

2 cups grated carrots (see Note)

1 Granny Smith apple, cored, peeled, and
  coarsely shredded

½ cup finely chopped pecans

2 tablespoons chopped fresh dill

3 large eggs

1 cup corn oil

1 tablespoon vanilla extract

Preheat the oven to 350°F. Butter 18 muffin cups or line with paper liners. Sift the flour, baking soda, cinnamon, ginger, cloves, and salt together into a large bowl. Add the sugar, then stir in the carrots, apple, pecans, and dill. In a medium bowl, whisk together the eggs, oil, and vanilla. Add the egg mixture to the flour mixture, stirring just until the batter is combined. Spoon the batter into the muffin cups, filling them three-quarters full.

Bake until a toothpick inserted into the center of a muffin comes out clean, 25 to 30 minutes. Cool the muffins in the pan on a wire rack for 5 minutes, then remove from the pan and cool on the rack.

MAKES 18 MUFFINS

N O T E : When you're in a hurry, pick up a bag of pre-grated carrots in the produce section of your supermarket. If you want the carrots to disappear into the muffins completely, give them a couple of chops with a chef's knife to make the shreds even smaller.

Cranberry-Orange Scones

Originally griddle-baked quick breads, scones are now usually made in the oven. And while they were once tri-angular and enriched with oats, they are now any shape at all, biscuitlike, and more often than not studded with bits of fruit, nuts, or even chocolate chips.

The Scots pronounce them "skahns" and they should know, since they invented them, but Americans pro-nounce it "skōne," the way the word is written. Either way, they're a nice alternative to breakfast muffins.

continued

3 cups all-purpose flour

½ cup superfine sugar

2 teaspoons baking powder

1 teaspoon baking soda

¼ teaspoon ground cloves

½ teaspoon kosher salt

1 tablespoon finely grated orange zest

12 tablespoons (1½ sticks) unsalted butter, chilled,
   cut into ½-inch cubes

¾ cup roughly chopped dried cranberries

1 cup cold buttermilk

Preheat the oven to 375°F.

Combine the flour, sugar, baking powder, baking soda, cloves, and salt in a medium bowl. Stir in the orange zest. Add the butter and rub it in with your fingertips until the mixture resembles coarse meal. Toss in the dried cranberries. Gradually stir in the buttermilk, mixing only until a dough is formed.

On a lightly floured work surface, roll out the dough into a 1-inch-thick round. Cut the dough into 8 triangles. Place the scones 2 inches apart on an ungreased baking sheet.

Bake until firm to the touch and golden, about 25 minutes. Transfer to a wire rack to cool.   **MAKES 8 SCONES**

Cinnamon–Sour Cream Pancakes

Light and fluffy as morning clouds, these are good either at brunch or supper. It's worth spending extra to get real maple syrup, not "pancake syrup." It comes in grades from AA (the pales) to C (the darkest and strongest-flavored). Heat the syrup gently over a burner so it won't cool off your hot pancakes.

2 large eggs, separated

1 cup sour cream

1 tablespoon granulated sugar

¼ teaspoon ground cinnamon

½ cup all-purpose flour

½ teaspoon baking powder

¼ teaspoon kosher salt

1 tablespoon unsalted butter

Unsalted butter and pure maple syrup, for serving

Whisk the egg whites in a medium bowl until soft peaks form. Set aside.

Whisk the egg yolks and sour cream together in a large bowl. Add the sugar and cinnamon and whisk until blended. Combine the flour, baking powder, and salt in a medium bowl. Stir the flour mixture into the batter, then gently fold in the egg whites.

Melt the butter in a 10-inch skillet over medium heat. In batches, ladle the batter into the skillet, making 4-inch cakes. Cook the pancakes until the small bubbles that form on the surface remain open when they pop. Turn and cook the second side until golden. Keep warm on a heated plate, while you cook the rest of the pancakes. Serve with butter and warm maple syrup. **MAKES TWELVE 4-INCH PANCAKES**

the CANNING SHELF

JAMS AND PRESERVES

The fruit and berry season comes on with such swift abundance that we can hardly believe our eyes. Immediately after the spring rains, the strawberries ripen, and then, before we know it, the succession of raspberries, blueberries, blackberries, gooseberries, peaches, plums, pears, and apples comes upon us like a never-ending parade.

We can't resist loading up at the farm stand, knowing that it won't go to waste, that by tomorrow morning we will have made a delicious jam or preserve out of our cache. The ladies at the farm stand know we have big plans for their fruit because of the huge amounts that we buy. They usually suppose it's for pies, and remark that the dinner must be a special one. We love the charmed expressions on their faces when we tell them we're making Blueberry-Cinnamon Jam or Plum Butter. They hold the art of canning in high regard.

The best preserves are kept simple, letting the ripe fruit show its clean crisp flavors. If too much spice or sugar is added, the taste becomes muddy and loses its vigor. The fruit must be at the height of ripeness, with no blemishes. Overripe fruit should never be used; only by canning perfect fruit will you have perfect preserves.

In the middle of summer, when this abundance could be taken for granted, it's easy to forget what a cold winter morning feels like, or how much we will savor the sweetness of perfectly ripened berries when the fields are empty and the orchards are dormant. Each time we open a new jar and taste the brightness of last season's fruit, we're thankful we took the time to put some by.

CANNING DIRECTIONS

We taught ourselves to can from the directions on the back of the mason jar box. Later we learned to make pickles, jams, and preserves with the help of a friend, Robert Stehling, who was born in North Carolina and came north to cook. We spent many nights with him putting up Home Ketchup by the caseful in a sort of assembly line. Every Wednesday night we turned the kitchen at Home Restaurant into a ketchup canning factory. After the last meal was served, big pots of water were heated to boiling, and by 1:30 in the morning we would have canned two hundred pint jars, enough to keep up with our increasing sales. While we were at it, we would also can dill pickles, spicy carrots, barbecue sauce, and whatever else caught our fancy. Robert now cooks at his own restaurant, Hominy Grill, in Charleston, South Carolina, where the dining room is lined with cupboards and shelves filled with homemade jams and pickles.

How Does Canning Work? When we put up food, we use the boiling water method (bottling under heat), which is considered the easiest and safest. When the ingredients in a jar are heated to 212°F, bacteria are killed and the food is sterilized. That's why it's important to process—leave the jars in boiling water—for the recommended time to ensure that the heat will reach the core of the jar and sterilize the entire contents. While the food is being processed, heat causes it to expand and forces the air out of the jar. When the jar is removed from the hot water and begins to cool, its contents begin to contract. There is now a vacuum inside, which causes the domed lid to be sucked down, forming a seal.

We like to use mason jars with flat metal lids and rims that twist on. Because cleanliness is paramount in canning, the flat metal lids lined with a rubber seal are discarded after one use and replaced by new ones, ensuring a perfect seal each time. The jars and rims, though, may be used over and over again, as long as they stay intact. For this reason, always inspect your jars for cracks and chips, especially on the sealing edges. Discard any that are damaged, as well as any rusted or dented metal rings.

Wash the jars in hot soapy water, rinse them thoroughly, and keep them submerged in hot water until you are ready to fill them. This will guard them against airborne bacteria.

Fill a large stockpot with water. This is the pot you will use to process the filled capped jars. Place a round rack in the bottom of the pot. The rack is important, because it allows boiling water to circulate under the jars. It should sit at least ½ inch above the bottom of the pot. Bring enough water to cover the jars by 1 inch to a boil.

Fill a medium saucepan with water, place the lids and rims in the water, and bring the water to a simmer—not a rolling boil, which could damage the rubber seal. Keep the lids and rims immersed in the water.

Just before you're ready to fill the jars, remove them from the hot water, drain them, and place them upright on a clean surface.

Fill the jars: If you're canning jam, jelly, or chutney, a wide-necked funnel designed specifically for canning will help guide the ingredients into the jars. Otherwise, a ladle will suffice. If you are canning pickles or fruits that need to be packed into the jars before you top them with a hot liquid, make sure that you achieve a "tight pack." This means positioning the ingredients in the jar with the least amount of air space between them. This will keep them from floating to the top of the jar when the liquid is added. Leave ½ inch of headroom—the space from the top of the ingredients to the top of the jar—for bulky ingredients such as pickles and fruits and ¼ inch of headroom for jams, jellies, and other preserves of similar consistency. Gently spin each jar to remove any air bubbles trapped inside.

With a clean towel that has been dipped in boiling water and wrung out, wipe the rims of each jar clean to remove any food particles.

Top each jar with a hot lid, rubber side down. Screw the metal rims down just to the point where they fit tightly—do not screw them down with force. Air needs to escape in processing, and there needs to be a little give for the expansion of the jar in processing.

Make sure the water in the stockpot is at a hard boil. Place the sealed jars upright on the rack in the boiling water, leaving a little space between each jar. If there is not enough water in the pot to cover the tops of the jars by 1 inch, add more boiling water. If the hard rolling boil is not maintained when you put in the jars, cover the stockpot with a lid until the water comes back to a hard boil. Start timing from that point.

Keep the jars in the boiling water for the recommended processing time. Then, remove the jars from the water and place them on a counter that's been covered with a towel. This will allow the jars to drip dry, and, if the counter is very cold, the towel will insulate them from a sudden temperature shock that could cause the glass to break.

Allow the jars to cool until you can handle them comfortably—about 30 minutes. Gently shake the jars, keeping them upright, to release any trapped air bubbles. Allow the jars to cool fully.

Check the tops to make sure you have achieved a seal. If the button on top of each lid is fully depressed, you have achieved a seal. If it isn't, you can attempt to reprocess the contents in a clean jar, or jars, with a new lid. Check to make sure you used the recommended headroom and processing time. If only one jar fails to seal, we usually store it in the refrigerator to enjoy in a few days time.

A Preserving Glossary

J a m Mashed fruit boiled with sugar until it thickens.

J e l l y The juice strained from a mashed fruit, boiled with sugar until it jells.

C o n s e r v e A combination of two or more fruits cooked until smooth. Nuts are sometimes added.

P r e s e r v e Usually one kind of food left whole or halved and put up in a sugar syrup.

B u t t e r A preserve made like jam, but reduced much longer, usually by cooking it for an hour or longer, until it reaches a glossy, spreadable consistency.

C h u t n e y A combination of fresh or dried fruits put up with vinegar, spices, and, occasionally, nuts.

Tips on Making Jam or Jelly

S k i m m i n g   t h e   J a m   o r   J e l l y Once the sugar has been dissolved into the mash of fruit, the jam or jelly should be brought to a full hard, rolling boil that can't be stirred down. While the mixture is boiling, skim the surface to remove the white froth. This step will make your jam or jelly prettier.

Testing the Jam or Jelly In order to decide if the jam or jelly is ready to be taken off the heat and processed, follow this two-step test:

Step 1. Dip a metal teaspoon into the boiling mixture. Remove the spoon and hold it horizontally over the pot, allowing the syrup to drip from it. If the syrup clings together before dripping from the spoon, you should proceed to the next step. If the syrup isn't thickened and drops easily, continue the hard boil, testing every 30 seconds or so. It should thicken in 2 to 3 minutes, although sometimes fruits harbor more water than expected and you won't get a jell for 15 minutes or longer.

Step 2. Drop about a teaspoonful of the syrup onto a chilled plate, and let it cool for about 30 seconds. Depress the center of the mound with your fingertip. Release. If the syrup does not close back on itself, the jam or jelly is ready to process.

Raspberry Jam

This scarlet jam will remind you of summer all winter long.

4 pounds fresh raspberries
½ cup fresh lemon juice
6 cups granulated sugar

Mash the raspberries with a potato masher in a large bowl. Place a strainer over another large bowl, ladle half of the pulp into the strainer, and push it through the strainer to remove the seeds. (This will keep the finished jam from being too seedy.)

Return the strained raspberries to the rest of the pulp and transfer it to a heavy 4-quart saucepan. Bring it to a gentle boil over medium heat. Stir in the lemon juice and sugar, increase the heat, and bring to a hard boil. Begin to check for jelling (see page 329).

When it is jelled, ladle it into 12 hot sterilized 4-ounce mason jars, leaving ¼-inch headroom. Wipe the rims and seal the jars. Process in a boiling water bath for 10 minutes.

MAKES TWELVE 4-OUNCE JARS

pectin Pectin is a natural substance found in ripe fruits. When the fruit is cooked with liquid and sugar, the pectin makes it thicken; if there's not enough natural pectin, more can be added in the form of fresh lemon juice or commercial pectin, either liquid or powdered.

Peach Jam

This recipe works equally well with nectarines.

4 pounds peaches, peeled, pitted, and cut into
  medium dice
1 cup water
½ cup fresh lemon juice
5 cups granulated sugar

Combine the peaches and water in a heavy 4-quart saucepan over medium heat and cook, stirring occasionally, until the fruit breaks down to a mash, about 30 minutes. Bring it to a gentle boil. Stir in the lemon juice and sugar, increase the heat, and bring to a hard boil. Begin to check for jelling (see page 329).

When it is jelled, ladle it into 8 hot sterilized half-pint jars, leaving ¼-inch headroom. Wipe the rims and seal the jars. Process in a boiling water bath for 10 minutes.

MAKES 8 HALF-PINT JARS

a peach sequence Early-season peaches are often firm to the touch and perfect for preserving as whole fruit. As the season progresses, different varieties arrive, each one softer and juicier. By August, the fruit at the farm stand fills the hot air with an incredible perfume. That's when we buy peaches to make jam.

GRANDMOTHER DROVER, PICKING BLUEBERRIES, 1986

Plainfield, Wisconsin, just north of Berlin, is

strawberry country. There, the soil changes from the rich

deep color that corn loves to a sandier, lighter humus

more suitable for crops like potatoes and strawberries.

Every spring, my mom would take us kids to the U-pick

fields, where we loaded up with bushels of ripe strawber-

ries for homemade jam. Once back home, Mom would sit

us down at the kitchen table. It was an orderly affair, a

production line, with strawberries moving across the

kitchen table to be stemmed and sliced and then put into

the big kettle, where they were boiled down in batches till

they turned into jam. I remember eating as many straw-

berries as I could before they went to the stove, but by

early afternoon we'd have dozens of pints of bright red

jam lining the kitchen counter. —DAVID

Mom Page's Strawberry Jam

5 pounds fresh strawberries, hulled
½ cup fresh lemon juice
8 cups granulated sugar

Mash the fruit with a potato masher in a large bowl and
transfer to a large heavy saucepan. Bring it to a rolling
boil over medium heat, about 45 minutes. Stir in the
lemon juice and sugar, increase the heat, and bring to a
hard boil that cannot be stirred down. Begin to check for
jelling (see page 329).

When it is jelled, ladle it into 10 hot sterilized half-pint
mason jars, leaving ¼-inch headroom. Wipe the rims and
seal the jars. Process in a boiling water bath for
10 minutes. MAKES 10 HALF-PINT JARS

Rose Hip Jam

Only after we found brambly wild roses growing on the beach did we remember seeing recipes for this jam in some old cookbooks.

1½ pounds ripe rose hips
6 cups water
½ cup fresh lemon juice
5 cups granulated sugar

Slice the green leafy crown from each rose hip with a paring knife, then cut the fruit in half. Place them with the water in a large heavy pot. Cover and simmer over medium heat until the fruit is softened, about 35 minutes. Mash the fruit with a potato masher, while continuing to simmer for 5 minutes longer.

Place a strainer over a large bowl. Ladle the rose hips into the strainer and push the pulp through the strainer with the back of the ladle to remove the skins and seeds. Discard the skins and seeds.

Return the rose hip pulp to the pot and bring to a boil over medium heat. Stir in the lemon juice and sugar, increase the heat, and boil hard for 2 minutes. Begin to check for jelling (see page 329).

When it is jelled, ladle it into 12 hot sterilized 4-ounce mason jars, leaving ¼-inch headroom. Wipe the rims and seal the jars. Process in a boiling water bath for 10 minutes.

MAKES TWELVE 4-OUNCE JARS

rosa rugosa On the beaches of Long Island, bushes of the wild rose Rosa Rugosa grow everywhere. They bloom with big floppy pink blossoms, but around mid-July, they begin to produce "hips," the round red-orange fruits that appear after the bloom. This is the crop we use for jam.

Blueberry-Cinnamon Jam

A touch of cinnamon in this jam brings out the richness of the berries.

2 quarts fresh blueberries, stemmed
1 teaspoon ground cinnamon
½ cup fresh lemon juice
4½ cups granulated sugar

Crush the blueberries with a potato masher in a large bowl. Stir in the cinnamon. Transfer the mixture to a heavy 6-quart pot and bring it to a gentle boil, stirring occasionally, over medium heat. Stir in the lemon juice and sugar, increase the heat, and boil hard for 3 minutes. Begin to check for jelling (see page 329).

When it is jelled, remove from the heat, skim, and let cool for 5 minutes. Ladle into 12 hot sterilized 4-ounce mason jars, leaving ¼-inch headroom. Wipe the rims and seal the jars. Process in a boiling water bath for 10 minutes.

MAKES TWELVE 4-OUNCE JARS

nantucket blueberries While we were visiting on Nantucket, a friend asked us to gather wild blueberries, telling us to keep our eyes peeled, since the bushes grow low to the ground. In the midst of what we thought was ordinary bramble, we realized we were surrounded by tiny blueberries at their peak. Nantucket berries are small with intense flavor, because they have to survive in a harsh environment; we bent down to sample the first sun-warmed berry and found it as sweet as blueberry jam out of the jar.

Mint Jelly

We disagree about mint jelly. David thinks it's awful; I love it. Not only did I always have it with leg of lamb when I was a kid, but I find it a good way to have jelly with dinner. This recipe makes a delicious jelly with big mint flavor and no green color. —BARBARA

3 cups finely chopped fresh mint
3½ cups water
1 (1¾-ounce) box pectin or 6 tablespoons liquid pectin
4 cups granulated sugar

Combine the mint and water in a 4-quart saucepan, bring just to a boil, and boil gently for 3 minutes. Remove the pan from the heat, cover, and let stand for 10 minutes.

Strain the warm mint liquid into another large saucepan; discard the mint. Bring the liquid to a gentle boil over medium heat. Stir in the pectin, increase the heat to medium-high, and bring to a hard boil. Stir in the sugar, return to a hard boil, and cook for 2 minutes. Begin to check for jelling (see page 329).

When it is jelled, ladle into 8 hot sterilized 4-ounce mason jars, leaving ¼-inch headroom. Wipe the rims and seal the jars. Process in a boiling water bath for 10 minutes.

MAKES EIGHT 4-OUNCE JARS

Plum Conserve

A conserve is similar to a chutney, in that it usually contains more than one fruit and often includes nuts. It's different, however, in that it's cooked until the fruits turn into a spreadable mash, unlike chutney, which remains chunky. This conserve is a delicious accompaniment to pies, pound cake, and ice cream and is just perfect with a creamy, soft-ripening cheese.

3½ pounds plums, pitted and quartered

5 cups granulated sugar

1½ cups dark raisins

1 teaspoon ground cinnamon

1 teaspoon ground ginger

1 teaspoon grated lemon zest

1 lemon, peeled, seeded, and cut into
  ¼-inch dice

1 cup chopped walnuts

Place the plums in a heavy 6-quart pot over medium heat. Cover and cook, stirring occasionally, until they release their juice, about 7 minutes. Remove the cover, bring to a boil, and stir in the sugar, raisins, cinnamon, ginger, lemon zest, and lemon pulp. Return to a boil and boil for 5 minutes. Stir in the walnuts and boil for 5 minutes longer. Remove from the heat, skim off any foam from the surface, and let stand for 10 minutes.

Ladle into 11 hot sterilized half-pint mason jars, leaving ¼-inch headroom. Wipe the rims and seal the jars. Process in a boiling water bath for 10 minutes.

MAKES 11 HALF-PINT JARS

Sweet Yellow Tomato Preserves

Early cookbooks have recipes for tomato jams, jellies, and preserves that were used as spreads for biscuits. Green and tiny yellow tomatoes were commonly cooked with loads of sugar. We prefer to pickle tart green tomatoes and use the sweeter yellow ones for preserving.

5 pounds small yellow tomatoes, such as yellow cherry
    or Sungold tomatoes
1 lemon, thinly sliced with peel
4 cups granulated sugar
3 tablespoons apple cider vinegar (5% acidity)
1 tablespoon kosher salt

Rinse the tomatoes, then prick each one 4 or 5 times with a needle. Place the tomatoes in a bowl, add the lemon, and pour the sugar over them. Cover and let stand for 4 hours.

Transfer the tomato mixture to a 10-quart pot and add the vinegar and salt. Cook uncovered over medium-low heat for 1 hour; gently stir 4 or 5 times but be careful not to burst the tomatoes.

Carefully drain the tomatoes, reserving the liquid. Pour the liquid into a saucepan and boil until it is reduced by half, about 30 minutes.

Pack the tomatoes and lemon slices into 7 hot sterilized half-pint mason jars. Ladle the hot liquid over them, leaving ¼-inch headroom. Wipe the rims and seal the jars. Process in a boiling water bath for 10 minutes.

MAKES 7 HALF-PINT JARS

yellow tomatoes These were new to us when we fell off the Midwest haywagon and first encountered California produce (although not quite so strange and inedible looking as prickly pear, cherimoya, and lotus root). Soon we were cooking happily with old-fangled and hybrid varieties such as Green Zebras, Yellow Currants, and Big Rainbows.

Plum Butter

Fruit butters take long cooking and laborious stirring. As the mashed fruit simmers and thickens, its sugars caramelize and the flavors are concentrated, providing a richness unmatched by the shorter cooking times of jellies and jams. Our deep jammy plum butter spreads on toast like silk.

4 pounds plums, cut lengthwise in half and pitted
2½ cups granulated sugar
1½ teaspoons ground ginger

Place the plums in a 6-quart pot and cook over low heat, stirring so that they don't scorch, until they break down to a mash, about 35 minutes. Remove the pot from the heat.

Place a wire strainer over a large bowl and ladle one-quarter of the pulp at a time into the strainer, pushing it through the strainer to remove the skins. Discard the skins. The strained pulp should measure about 5 cups.

Combine the pulp, sugar, and ginger in a heavy 4-quart saucepan and cook over medium heat until the fruit is thickened and resembles a glassy spread, about 1½ hours. It is important to stir every 5 minutes to keep the fruit from scorching.

continued

Ladle into 4 hot sterilized half-pint mason jars, leaving ¼-inch headroom. Wipe the rims and seal the jars. Process in a boiling water bath for 10 minutes.

MAKES 4 HALF-PINT JARS

a little history Fruit butters were made by early settlers not only because fruits were a large part of their diet, but also because the long cooking time brought out the natural sweetness of the fruit, a help when sugar was hard to get. We can guess that Indians also made fruit butter, since we know they made fruit leather, which is fruit butter even further reduced to a thick paste and dried in sheets.

BUD PAGE AND HIS GRANDMA, 1930

Apple Butter

We've held back the spices in our apple butter so that the sweet apple flavor can shine through. It may seem like an awful lot of apples, but after they're cooked, you'll wind up with just ten cups of apple butter—not a lot for a whole winter's worth of hot buttered toast. And, of course, you can cut the recipe in half.

18 pounds McIntosh apples, cored, peeled, and sliced
½ cup fresh lemon juice
5 cups granulated sugar
2 tablespoons apple cider vinegar (5% acidity)
1 tablespoon kosher salt
1 teaspoon ground cinnamon

Place the apples and lemon juice in a large heavy stockpot over medium heat and cook, stirring occasionally, until the fruit breaks down to a mash, about 45 minutes. Stir in the sugar, vinegar, salt, and cinnamon. Cook at a gentle boil, stirring often, until the mash is thickened and a toasty brown color, about 3½ hours.

Ladle into 11 hot sterilized half-pint mason jars, leaving ¼-inch headroom. Wipe the rims and seal the jars. Process in a boiling water bath for 10 minutes.

MAKES 11 HALF-PINT JARS

WHOLE FRUITS

Spiced Peaches

In the Midwest, we didn't have peach trees, so as young-sters neither of us ever tasted homemade canned peaches. Years later, living in a warmer climate, we put up our own, and ever since we've held them in high esteem. Use early, firm peaches for this recipe.

6 pounds firm peaches
6 cups granulated sugar
6 cups water
1 teaspoon minced crystallized ginger (see Note)
2 (3-inch) cinnamon sticks, broken into 4 pieces each
8 allspice berries

Score each peach with a shallow X on the underside. Fill an 8-quart pot with water and bring it to a gentle boil. Fill a large bowl with ice water. Dip the peaches 4 at a time into the boiling water and scald them for about 30 seconds, then plunge them into the ice water to cool. Slip the skins off, halve the peaches, and gently remove the pits.

Combine the sugar, water, ginger, cinnamon sticks, and allspice berries in a 6-quart pot over medium heat. Simmer until the sugar dissolves, about 15 minutes.

Pack the peaches into 8 hot sterilized pint mason jars. Ladle the hot syrup over them and evenly distribute the spices among the jars. Leave ¼-inch headroom. Wipe the rims and seal the jars. Process in a boiling water bath for 20 minutes.　　　　　　**MAKES 8 PINT JARS**

NOTE: Crystallized ginger is another name for candied ginger, which you can buy in supermarkets and good candy shops. It's made by cooking pieces of fresh ginger in a sugar syrup, then coating them with more sugar. The recipe uses very little, but we think it makes a difference.

Spiced Seckel Pears

You see these tiny brown, often-hard pears in late fall. Some people call them winter pears because they hang on the trees long into autumn and, when they're picked, soften slowly into the holiday season. Seckel pears are great for stewing and canning whole because they hold their shape so well.

These pears are first lightly brined, then poached in heavy syrup, making a vibrant after-dinner treat. We serve them right out of the jar with a little of their syrup and a plate of Sugar Cookies (page 410).

FOR THE BRINE

1 gallon water

2 tablespoons apple cider vinegar (5% acidity)

2 tablespoons kosher salt

24 Seckel pears (about 3 pounds)

FOR THE SYRUP

2 quarts water

6 cups granulated sugar

½ cup fresh lemon juice

1 teaspoon minced crystallized ginger

½ vanilla bean, split lengthwise

1 (3-inch) cinnamon stick, broken into 6 pieces

continued

Combine the water, vinegar, and salt in a large bowl. Peel the pears, keeping them whole, with the stems on, and drop them into the brine as soon as you complete each one. Let the pears sit in the brine about 30 minutes while you prepare the syrup.

Combine all the syrup ingredients in a 4-quart saucepan and simmer over low heat until the sugar is dissolved, about 10 minutes.

Transfer the syrup to a large stockpot and return to a simmer. Remove the pears from the water and rinse them. Place the pears in the syrup and simmer for about 5 minutes, until the pears are warmed through. Remove from the heat; remove the vanilla bean and discard it.

Gently remove the pears from the syrup and pack them in 6 hot sterilized pint mason jars, 4 pears to a jar: Placing 2 pears upright and 2 upside down will allow for a properly tight pack. Ladle the hot syrup over them, evenly distributing the cinnamon sticks and leaving ¼-inch headroom. Wipe the rims and seal the jars. Process in a boiling water bath for 20 minutes.　　MAKES 6 PINT JARS

Bourbon Cherries

A perfect garnish for Manhattan cocktails, these can also be enjoyed by themselves. They soak up a fair amount of the liquid in the jar, so they pack quite a punch. Because of the alcohol, there's no need to process these in a boiling water bath. If, however, you prefer a poached-fruit texture in your dessert fruit, process them for ten minutes.

1 cup superfine sugar

1½ cups water

4 pints black Montmorency cherries, stemmed

2 (1-liter) bottles Kentucky bourbon

Place 2 tablespoons sugar and 3 tablespoons water into each of 8 sterilized pint mason jars. Fill the mason jars with the cherries, packing them tightly but being careful not to crush them. Fill each jar with bourbon, leaving ½-inch headroom. Seal the jars and shake them to dissolve the sugar. Store them in a dark place for 3 months.

MAKES 8 PINT JARS

cherry cordial Every year, we put up bourbon cherries. We sit at the kitchen table surrounded by mason jars, cherries, and a couple of bottles of Kentucky bourbon. All afternoon we pack the cherries into the jars, topping them off with bourbon, and marvel at the beauty of what we've done. There's been many a dinner when we snacked on these long after we thought we were finished eating and drinking.

CHUTNEYS

Green Tomato–
Apple Chutney

Tomatoes provide a whole second crop once the weather turns cold and the unripe, apple-hard green fruits are brought in. They can either be fried or preserved in chutneys, relishes, and chowchow.

4½ pounds green tomatoes

1 pound apples, cored, peeled, and cut into ½-inch dice

1 pound onions, cut into ¼-inch dice

¾ cup diced shallots (⅛-inch dice)

1 leek, thinly sliced

1 teaspoon minced hot chiles

1 cup apple cider vinegar (5% acidity)

1 cup olive oil

2 tablespoons kosher salt

1 tablespoon granulated sugar

1 teaspoon minced ginger

1 teaspoon ground turmeric

¼ teaspoon ground allspice

Core the tomatoes, cut them into quarters, and scoop out the seeds. Discard the seeds and dice the tomatoes.

Place all the ingredients in an 8-quart pot over medium heat and bring to a gentle boil. Continue to cook for 5 minutes, stirring occasionally.

Laddle the chutney into 11 hot sterilized half-pint mason jars, leaving ¼-inch headroom. Wipe the rims and seal the jars. Process in a boiling water bath for 10 minutes.

MAKES 11 HALF-PINT JARS

a natural combination The first harvest of fall apples happens just when we're loaded up with baskets of green tomatoes. Early in the morning we drive up to Wickham's Farm Stand in Cutchogue, New York, and pick out the best of the apples that came in that day. Soon we're home chopping what seem to be mountains of green tomatoes, apples, and onions.

Rhubarb Chutney

The snappy flavor of rhubarb is one of the first culinary signs that spring is here. Because the season is so short that it's often gone before we've had our fill, we've learned to make chutney so we can enjoy rhubarb throughout the year.

4 pounds rhubarb, trimmed and cut into 1-inch pieces

4 cups diced yellow onions (¼-inch dice)

2 cups golden raisins

2 cups apple cider vinegar (5% acidity)

2 cups granulated sugar

2 tablespoons minced ginger

2 teaspoons dry mustard

2 teaspoons kosher salt

1 teaspoon red pepper flakes

Combine all the above ingredients in a heavy 6-quart pot and bring to a boil. Gently boil the mixture for about 40 minutes, stirring occasionally. The rhubarb will break apart.

Ladle into 14 hot sterilized half-pint mason jars, leaving ½-inch headroom. Wipe the rims and seal the jars. Process in a boiling water bath for 10 minutes.

MAKES 14 HALF-PINT JARS

PICKLES, RELISHES, AND VEGETABLES

We always offer one of our homemade pickles or relishes

at the restaurant. It could be our Firecracker Relish

or Grandmother Drover's Dill Pickles or the Bourbon

Cherries that we drop into Manhattans. It's part of our

feeling that American food isn't about using butter-rich

sauces, but rather about setting off the natural tastes

of a food with vibrant relishes, preserves, chutneys,

and pickles.

There's something very American about opening the

pantry door and seeing all those mason jars full of things

that you've put up for the winter. We think of it as part of

living in a region where the growing season is short, and

where you know you'd better have enough food to last

you through the cold months ahead.

Pickled Peppers

These peppers get incredibly spicy and vinegary as they sit on the shelf, but it takes about three months for that to happen. Don't be dismayed if at first they don't live up to your expectations. Put them away in a dark cupboard and don't take them out until they're thoroughly brined.

3 pounds mixed green and red bell peppers

6 cups water

3 cups apple cider vinegar (5% acidity)

2 tablespoons yellow mustard seeds

2 tablespoons fennel seeds

2 tablespoons coriander seeds

1 tablespoon celery seeds

1 tablespoon kosher salt

1 tablespoon granulated sugar

1 teaspoon black peppercorns

1 teaspoon red pepper flakes

Remove the stems, seeds, and pith from the peppers and slice the peppers lengthwise into 1-inch-wide strips. Set aside.

Bring the remaining ingredients to a boil in a 4-quart pot. Boil for 5 minutes.

Pack the peppers into 4 hot sterilized pint mason jars. Ladle the boiling pickling liquid over them, evenly distributing the spices among the jars and leaving ½-inch headroom. Wipe the rims and seal the jars. Process in a boiling water bath for 10 minutes.

These peppers are best when allowed to sit for 3 months, allowing the spicy brine to soak into the peppers.

MAKES 4 PINT JARS

Green Tomato Pickles

When sweetness and spice are properly balanced in these firm pickles, their bright flavor shines through. Adding carrots and onions turns them into a small salad that we serve with sandwiches or slices of cold ham or chicken.

*6 pounds medium green tomatoes, cored, quartered, and
   seeded*

1½ pounds yellow onions, thinly sliced

1 large carrot, peeled and cut into 16 (3-inch) strips

FOR THE BRINE

½ cup kosher salt

FOR THE PICKLE

4 cups water

2 cups apple cider vinegar (5% acidity)

½ cup granulated sugar

2 teaspoons yellow mustard seeds

2 teaspoons celery seeds

2 teaspoons black peppercorns

1 lemon, thinly sliced crosswise

8 fresh dill sprigs

Combine the tomatoes, onions, and carrots in a large glass or ceramic bowl, toss with the salt, cover, and let stand overnight, about 8 hours. Rinse and let drain.

Bring the water, vinegar, sugar, mustard seeds, celery seeds, and peppercorns to a boil in a large pan. Boil for 5 minutes.

Pack the tomatoes, onions, carrots, lemon slices, and dill into 8 hot sterilized pint mason jars. Ladle the pickling liquid over them, evenly distributing the spices among the jars and leaving ½-inch headroom. Wipe the rims and seal the jars. Process in a boiling water bath for 10 minutes.

MAKES 8 PINT JARS

pickle day Tuesday is the day we do our pickling and jam making, which means that on Mondays we make the eight-mile drive out to Latham's Farm Stand in Orient, New York, to select our produce. Somehow we always leave with armloads more than we intended, which means we have quite a busy Tuesday ahead of us.

Pickled Okra

Most people know okra only as the vegetable whose gelatinous texture thickens gumbos, but the green pods are delicious when they're made into bright green pickles.

4 cups water

2 cups apple cider vinegar (5% acidity)

¼ cup granulated sugar

2 tablespoons yellow mustard seeds

2 tablespoons fennel seeds

1 tablespoon celery seeds

2 tablespoons kosher salt

1 teaspoon red pepper flakes

2 pounds okra

6 shallots, peeled and cut in half

1 red bell pepper, cut into 12 strips

continued

the canning shelf

Bring the water, vinegar, sugar, mustard seeds, fennel seeds, celery seeds, salt, and red pepper flakes to a boil in a 4-quart pot. Boil for 5 minutes.

Pack the okra, shallots, and red pepper strips into 6 hot sterilized pint mason jars. Ladle the boiling pickling liquid over them, evenly distributing the spices among the jars, leaving ½-inch headroom. Wipe the rims and seal the jars. Process in a boiling water bath for 10 minutes.

MAKES 6 PINT JARS

Watermelon Pickles

We had never tasted watermelon pickles until we made them for ourselves, but since then, they've held a special place in our hearts. Although they're probably the most labor-intensive of all pickles, they're well worth the trouble. Apart from their uniqueness, they're sweet and citrusy and retain a pleasing crunch.

FOR THE BRINE

¾ cup kosher salt

6 cups cold water

1 large watermelon

FOR THE PICKLE

1 tablespoon whole cloves

1 (3-inch) cinnamon stick

1 teaspoon minced crystallized ginger

⅛ teaspoon ground nutmeg

5 cups water

7 cups granulated sugar

3 cups apple cider vinegar (5% acidity)

For the brine, dissolve the salt in the water in a large glass or ceramic bowl. To prepare the rind, quarter the watermelon and scoop out the pink flesh, making sure to scrape all of the pink flesh from the green inner rind. Save the pink flesh for another use. Peel the hard dark green outer skin away and discard it. Cut the remaining light green inner rind into strips about 1 inch wide and 2 inches long. Measure 3 quarts cut rind and add it to the salted water. Let stand for 5 hours.

Drain and rinse the rind under cold running water. Place it in an 8-quart pot, cover with fresh water, and simmer for 10 minutes over medium heat. Drain and rinse under cold water. Transfer to a large ceramic or glass bowl.

For the pickle, tie the spices together in a piece of cheesecloth. Bring the spice bag, water, sugar, and vinegar to a boil in an 8-quart pot. Reduce the heat and simmer uncovered for 5 minutes. Remove the spice bag and discard it. Pour the hot liquid over the rind and let stand for 12 to 24 hours.

Remove the rind from the liquid and bring the liquid to a boil.

Place the rind in 12 hot sterilized half-pint mason jars. Fill the jars with the hot liquid, leaving ¼-inch headroom. Wipe the rims and seal the jars. Process in a boiling water bath for 10 minutes.   **MAKES 12 HALF-PINT JARS**

an american antipasto We've always loved the robust flavor and staunch texture of American country ham. When David happened to recall the classic Italian antipasto of summer melon slices wrapped in prosciutto, it dawned on him that bits of watermelon pickle would be wonderful wrapped in dry-cured smoked ham. It turned out that these two very American ingredients are as much at home with each other as the Italian ingredients are.

GRANDMOTHER DROVER AND HER FRIEND,
LAURA, PUTTING UP CORN, 1986

Grandpa Drover was a packrat. His sheds

were filled with old workbenches stacked high with tools,

bottles, basins, and myriad treasures cluttered the floor.

He also couldn't stop planting vegetable gardens.

When Grandma Drover entered her eighties, she

insisted that Grandpa cut back on his gardening: She

simply couldn't can it all. However, her demands went

unheeded, and every summer, she canned bushels of

beans and brined pounds of pickles. This is how she did it.

—DAVID

Grandmother Drover's
Dill Pickles

4 pounds pickling cucumbers

FOR THE BRINE

¾ cup kosher salt

1 gallon cold water

FOR THE PICKLE

5 cups water

3 cups apple cider vinegar (5% acidity)

⅓ cup kosher salt

2 tablespoons granulated sugar

3 tablespoons yellow mustard seeds

2 tablespoons coriander seeds

½ teaspoon red pepper flakes

1 large white onion, thinly sliced

21 fresh dill sprigs

Slice the cucumbers lengthwise in half or into quarters.

For the brine, dissolve the salt in the water in a large bowl. Place the cucumbers in a large ceramic or glass bowl, pour the salted water over them, and let them stand overnight, about 8 hours.

For the pickle, bring the water, vinegar, salt, sugar, mustard seeds, coriander seeds, and red pepper flakes to a boil in an 8-quart pot.

Drain the cucumbers, discarding the brine; do not rinse the cucumbers.

Pack the cucumbers, onion, and dill into 7 hot sterilized pint mason jars. Ladle the boiling pickling liquid over them, evenly distribute the spices among the jars and leave ½-inch headroom. Wipe the rims and seal the jars. Process in a boiling water bath for 10 minutes.

MAKES 7 PINT JARS

the canning shelf

Olive Oil Pickles

When we tell people the secret ingredient is olive oil, they can't believe it. This recipe can be halved, but we like to make lots so we can give them as gifts.

7 pounds carrots, peeled and sliced ¼ inch thick

14 pounds pickling cucumbers, sliced ¼ inch thick

6 pounds yellow onions, sliced ¼ inch thick

3 cups kosher salt

4 quarts white wine vinegar

2¾ cups olive oil

1 cup celery seeds

1½ cups yellow mustard seeds

¼ cup red pepper flakes

Bring a pot of salted water to a simmer and blanch the carrots for 3 minutes. Rinse the carrots under cold running water. Place the carrots, cucumbers, and onions in a large bowl and toss them with the salt. Let the mixture stand overnight, about 8 hours.

Drain and rinse the vegetables and return them to the bowl. Pour the vinegar over them and let stand for 3 to 4 hours.

Drain the vinegar into a saucepan, add the olive oil, celery seeds, mustard seeds, and red pepper flakes to the vinegar and bring to a boil.

Pack the cucumbers, carrots, and onions into 16 hot sterilized pint mason jars. Ladle the boiling pickling liquid over them, evenly distributing the spices among the jars, and leave ½ inch headroom. Wipe the rims and seal the jars. Process in a boiling water bath for 10 minutes.

MAKES 16 PINT JARS

Preserved Grape Leaves

We like to cook whole fish wrapped in brined grape leaves, with bits of herbs and lemon slices tucked into the package. Although we often buy the leaves already brined, we're always on the lookout for wild grapevines when we go out foraging in the spring. Then we pick the tender green leaves, take them home, and process them ourselves.

30 large grape leaves

FOR THE BRINE
5 cups water
1 cup coarse sea salt

Blanch the leaves in batches of 5 at a time in boiling water for 20 seconds. Let them dry flat on kitchen towels or paper towels.

For the brine, combine the water and salt in a large saucepan over medium heat and bring it to a boil.

Stack 10 grape leaves in each of 3 stacks, roll, and place in 3 hot sterilized pint mason jars, folding and tucking in any leaves that protrude from the top. Fill the jars with the hot brine, leaving ¼-inch headroom. Wipe the rims and seal the jars. Process in a boiling water bath for 5 minutes.

When you use the leaves, rinse them well to remove the brine. **MAKES 3 PINT JARS**

Firecracker Relish

Don't let the simplicity of the ingredients belie the tastiness of the end product; this relish has the perfect balance of sweet and spicy. Bright red and glassy, it adds a piquant kick to many dishes. We love it on leg of lamb and grilled tuna.

3 pounds red bell peppers, cut into ¼-inch dice

2 tablespoons red pepper flakes

2 tablespoons minced garlic

1 tablespoon Home Spice Mix (page 26)

1 teaspoon ground ginger

3 cups granulated sugar

1 cup apple cider vinegar (5% acidity)

Combine the bell peppers, pepper flakes, garlic, spice mix, and ginger in a large bowl, cover, and let stand at room temperature for 5 hours.

Combine the pepper mixture with the sugar and vinegar in an 8-quart pot over medium heat and bring to a gentle boil. Reduce the heat to medium-low and gently boil until the relish becomes thick and glassy, about 1¾ hours.

Ladle the hot relish into 4 hot sterilized half-pint mason jars, leaving ¼-inch headroom. Wipe the rims and seal the jars. Process in a boiling water bath for 15 minutes.

MAKES 4 HALF-PINT JARS

Green Tomato–
Cucumber Relish

When the weather threatens frost and it looks as though the tomatoes on the vine will never have a chance to ripen, we go out and pick them still hard and green and make this tart relish.

2½ pounds green tomatoes

1½ pounds cucumbers, peeled, seeded, and cut into
   ¼-inch dice

1½ pounds green bell peppers, cut into ¼-inch dice

¾ pound yellow onions, cut into ¼-inch dice

½ cup kosher salt

2 cups granulated sugar

1 cup apple cider vinegar (5% acidity)

¼ cup all-purpose flour

1 tablespoon ground turmeric

2 teaspoons dry mustard

Core the tomatoes and cut them in half. Scoop out the seeds and discard them. Cut the tomatoes into ½-inch dice.

Combine the tomatoes, cucumbers, green peppers, onions, and salt in a glass or ceramic bowl. Cover and refrigerate overnight, about 8 hours.

Transfer the mixture to a large pot and bring to a gentle boil over medium heat. Remove from the heat and drain immediately, reserving ½ cup of the liquid.

Return the drained vegetables to the pot, add the sugar and vinegar, and bring to a gentle boil. Whisk the flour, turmeric, and dry mustard into the reserved liquid. Add the flour mixture to the vegetables, return to a gentle boil, and cook until the relish is thickened, about 5 minutes.

Ladle the hot relish into 5 hot sterilized pint mason jars or 10 half-pint jars. Wipe the rims and seal the jars. Process in a boiling water bath for 10 minutes. **MAKES 5 PINT JARS**

GRANDMOTHER McCALL
(SECOND FROM RIGHT), AT 16, 1921

This is the relish my grandmother made every single summer. When she died, the recipe died with her, and although we did the best we could to reproduce it, we couldn't get it quite right. Then, at Uncle Gene's funeral, an aunt handed me a sheet of paper that had the original recipe written on it. It turns out that we had completely forgotten the cabbage. —BARBARA

Grandmother McCall's
Relish

12 medium green bell peppers, finely chopped

12 medium red bell peppers, finely chopped

10 medium yellow onions, finely chopped

1 small head green cabbage, finely chopped

¾ cup kosher salt

Boiling water to cover

4 cups apple cider vinegar (5% acidity)

4 cups granulated sugar

2 tablespoons celery seeds

2 tablespoons yellow mustard seeds

Place the peppers, onions, and cabbage in a large bowl and toss with the salt. Add just enough boiling water to cover the vegetables and let stand for 15 minutes.

Transfer the vegetables to a colander and drain well, pressing out any excess liquid with the back of a spoon. Transfer to a large stainless-steel pot, add the vinegar, sugar, celery seeds, and mustard seeds, and bring to a boil over medium heat. Boil for 15 minutes, stirring often.

Ladle the relish into 6 hot sterilized pint mason jars, leaving ¼-inch headroom. Wipe the rims and seal the jars. Process in a boiling water bath for 10 minutes.

MAKES 6 PINT JARS

Stewed Tomatoes

We can't resist buying bushels of tomatoes at farmers' markets and putting them up to enjoy over the winter. Homemade are so much better than canned stewed tomatoes. Since these are already seasoned, all you have to do is heat and serve them. We like to simmer chicken breasts in them. Yellow tomatoes have a beautiful color, and because they're low in acidity, we think they work well with more delicate fish and shellfish.

17 pounds ripe red or yellow tomatoes

1 tablespoon olive oil

2 cups diced celery (¼-inch dice)

1 cup diced onions (¼-inch dice)

1 cup diced green bell peppers (¼-inch dice)

½ cup apple cider vinegar (5% acidity)

2 tablespoons kosher salt

18 large fresh basil leaves

Fill a 10-quart pot with water and bring to a gentle boil. Fill a large bowl with ice water. Cut a shallow X on the underside of each tomato, then core the tomatoes. Scald the tomatoes 4 at a time in the boiling water for about 20 seconds, then plunge them into the ice water until they cool. Remove them from the water and slip the skins off, discarding the skins.

Cut the tomatoes crosswise in half and scoop out the seeds, discarding the seeds. Quarter the larger tomatoes.

Heat the olive oil in a 12-inch skillet over medium heat. Add the celery, onions, and green peppers and cook until they are softened, about 5 minutes.

Combine the vegetables with the tomatoes in a large stockpot over medium heat. Add the vinegar and salt and bring to a gentle boil, stirring occasionally. Cook until the tomatoes are warmed through, about 15 minutes. Be careful not to stir too often, to keep the tomatoes from breaking down.

Ladle the hot tomatoes into 9 hot sterilized pint mason jars and add 2 basil leaves to each jar. Top with the remaining hot liquid, leaving ½-inch headroom. Wipe the rims and seal the jars. Process in a boiling water bath for 20 minutes.   MAKES 9 PINT JARS

SOMETHING SWEET

CAKES

Pound Cake   369

Toasted Angel Food Cake   370

Frozen Lemon Icebox Cake
with Strawberry Sauce   374

Devil's Food Cupcakes   376

Sour Cream Coffee Cake   377

Strawberry Shortcake   378

PUDDINGS

Chocolate Pudding   382

Butterscotch Pudding   384

Persimmon Pudding   385

Native Pudding   387

Bread Pudding with Pear-Rum Sauce   388

PIES

Rustic Apple Pie   392

Bourbon Pecan Pie   393

Honey Pumpkin Pie   394

Buttery Pie Dough   395

CRISPS AND COBBLERS

Peach-Blueberry Crisp   397

Strawberry-Rhubarb Crisp   398

Apple Cobbler with
Dropped Cheddar-Biscuit Topping   400

DESSERTS

Desserts figure prominently in our memories of childhood. With good reason: Americans do dessert better than anyone else. People from other countries are always saying, "Oh, we just have fruit or a bite of cheese at the end of the meal, but you Americans like sweets," to which our answer is, "Yes, indeed, we do."

American desserts are both simple and sophisticated. Nothing could be as unpretentious as a pie, but to make a great apple pie takes some deftness and skill and sensitivity to the ingredients. How tart are the apples? How fresh is the flour? Is the kitchen warm or cold? That's why to make a good dessert you have to be in practice, to be making desserts consistently. Luckily, that's no hardship.

CAKES

Sometimes cakes are for special events, like weddings and birthdays. In the Page family, every birthday was celebrated with a tall angel food cake made by Grandma Page. But cakes can also be midmorning treats, just a slice of toasted pound cake or a wedge of coffee cake with a cup of coffee.

Pound Cake

We use this recipe as a foundation for many different pound cakes, adding citrus zest or finely chopped nuts, splitting the cooled cake into two layers and spreading homemade preserves between the layers. We also toast leftover slices for breakfast.

½ pound (2 sticks) unsalted butter, softened
1⅔ cups granulated sugar
5 large eggs, lightly beaten
2 cups cake flour
¼ teaspoon salt

Preheat the oven to 300°F. Butter and flour a deep 8-inch round cake pan or an 8 x 4-inch loaf pan.

In a large mixing bowl, beat together the butter and sugar until the mixture is light yellow and fluffy. Beat in the beaten eggs half at a time and continue to beat until the mixture forms a slowly dissolving ribbon when the whisk is lifted. Beat in the cake flour and salt half at a time until the mixture is smooth.

Pour the batter into the cake pan and bake until a toothpick inserted into the center comes out clean, about 1½ hours. Let cool in the pan on a rack for 45 minutes.

SERVES 8

FRUITY POUND CAKE Add ½ cup fruit, such as blueberries or diced peaches, or 1 tablespoon minced lemon zest to the batter.

pound cake Pound cake doesn't weigh a pound or cost a pound; it gets its name from the quantities of the ingredients that go into it. In Amelia Simmons's *American Cookery,* the first American cookbook, the recipe calls for "1 pound of sugar, 1 pound of butter, 1 pound of flour, 1 pound, or 10, eggs." A sizable cake, but an easy recipe to remember.

Toasted Angel Food Cake

Angel food cake has had a recent revival of popularity, probably because it's made without butter or egg yolks. We think it tastes best when the slices are toasted.

2 cups egg whites (from about 15 large eggs),
  at room temperature
½ teaspoon salt
2 teaspoons cream of tartar (see Note)
1½ cups superfine sugar
1 teaspoon almond extract
1 teaspoon vanilla extract
1 cup sifted cake flour

Preheat the oven to 350°F.

In the bowl of an electric mixer, beat the egg whites at medium-high speed until foamy. Add the salt and cream of tartar and continue beating until soft peaks form. Gradually add the sugar and beat until stiff peaks form. Beat in the almond and vanilla extracts. Gently fold in the cake flour in three additions, mixing only to combine.

Pour the batter into an ungreased 10 x 4-inch tube. Bake until the top of the cake is golden brown, about 50 minutes. Invert the pan onto a slender bottleneck, such as a wine bottle, and let cool completely.

Run a thin sharp knife around the sides of the pan and the center tube to release the cake, then turn cake out onto a plate.

To serve, cut the cake into 1¼-inch-thick wedges and lightly toast them in the oven or on a griddle. Place 2 slices on each plate, and serve with fruit or sorbet.

SERVES 8

NOTE: Angel food cakes depend on the air that's beaten into the egg whites for their rising. Adding cream of tartar, or tartaric acid, helps to increase the volume of the beaten whites and make them stable. Baking powder contains some cream of tartar: The added acid makes bubbles of carbon dioxide that help the batter rise.

Nana's birthday cake A private room had

been arranged for, along with a two-tiered chocolate

birthday cake, to celebrate my nana Leila's fiftieth birth-

day. A couple of weeks before the party, my mother and

father decided to marry. However, due to the fact that my

mother was seventeen and Roman Catholic and my

father was twenty-three and Protestant, talk of marriage

had been forbidden.

Feeling desperate and in love, they borrowed a friend's car

and drove from New Jersey to Elkton, Maryland, where they

were secretly married. Although they returned to New

Jersey intent on keeping their marriage a secret, they worried that the secret would come out at Nana's birthday party.

The day before the party, my parents decided it was time for reckoning. Theirs was a huge decision; not only would they most certainly be ostracized from the family, but my mother would lose her appointment as Miss Atlantic City, a title given the city's most beautiful and talented unmarried young woman.

To their surprise, the families were delighted with the news—although shocked—and congratulations and cocktails were passed about. In the midst of the festivities, everyone decided that Nana's birthday party would be a joint celebration. Nana's chocolate birthday cake was transformed into a wedding cake and two knives cut it simultaneously. My nana unselfishly gave away her party, her cake, and her only son, and to this day my mother is still a beauty queen in everyone's eyes.   —BARBARA

Frozen Lemon Icebox Cake
with Strawberry Sauce

We no longer make the refrigerated whipped cream icebox cake whose recipe is printed on boxes of chocolate wafers found on every grocer's shelf (although that one was also delicious). Instead, on hot summer nights this deliciously tart and sweet frozen cake is the perfect treat to cool you down.

FOR THE CAKE

2 cups vanilla wafer crumbs (see Note)

8 tablespoons (1 stick) unsalted butter, melted

6 large eggs, separated

¼ teaspoon salt

Grated zest of 1 lemon

½ cup fresh lemon juice

1 (14-ounce) can condensed milk

½ teaspoon cream of tartar

½ cup granulated sugar

FOR THE SAUCE (MAKES 1½ CUPS)

1 pint ripe strawberries, hulled

Fresh lemon juice to taste

Superfine sugar to taste

For the cake, preheat the oven to 350°F.

Place the wafer crumbs in a small bowl and stir in the melted butter. Press this mixture into the bottom and up the sides of a 10-inch springform pan. Bake until golden, 12 to 15 minutes. Let the crust cool completely.

Place the egg yolks in a mixer bowl and beat on medium speed until thick and pale, 4 to 5 minutes. Beat in the salt, lemon zest, and lemon juice. Slowly add the condensed milk, continuing to beat for about 1 minute.

In a separate mixer bowl, beat together the egg whites and cream of tartar until foamy. Gradually beat in the sugar, then continue to beat to a stiff meringue.

With a spatula, fold half of the meringue into the lemon mixture and pour it into the cooled baked crust. Spread the remaining meringue evenly over the filling.

Bake until the top is lightly browned, about 20 minutes. Let cool on a wire rack.

Using a small knife dipped in hot water, loosen the meringue from the sides of the pan, but do not release the side. Cover with plastic wrap and freeze for at least 4 hours, or overnight.

For the sauce, purée the berries in a food processor or blender with a bit of lemon juice until smooth. Strain to remove the seeds. Stir in sugar and more lemon juice to taste. Cover and refrigerate until needed.

To serve, remove the side of the pan, cut into wedges, and serve frozen with the sauce.   SERVES 12

NOTE: To make cookie crumbs, either drop the cookies through the tube of a food processor with the motor going, or lay them on a counter and crush them with a rolling pin. Covering the cookies with a sheet of waxed paper will help prevent the crumbs from flying all over the kitchen.

Devil's Food Cupcakes

I make a devil's food cake for David every Valentine's Day. At other times of the year, when he has been especially well behaved, I make him these. This quick and easy recipe makes a frosting as rich and chocolaty as much more complicated preparations. —BARBARA

FOR THE CUPCAKES

4 ounces unsweetened chocolate

2 cups granulated sugar

1½ cups all-purpose flour

¾ teaspoon baking soda

½ teaspoon salt

1 cup hot brewed coffee

½ cup sour cream

½ cup vegetable oil

2 large eggs, lightly beaten

FOR THE FROSTING (MAKES 1 CUP)

4 ounces unsweetened chocolate

¾ cup evaporated milk

1 cup confectioners' sugar

¼ teaspoon kosher salt

For the cupcakes, preheat the oven to 350°F. Line 16 muffin cups with liners.

Melt the chocolate in a double boiler over hot, not simmering, water. Remove the pan from the heat.

Sift the sugar, flour, baking soda, and salt together into a large bowl. In a medium bowl, whisk together the hot coffee, sour cream, and vegetable oil. Gradually whisk in the eggs, then stir in the chocolate. Add the wet ingredients to the dry ingredients and stir until the ingredients are smoothly blended.

Fill the cupcake liners about two-thirds full. Bake until a toothpick inserted in the center of a cupcake comes out clean, 20 to 25 minutes. Cool completely on a wire rack.

For the frosting, melt the chocolate in a double boiler over hot, not simmering, water. Place the milk, sugar, and salt in a medium bowl and stir until the sugar is dissolved, about 2 minutes. Add the chocolate in a slow stream and mix until thoroughly blended. Refrigerate for about 30 minutes before using. Frost the cupcakes with the frosting.   **MAKES 16 CUPCAKES**

Sour Cream Coffee Cake

We've never seen a community cookbook that didn't have a recipe for a cinnamon-layered coffee cake like this one, but we think ours is the best. We make this for breakfast whenever we have guests staying over at our house, and inevitably they leave with a copy of the recipe.

3 cups all-purpose flour

2 teaspoons baking powder

1 teaspoon baking soda

¼ teaspoon ground nutmeg

¼ teaspoon salt

1 cup (firmly packed) dark brown sugar

2 teaspoons ground cinnamon

¾ cup chopped walnuts

¾ pound (3 sticks) unsalted butter, softened

1¼ cups granulated sugar

1 teaspoon vanilla extract

3 large eggs

1½ cups sour cream (see Note)

continued

something sweet

Preheat the oven to 325°F. Butter and flour a 12 x 9 x 2-inch baking pan.

Sift together the flour, baking powder, baking soda, nutmeg, and salt into a medium bowl. In a small bowl, mix together the brown sugar, cinnamon, and nuts.

In a large bowl, using an electric mixer, beat the butter and sugar until light and fluffy. Add the vanilla. Add the eggs one at a time, beating well after each addition. Beat in the sour cream. On low speed, gradually add the flour mixture, beating just until the ingredients are combined.

Spoon one third of the batter into the prepared pan and sprinkle one third of the nut mixture on top. Repeat this step twice with the remaining batter and nut mixture. Bake until a toothpick inserted into the center of the cake comes out clean, about 50 minutes. Cool the cake in the pan for 10 minutes, then serve.   SERVES 6 TO 8

N O T E : Sour cream has about 20 percent fat, around the same as light cream. The tangy taste comes from the addition of lactic acid cultures. Don't try to substitute reduced or nonfat sour cream in baking recipes.

Strawberry Shortcake

If we had our way, we'd always make strawberry shortcakes entirely out of wild strawberries. The scarcity of these little jewels makes this impossible, but summer-ripe berries do very well. You sometimes see sponge cake used as a base for strawberry shortcake. That's not how it's done in our kitchen, where we consider the crumbly dough of old-fashioned biscuits the perfect receptacle for the deep red berry juice.

FOR THE BISCUITS

2¾ cups all-purpose flour

2 tablespoons plus 1 teaspoon granulated sugar

1 tablespoon plus 1 teaspoon baking powder

1 teaspoon salt

7 tablespoons unsalted butter, well chilled,
   cut into ½-inch pieces

1 cup plus 2 tablespoons heavy cream

¼ teaspoon vanilla extract

FOR THE STRAWBERRIES

2 pints ripe strawberries, hulled and sliced

2 tablespoons granulated sugar

2 teaspoons fresh lemon juice

FOR THE WHIPPED CREAM

1 cup heavy cream, chilled

1 tablespoon granulated sugar

½ teaspoon vanilla extract

Preheat the oven to 375°F.

Sift together the flour, 2 tablespoons of the sugar, the baking powder, and salt into a mixing bowl. Add the butter and beat on low speed for 1 to 2 minutes, until the mixture has the consistency of coarse meal. Continue mixing and slowly add 1 cup of the cream and the vanilla. Mix just until the dough comes together. Turn the dough out onto a lightly floured work surface and knead until it comes together in a ball, about 1 minute; be careful not to overwork it.

On a lightly floured surface, roll the dough out into a rectangle about ¾ inch thick. Cut out 2½-inch rounds with a biscuit cutter and place them ¾ inch apart on an ungreased baking sheet. The dough scraps can be brought together, rerolled, and cut. Brush the remaining 2 table-spoons cream on the top of the biscuits and sprinkle with the remaining 1 teaspoon sugar.

Bake until the biscuits are golden brown, 25 to 30 minutes. Let cool completely on a wire rack.

While the shortcakes are baking, prepare the strawberries and whipped cream.

Toss the strawberries in a large bowl with the sugar and lemon juice. Place the strawberries in the refrigerator and let them macerate for 30 to 40 minutes. (This same method can be used with other berries as they come into season, such as blueberries, raspberries, and blackberries.)

For the whipped cream, combine all the ingredients in a large bowl and whip to soft peaks. (The trick to whipping heavy cream by hand is to use a good-quality whip and to whip the cream in a cold stainless-steel bowl over a second bowl filled with ice.)

For the assembly, cut the shortcakes horizontally in half. Drizzle ½ cup of the liquid from the strawberries onto 8 small dessert plates. Place the bottom of the shortcakes on the plates, top with a layer of whipped cream, followed by some of the strawberries and their syrup, and finish with more whipped cream. (Make sure that each shortcake has plenty of syrup from the strawberries.) Add the top of the shortcake, the remaining strawberries, and the remaining whipped cream. Serve immediately. SERVES 8

BOATING IN WISCONSIN, 1990

Wild strawberries I first tasted wild strawberries

when David and I were in Wisconsin in search of a fish boil,

a local tradition where huge cauldrons of fish, potatoes,

and onions are boiled for a hungry crowd. We were walk-

ing in the shallow water at the edge of Lake Michigan

when David began to rummage around the edge of the

pine woods. Scattered throughout the underbrush were

tiny strawberry plants with a crop of ripe wild strawberries.

I popped one into my mouth and it tasted like a whole pint

of strawberries had been condensed in one tiny berry. We

happily raided the whole treasure trove. —BARBARA

PUDDINGS

When we were planning Home Restaurant, we asked ourselves what we meant by "home cooking"—and pudding was the first thing that came to mind. It just feels like home: sensual and comforting but not at all to be taken for granted. And it's something you can rely on, just as long as you treat it with kindness.

Chocolate Pudding

This is now the single most requested recipe by our customers. We're always surprised at how many people order dessert, considering they've already had a lot to eat. But it seems there's always room for chocolate.

4 cups heavy cream
5 ounces bittersweet chocolate (see Note), finely chopped
6 large egg yolks
½ cup granulated sugar
1 teaspoon vanilla extract
Pinch of salt

Preheat the oven to 325°F.

Bring the heavy cream to a simmer in a large heavy saucepan, then remove the pan from the heat.

Place the chocolate in a large stainless-steel bowl, add 1 cup of the warm cream, and let stand until the chocolate is melted. Stir the chocolate mixture until it is smooth, then stir in the remaining cream.

In a separate large bowl, whisk together the egg yolks, sugar, vanilla, and salt. Gradually whisk in the chocolate mixture. Strain the pudding through a fine-mesh strainer and skim off the froth on the top.

Pour the pudding into eight 6-ounce ovenproof ramekins. Place them in a deep baking pan and put the pan in the oven. Add enough hot water to the pan to reach halfway up the sides of the ramekins, then cover the pan with aluminum foil. Bake the puddings for about 50 minutes. When gently shaken, they should look set around the edges but not quite set in a quarter-size area at the center.

Remove the ramekins from the water bath and let cool at room temperature. Refrigerate for several hours, or overnight. Serve chilled.   SERVES 8

N O T E : Bittersweet chocolate has sugar, vanilla, and lecithin added to the pure chocolate liquor and cocoa butter. Although semisweet usually has more sugar, the two are pretty much interchangeable in recipes.

Butterscotch Pudding

It took a surprising amount of work to get this pudding to the point when it had a perfect balance of deep caramel flavor and creamy velvety texture. The payoff is a dessert that's been a customer favorite for years.

6 large egg yolks

1 cup whole milk

2 cups heavy cream

¼ cup (firmly packed) dark brown sugar

¾ cup granulated sugar

¼ cup water

1 teaspoon salt

1 teaspoon vanilla extract

Place the egg yolks in a large bowl and lightly whisk them together.

Whisk together the milk, cream, and brown sugar in a heavy saucepan and heat over medium-high heat until small bubbles form around the edge. Remove from the heat.

Dissolve the granulated sugar in the water in a large heavy saucepan over low heat. Increase the heat to high and cook the sugar without stirring until it is golden amber in color. Carefully and slowly pour the hot cream mixture into the caramel and stir with a long wooden spoon or whisk; the caramel will bubble up and steam as you begin to combine them. Gently and slowly whisk the caramel cream into the egg yolks. Stir in the salt and vanilla. Strain the pudding and refrigerate it until cooled, about 30 minutes. Skim off any air bubbles.

Preheat the oven to 300°F.

Pour the pudding into six 6-ounce ramekins. Place them in a deep baking pan and put the pan in the oven. Add enough hot water to the pan to reach halfway up the sides of the ramekins, then cover the pan with aluminum foil. Bake the puddings for about 50 minutes. When gently shaken, they should look set around the edges but not quite set in a quarter-size area at the center.

Remove the ramekins from the water bath and let cool to room temperature. Refrigerate for several hours, or overnight. Serve chilled.   SERVES 6

butterscotch   What we call "butterscotch" is a flavor that blends butter and brown sugar, which in turn gets its flavor from the addition of molasses. The hard candy called butterscotch is made with brown sugar rather than the white sugar that's cooked to make toffee.

Persimmon Pudding

Common in the Midwest, persimmon pudding has a texture that resembles wet cake. The first time we had it, we thought it was undercooked, but since everyone else was spooning it up and asking for seconds, we understood it was a one-of-a-kind treat. It's best served hot, since it falls on cooling.

continued

6 ripe persimmons (to yield 1 cup pulp)

1 cup (firmly packed) brown sugar

1 cup whole milk

4 tablespoons (½ stick) unsalted butter, melted

¼ cup Kentucky bourbon

1 large egg, separated

1 cup all-purpose flour

2 teaspoons baking powder

¼ teaspoon salt

¼ teaspoon ground cinnamon

¼ teaspoon ground allspice

¼ teaspoon ground ginger

⅛ teaspoon ground nutmeg

Sweetened whipped cream, for serving

Preheat the oven to 350°F. Butter an 8-inch square or 9-inch round baking dish.

Cut the persimmons in half and scoop out the pulp; discard the skin. Force the pulp through a strainer to remove any tough membranes. Stir the persimmon, brown sugar, milk, butter, and whiskey together in a large bowl. Whisk the egg yolk in a small bowl and stir it into the persimmon mixture.

Sift the flour, baking powder, salt, and spices together into a small bowl. Add the flour mixture half at a time to the persimmon mixture and stir until smoothly blended.

In a small bowl, whisk the egg white to stiff peaks. Fold it into the batter with a spatula.

Pour the batter into the buttered baking dish and bake for 1 hour. Serve immediately, scooping portions into small bowls and topping with freshly whipped cream.

SERVES 4

persimmons Persimmons come into season around the winter holidays. In October and November, bright orange fruits dangle from every branch of the persimmon tree, waiting for the first frosts that legend says ripen the fruit. The frost actually has nothing to do with the ripening process, which happens by itself around early November, when the fruit is so soft it feels as though there's nothing but water under the skin.

Native Pudding

This is the dessert we made for a dinner at the James Beard House honoring Amelia Simmons, who wrote the first American cookbook in 1796—a hundred years before Fannie Farmer. Simmons's recipe, though, was heavier than ours due to the fact that Indians and early settlers depended on it for sustenance rather than enjoying it as a delicate dessert.

3 cups whole milk
¼ cup molasses
⅓ cup fine yellow cornmeal
2 large eggs
¼ cup granulated sugar
2 tablespoons unsalted butter, softened
½ teaspoon ground ginger
½ teaspoon ground cinnamon
¼ teaspoon salt

Preheat the oven to 300°F.

Stir together the milk, molasses, and cornmeal in a 4-quart saucepan. Heat, stirring constantly, over medium-low heat until thickened, about 10 minutes. Remove from the heat.

Whisk together the eggs, sugar, butter, spices, and salt in a medium bowl. Gradually stir the egg mixture into the warm cornmeal mixture.

Pour the pudding into six 6-ounce ramekins. Place them in a deep baking pan and put the pan in the oven. Add enough hot water to the pan to reach halfway up the sides of the ramekins, then cover the pan with aluminum foil. Bake until set, 1½ to 2 hours.

Remove the ramekins from the water bath and let cool slightly. Serve warm. **SERVES 6**

Bread Pudding with Pear-Rum Sauce

Bread pudding comes from frugal kitchens. Like French toast and Tuscan bread salad, it had a humble beginning as a way to use up day-old bread. And, like them, it can make a very satisfying dish all by itself. It can range from dense and chunky to a smooth-textured custardy dessert. Ours is fluffy because we whip the egg whites and fold them into the custard at the last minute.

6 cups cubed white bread, without crusts (1-inch cubes)
1 cup peeled, cored, and diced pear (½-inch dice)
1 cup dark raisins
¼ teaspoon ground cinnamon
⅛ teaspoon ground nutmeg
⅛ teaspoon ground ginger
3 large eggs, separated
¾ cup granulated sugar

3 cups whole milk

2 tablespoons molasses

¼ teaspoon vanilla extract

¼ teaspoon salt

Pear-Rum Sauce (recipe follows)

Preheat the oven to 350°F. Butter six 8-ounce ramekins.

If the bread cubes are very moist, dry them in a 300°F oven for about 10 minutes, being careful not to let them brown (the center of the cubes should still be moist).

Combine the bread, pear, raisins, and spices in a large bowl.

Beat the egg yolks and sugar in a mixer bowl until light yellow and fluffy.

Heat the milk, molasses, vanilla, and salt in a saucepan until small bubbles form around the edge of the pan. Slowly pour the heated milk mixture into the egg yolk mixture while stirring constantly.

Whisk the egg whites in a medium bowl to soft peaks. Gently fold the egg whites into the egg yolk mixture with a spatula, being careful not to deflate the whipped egg whites.

Divide the bread mixture among the 6 ramekins. Pour the custard over the bread, dividing it equally. Bake until the top is golden, about 25 minutes. Serve immediately, drizzled with the pear sauce.   SERVES 6

continued

❖ PEAR-RUM SAUCE ❖

3 pears, peeled, cored, and cut into ½-inch dice

1 cup rum (we use Mount Gay)

3 tablespoons unsalted butter

2 tablespoons molasses

⅛ teaspoon ground cinnamon

Place all the ingredients in a heavy saucepan and heat over low heat until the pears soften and the sauce thickens, about 20 minutes. Serve warm. (The sauce can be made ahead of time and refrigerated. Reheat over low heat before serving.)   **MAKES 3 CUPS**

GRANDPA SHINN (CENTER), AT SLOPPY JOE'S IN HAVANA
DURING PROHIBITION, 1930

PIES

Every Thanksgiving we serve pumpkin and apple pies, and no matter where the customers come from, half will order one and half the other. It's not a tradition we'd dare mess with, because pies are the most American dessert—maybe the most American food—there is. They're so big and thick, so bountiful, that they seem to sum up the whole American food experience.

Lately, we've noticed that restaurant chefs have been serving individual pies, probably figuring that the classic triangular slice is too rough and homemade-looking. We object. We think an individual pie gives you too much crust and too little sweet juicy fruit filling to be satisfying.

Rustic Apple Pie

The folded-in crust on this homey pie makes it simple to put together, even for cooks who think they can't handle pastry well.

¾ cup (firmly packed) light brown sugar

3 tablespoons all-purpose flour

½ teaspoon ground cinnamon

½ teaspoon ground cardamom

¼ teaspoon ground nutmeg

Pinch of salt

2 pounds Granny Smith apples, cored, peeled, and sliced ¼ inch thick (see Note)

1 tablespoon fresh lemon juice

Buttery Pie Dough (page 395)

1½ tablespoons unsalted butter, melted

2 tablespoons superfine sugar

Preheat the oven to 400°F.

Combine the brown sugar, flour, cinnamon, cardamom, nutmeg, and salt in a small bowl.

In a large bowl, toss the apples with the lemon juice. Sprinkle the sugar mixture over the apples and toss well until the apples are evenly coated.

On a lightly floured work surface, with a floured rolling pin, roll the dough out into a 16-inch circle, occasionally lifting the dough and giving it a quarter turn (this helps keep it round). Lightly flour the dough and fold it in half, then lift it into a 9-inch pie plate, with the fold at the center. Unfold the dough and gently fit it into the plate, allowing the excess dough to hang over the sides.

Spread the apple filling in the pie plate and fold the excess dough over it, pleating the dough as necessary. Brush the dough with the melted butter and sprinkle with the superfine sugar.

Bake until the apples are tender and crust is brown, about 45 minutes. Serve warm.   SERVES 8

NOTE: In the autumn months, different apple varieties come into season in succession, making for exceptional pie baking. We ask for Granny Smiths in this recipe because they're firm, tart, and available all year round, but if you're near an apple orchard, find out what they've been picking that week and combine two or more baking apple varieties for an interesting taste profile. We also like to use Gravenstein, Jonamac, Empire, and Rome apples.

Bourbon Pecan Pie

You can't get more Southern than this recipe, with its pecans, corn syrup, and heady taste of bourbon. Serve it warm, with a big scoop of vanilla ice cream melting on the plate alongside it.

3 large eggs

1 cup dark corn syrup

½ cup (packed) light brown sugar

3 tablespoons unsalted butter, melted and cooled

3 tablespoons Kentucky bourbon

1 teaspoon vanilla extract

½ teaspoon ground cinnamon

3 cups chopped pecans

1 (9-inch) pie shell made with Buttery Pie Dough
  (page 395), unbaked

continued

Preheat the oven to 325°F.

In a large bowl, whisk together the eggs, corn syrup, and brown sugar. Add the melted butter and whisk until it is thoroughly combined. Whisk in the bourbon, vanilla, and cinnamon. Stir in the pecans.

Pour the filling into the pie shell. Bake until the filling is set, about 50 minutes. Let the pie cool completely before serving.   SERVES 8

pecans These thin-shelled oval nuts grow in the Southeast, especially in Georgia and Texas. Their high fat content makes them taste buttery but also causes them to turn rancid quickly, so store them in the refrigerator or freezer.

Honey Pumpkin Pie

Thanksgiving is no time for a new-fangled, thin, tartlike pumpkin pie. Instead, we make this real old-fashioned country recipe with a filling that's inches high and has just enough cream to make it smooth. One tip: When you take the pie out of the oven, there should be a three-inch circle in the center that's still wobbly. If you bake it longer, it will be overcooked, and you'll have a crack down the center of the pie.

1 (16-ounce) can pumpkin purée

⅓ cup granulated sugar

⅓ cup (firmly packed) light brown sugar

⅓ cup honey

3 large eggs, lightly beaten

1 tablespoon cornstarch

2 teaspoons ground cinnamon

1 teaspoon ground ginger

¼ teaspoon salt

1 cup heavy cream

1 (9-inch) pie shell made with *Buttery Pie Dough*
   (page 395), unbaked

Preheat the oven to 350°F.

Place the pumpkin purée in a large bowl and stir in the granulated sugar, brown sugar, and honey. Add the eggs, then stir in the cornstarch, ginger, cinnamon, and salt. Stir in the cream.

Pour the filling into the prepared pie shell. Bake until the edges of the filling are firmly set but the center jiggles slightly when shaken, about 1 hour and 15 minutes. Allow the pie to cool to room temperature and serve. **SERVES 8**

Buttery Pie Dough

This is our all-purpose recipe for single-crusted pies.

2 cups all-purpose flour

2 tablespoons granulated sugar

1 teaspoon salt

12 tablespoons (1½ sticks) unsalted butter,
   cut into ½-inch cubes

3 to 4 tablespoons ice water

Sift the flour, sugar, and salt into a medium bowl. Cut in the butter with a fork or pastry blender until the mixture resembles coarse meal. Gradually add 3 tablespoons of the ice water, stirring just until a dough begins to form; you may need to add more water if the dough seems dry. Form the dough into a disc.

continued

On a lightly floured surface, using a floured rolling pin, roll out the dough to a 14-inch round about ½ inch thick. Carefully fold the dough in half and place it in a 9-inch pie dish. Unfold the dough and fit it into the dish, allowing the excess dough to hang over the sides. Gently press the dough against the edge of the pie plate, then trim off the excess dough.   **MAKES ONE 9-INCH PIE CRUST**

pastry tips To make good pastry, you have to work quickly. The longer it takes, the more flour will be absorbed, and you want to use the least amount of flour possible both at the start and for dusting and rolling it out. We rub the butter into the flour with our fingers, but that can be tricky, because the heat of your hand can melt the butter unless you go very fast. The cold tines of a fork or wires of a pastry cutter are probably a safer tool to use until you gain experience.

an impromptu oven When we had friends over for a spring barbecue recently, we realized we didn't have anything for dessert. This was a problem, seeing that our kitchen was being renovated and our only option was the Weber grill. After two months of grilling out and washing dishes with the garden hose, we were sick of not having down-home desserts to finish off our meals. Then we remembered our cast-iron Dutch oven and decided to try making a crisp in it, cooking it over the coals. With some trepidation, we decided to forget about culinary perfection and cook like Scouts. Although it tasted a little smoky, that strawberry crisp was absolutely delicious, and we've since made other Dutch oven crisps on the barbecue, even though we now have a working kitchen.

CRISPS AND COBBLERS

Crisps are among the easiest desserts to make. All you need is your favorite combination of fruits and a crumb topping to sprinkle on top. When we have last-minute dinner company, we simply place a crisp in the oven when we sit down to eat and, by the time we're done with our main dish, it's bubbling away.

Peach-Blueberry Crisp

Another natural combination, since peaches and blue-berries show up in farm stands at the same time.

4 large ripe peaches
1 pint fresh blueberries
2 tablespoons all-purpose flour

FOR THE TOPPING
½ cup all-purpose flour
½ cup (packed) dark brown sugar
½ teaspoon ground cinnamon
¼ teaspoon ground nutmeg
⅓ cup (5⅓ tablespoons) unsalted butter, well chilled
⅓ cup slivered almonds

continued

Preheat the oven to 375°F. Butter a 9 x 6-inch baking dish.

Immerse the peaches in a large pot of boiling water for 15 seconds. Drain and immediately cool in ice water. Slip off the skins, pit, and cut into 1-inch-thick slices.

Combine the peaches and blueberries in a large bowl. Add the 2 tablespoons flour and lightly toss together. Spread the mixture evenly in the baking dish.

For the topping, combine the ½ cup flour, the brown sugar, cinnamon, and nutmeg in a small bowl. Add the butter and work it into the flour mixture with your fingertips until the mixture is crumbly.

Cover the peaches and blueberries with the topping and sprinkle the almonds evenly on top. Bake for 30 minutes. Serve hot, with vanilla ice cream.   **SERVES 6**

combining fruits   Our rule of thumb is to use fruits that are in season at the same time and to keep the combinations simple. If you use more than two fruits in a crisp, the flavors will become muddy and lose their individuality.

Strawberry-Rhubarb Crisp

This is one of those natural seasonal combinations, the sweet berries modifying the tartness of the rhubarb. It's a good example of how using foods that ripen at the same time makes sense in the kitchen.

FOR THE TOPPING

¾ *cup all-purpose flour*

¼ *cup granulated sugar*

¼ *cup (packed) light brown sugar*

¼ *teaspoon ground cinnamon*

⅛ teaspoon ground nutmeg

2 tablespoons unsalted butter, chilled

1 tablespoon fresh lemon juice

FOR THE FILLING

4 cups halved ripe strawberries

2 cups sliced rhubarb (1-inch pieces)

½ cup granulated sugar

⅓ cup all-purpose flour

¼ teaspoon ground mace

1 teaspoon vanilla extract

Preheat the oven to 350°F.

For the topping, stir together the flour, both sugars, and the spices in a bowl. Add the butter and work it into the flour mixture with your fingertips until it is crumbly. Stir in the lemon juice. The mixture will remain crumbly. Set aside.

For the filling, combine all the ingredients in a large bowl. Transfer to a 9 x 6-inch baking pan and spread evenly. Sprinkle with the crumb topping.

Bake until the top is browned and the filling is bubbling, 40 to 45 minutes. Serve warm or at room temperature, with vanilla ice cream or lightly sweetened whipped cream.   SERVES 6

r h u b a r b Rhubarb used to be called pieplant because it was so often baked into pies. We don't eat the leaves, which can be toxic, just the celery-green and pink stalks (trimmed but not peeled), which are so tart that they require lots of sugar to make them good to eat. In this country, rhubarb is often paired with strawberries, but in England, it's cooked with sugar and ginger.

Apple Cobbler with Dropped Cheddar-Biscuit Topping

In restaurants in the Midwest, when you order warm apple pie, the waitress asks if you want it with or without cheese, meaning a slice of Cheddar melted over the top. You don't see that in the East, so this warm cobbler topped with cheddar biscuits is our tip of the hat to a midwestern tradition. The biscuits, by the way, can be made on their own and served with breakfast bacon and eggs.

3 tablespoons unsalted butter

1 (3-inch) cinnamon stick

1 teaspoon finely grated lemon zest

10 medium Granny Smith apples, cored, peeled,
  and thinly sliced

¾ cup (packed) light brown sugar

1 recipe Cheddar Biscuits dough (page 313)

¼ cup superfine sugar

Melt the butter in a large deep skillet over medium heat. Add the cinnamon stick and lemon zest, then add the apples, tossing to coat them evenly with butter. Sprinkle the brown sugar over the apples and continue tossing them in the skillet until the sugar is evenly distributed. Cook, stirring, until the sugar has dissolved, about 5 minutes. Remove the skillet from the heat and discard the cinnamon stick.

Spread the apples in a 13 x 9 x 2-inch baking dish. Let cool to room temperature.

Preheat the oven to 375°F.

Drop the biscuit dough by tablespoonsful onto the cooled apples, covering them completely. Sprinkle the superfine sugar over the top.

Bake until the top is golden brown, about 30 minutes. Serve the cobbler warm or at room temperature, with vanilla ice cream.　　　　　SERVES 12

grunts There's lots of confusion about the difference among cobblers, grunts, and other early American deep-dish desserts. A cobbler is different from a crisp because it has a sugar-sprinkled biscuit crust, which some cook must have thought looked like cobblestones. Grunts were supposedly named for the noise the fruit makes when it cooks and bubbles under the biscuit crust.

GRANDMOTHER PAGE WITH
JOANNE (DAVID'S SISTER), 1958

something sweet

FRUIT DESSERTS

Everyone likes desssert, but we've learned that there are

chocolate people and fruit people. The first always order

the brownie sundae; the second will say they don't want

dessert but then add, "Well, maybe just a baked apple."

Pale Ale Apple Fritters

Fritters appear in the oldest American cookbooks. Called *beignets* in New Orleans, these deep-fried batter-dipped foods can be made with fruit, seafood, or vegetables and are almost always served hot.

The aroma that fills the house when we make apple fritters tempts us to sneak a few before our guests eat up the whole batch. These are delicious served with vanilla ice cream.

5 Granny Smith apples, cored, peeled, and sliced
    into ½-inch-thick rings
½ cup apple brandy
½ cup superfine sugar
1¼ cups all-purpose flour
½ teaspoon salt
1 cup pale ale
¼ cup whole milk
Canola or other vegetable oil, for deep-frying
Confectioners' sugar, for dusting

Place the apples in a large bowl and toss with the brandy and sugar. Cover and refrigerate for at least 1 hour and up to 4 hours.

Meanwhile, sift together the flour and salt into a medium bowl. Gradually whisk in the pale ale and milk, whisking until the batter is completely smooth. Cover the batter with plastic wrap and allow it to rest in the refrigerator for at least 30 minutes and up to 2 hours.

Heat the canola oil in a deep heavy pot over medium-high heat until it reaches 360°F. While the oil is heating, line a baking sheet or plate with paper towels. When the oil is hot, dip a few apple rings, one at a time, into the batter, coating generously, then shake off the excess batter and drop into the oil. Fry until golden brown on the first side, about 1 minute, then flip each fritter over, using a slotted spoon, and fry until golden brown on the second side. Transfer to the lined baking sheet to drain and repeat until all of the fritters are cooked. Dust the fritters with confectioners' sugar and serve immediately. SERVES 8

MY PARENTS, 1948

On a cold Saturday afternoon, my mom

would core and stuff apples with butter and sugar, and

put them in a glass pan with a little water, and bake them

for what seemed forever. Occasionally, she would open

the door and baste the apples with the sugary syrup in the

bottom of the pan. Finally, they'd be ready to eat around

4 P.M., just in time to ruin everyone's appetite for dinner.

This is our fail-proof recipe. —BARBARA

Mom Shinn's Baked Apples

6 red baking apples, such as Empire or Jonamac

4 tablespoons (½ stick) unsalted butter, softened

1 cup dark raisins

½ cup dried cranberries

¼ cup chopped walnuts

¼ cup honey

1 tablespoon granulated sugar

1 teaspoon ground cinnamon

Preheat the oven to 350°F.

Core the apples from the top, leaving the base intact; this will form a hollow for the stuffing.

Brush the outside of the apples with the softened butter. Combine the remaining ingredients and stuff the apples with the mixture.

Set the apples on a baking sheet and bake until tender, 45 to 60 minutes. Serve warm, with ice cream.   SERVES 6

Honeydew Fruit Salad

On a hot August afternoon, this is the most refreshing dessert imaginable.

Juice of 2 medium limes
6 large fresh mint leaves, thinly slivered
1 large honeydew melon

Combine the lime juice and mint ribbons in a medium bowl and set aside.

Slice the melon in half and scoop out the seeds. Slice off the rind and cut the melon into 1-inch cubes. Add to the lime juice mixture, tossing to coat. Serve immediately, or refrigerate until ready to serve.　　**SERVES 5**

l i m e   j u i c e For some reason, limes really hold onto their juice. It helps if you press and roll them under your hands, breaking down the membranes inside, before you cut them. If you have an old-fashioned juice reamer, that will help too.

GRANDFATHER PAGE WITH HIS BROTHERS
AND SISTER ON A WATERMELON BREAK, 1913

Citrus-Berry Salad

Vanilla adds an indefinable richness to tart grapefruit sections.

4 large pink grapefruits
1 vanilla bean
1 cup fresh blueberries
10 small fresh mint leaves

Using a sharp knife, peel the grapefruits, removing all the bitter white pith. Working over a bowl to catch the juices, slice between the membranes to release the grapefruit sections, allowing them to drop into the bowl.

Using a paring knife, split the vanilla bean lengthwise in half. Using the back of the knife, scrape the pulp out of the vanilla pod and add it to the grapefruit sections. Toss the grapefruit until the vanilla pulp is evenly distributed. Stir in the blueberries and mint and serve, or refrigerate and serve chilled.   **SERVES 4**

vanilla beans Actually the pods of a species of orchid, vanilla beans are as native to the Americas as corn, potatoes, and peppers are. These days, most vanilla beans come from Madagascar and the area around it.

Strawberry Soup

Strawberries are best used the day they are picked. When our local strawberry crop is abundant and we've made all the jams, crisps, and shortcakes that we can, we make this icy chilled soup. The purée remains vibrant and flavorful for a few days.

1 quart fresh strawberries, hulled and halved
½ cup water
¼ cup granulated sugar
½ teaspoon fresh lemon juice
4 fresh mint leaves

Place half of the berries, the water, and sugar in a 2-quart saucepan over low heat. Bring the mixture to a simmer and cook until the berries are soft and the juices are bubbly and thickened, about 5 minutes. Remove from the heat.

Purée the remaining berries with the cooked berry mixture and lemon juice in a food processor or blender until smooth. If the soup seems too thick, add a little water. Strain through a fine-mesh strainer. Be sure to press on the solids to extract all the juices from the berries. Cover and refrigerate until very cold, preferably overnight.

To serve, ladle the soup into 4 chilled shallow bowls and garnish with the mint leaves. **SERVES 4**

fruit soups Fruit soups are traditional in Scandinavia and Eastern Europe, where they're eaten at the start of the meal. There's been a vogue for them recently in this country, but here they're served as dessert on days when the temperature reaches tropical proportions.

COOKIES

When we opened Home Restaurant, it took a while for people to realize we were here. One way we got them to come in and try us was to give away cookies outside the front door. We'd hand them a cookie and they'd walk off eating it, not quite meeting our eyes, in a very New York way. They'd get halfway down the block and we'd see them stop, turn around, and say "This is great"—and they'd come back to make a reservation to eat with us.

OUR WINDOW ON THE WORLD

Sugar Cookies

Cookies are the first dessert most people learn to make, and everyone loves them. These delicate wafers with pale golden edges are perfect to serve with sorbets, pudding, or our Spiced Seckel Pears (page 343). When we've made an extra-large batch of these cookies, we sometimes spread a thin layer of melted chocolate on the underside of half of them and sandwich the cookies together.

4 tablespoons (½ stick) unsalted butter, softened

⅓ cup plus 1 tablespoon granulated sugar

1 large egg

1½ teaspoons whole milk

¼ teaspoon vanilla extract

½ cup sifted all-purpose flour

⅛ teaspoon salt

⅛ teaspoon baking powder

Preheat the oven to 375°F. Butter 2 cookie sheets.

Place the butter and ⅓ cup of the sugar in a large mixer bowl and beat until the mixture is light yellow and fluffy, about 3 minutes. Add the egg, milk, and vanilla and beat for 3 minutes longer.

Combine the flour, salt, and baking powder in a separate bowl. Add it to the butter mixture and beat on low speed until the ingredients are well blended, about 1 minute.

Drop the cookie dough by the tablespoon 2 inches apart onto the buttered cookie sheets. Sprinkle the tops with the remaining 1 tablespoon sugar. Bake until the edges become golden brown, about 10 minutes. Transfer to wire racks to cool.　　**MAKES 24 COOKIES**

Butter Cookies

For many of us, our lives are so chaotic around holiday time that it seems impossible to slow down and enjoy the season. But if we stop for just a minute and take a bite of a wreath- or star-shaped sugar cookie, the crumbly buttery mouthful brings back memories of past celebrations and revives the spirit of the season. These rich butter cookies are the ones we frost and decorate for the holidays.

8 tablespoons (1 stick) unsalted butter, softened

½ cup granulated sugar

1 large egg yolk

1 cup all-purpose flour

¼ teaspoon baking powder

⅛ teaspoon kosher salt

Place the butter and sugar in a large mixer bowl and beat until the mixture is light yellow and fluffy. Add the egg yolk and mix until blended.

Combine the flour, baking powder, and the salt in a separate bowl. Add to the butter mixture and beat on low speed until smooth. Cover the bowl with plastic wrap and refrigerate the dough until it is firm enough to roll out, 30 to 60 minutes.

Preheat the oven to 350°F.

On a well-floured surface, roll out the dough about ⅛ inch thick. Using cookie cutters, cut the dough into desired shapes and arrange them about 1 inch apart on ungreased cookie sheets.

Bake the cookies until the edges are pale golden, about 8 minutes. Cool on wire racks. **MAKES ABOUT 30 COOKIES**

Peanut Butter Cookies

Peanut butter cookies are our favorite midnight snack. Actually, they're also a favorite of a pesky raccoon that visits our pantry once a week in our home on Long Island. It's nice to know we're surrounded by gourmets.

1½ cups all-purpose flour

½ teaspoon baking powder

½ teaspoon salt

8 tablespoons (1 stick) unsalted butter, softened

½ cup smooth or chunky peanut butter

½ cup granulated sugar

½ (packed) light brown sugar

1 large egg

1 teaspoon vanilla extract

Preheat the oven to 350°F.

Combine the flour, baking powder, and salt in a small bowl.

In a large bowl, with an electric mixer, beat together the butter, peanut butter, and both sugars until light and fluffy, about 3 minutes. Add the egg and vanilla and beat for 2 minutes. On low speed, gradually add the flour mixture, beating until the ingredients are thoroughly combined.

Roll portions of the dough (about 1 tablespoonful per cookie) into balls, slightly flatten, and place 2 inches apart onto ungreased cookie sheets. Using the back of a fork, lightly press a crisscross pattern into each cookie.

Bake the cookies until the edges are lightly browned, 10 to 12 minutes. Cool on the cookie sheets on wire racks.

MAKES 36 COOKIES

Coconut Macaroons

We often have one or two of these coconut macaroons with our morning coffee. We use superfine sugar to make lemonade, macaroons, and meringues because it dissolves so quickly. If you don't have superfine, give granulated sugar a whir in your food processor.

4 large egg whites

1⅓ cups superfine sugar

¼ cup all-purpose flour

½ teaspoon salt

1 tablespoon vanilla extract

1 teaspoon coconut extract

4 cups unsweetened shredded coconut

Position a rack in the upper third of the oven and preheat the oven to 300°F.

In the bowl of an electric mixer, beat the egg whites on medium-high speed until they form stiff peaks. Gradually beat in the superfine sugar, then beat in the flour, salt, vanilla, and coconut extracts, mixing only to combine. Stir in the shredded coconut.

Using an ice cream scoop, form 12 mounds of dough 3 inches apart on 2 ungreased cookie sheets. Bake one sheet at a time until golden brown, 15 to 20 minutes. Allow the macaroons to cool completely on the cookie sheets on wire racks before removing them.

MAKES 12 LARGE MACAROONS

something sweet

Chocolate-Cherry
Chunk Cookies

The cookie version of chocolate-covered cherries.

5 ounces semisweet chocolate, coarsely chopped

3 cups all-purpose flour

1½ cups unsweetened cocoa powder

2 teaspoons cream of tartar

½ teaspoon baking powder

½ teaspoon salt

12 tablespoons (1½ sticks) unsalted butter, softened

1¼ cups granulated sugar

¾ cup (packed) light brown sugar

3 large eggs

½ cup dried cherries

½ cup white chocolate chips

Preheat the oven to 350°F.

Melt the chocolate in a double boiler over hot, not simmering, water. Set aside.

Sift together the flour, cocoa powder, cream of tartar, baking powder, and salt into a medium bowl.

In a large bowl, using an electric mixer, beat together the butter and both sugars on medium-high speed until light and fluffy, about 3 minutes. Gradually beat in the melted chocolate. Beat in the eggs one at a time, beating well after each addition. On low speed, beat in the flour. Stir in the cherries and chips. The dough will be stiff.

Form the dough into golf ball–size portions, flatten them between your palms, and place 1 inch apart on ungreased cookie sheets. Bake until the centers of the cookies are set, about 15 minutes. Cool on the cookie sheets on wire racks.   MAKES 36 COOKIES

Raspberry Buttons

An elegant version of old-fashioned thumbprint cookies. Raspberry jam or preserves is the traditional topping for these cookies, probably because of its bright red color. If your family prefers strawberry, apricot, or even marmalade, go ahead and use it.

2 cups all-purpose flour
¼ teaspoon salt
½ pound (2 sticks) unsalted butter, softened
½ cup granulated sugar
1½ teaspoons vanilla extract
½ cup seedless raspberry preserves

Combine the flour and salt in a small bowl.

In a large bowl, using an electric mixer, beat the butter and sugar on medium speed until light and fluffy, about 2 minutes. Beat in the vanilla. On low speed, gradually beat in the flour mixture. Shape the dough into a disc, wrap it in plastic wrap, and chill for 1 hour.

Preheat the oven to 350°F.

On a lightly floured surface, roll out the dough ½ inch thick. With a 1½-inch round cookie cutter, cut out circles of dough and place 2 inches apart on ungreased cookie sheets. Using the back of a spoon, press a shallow well into the center of each cookie. Fill each well with about a teaspoonful of raspberry preserves.

Bake the cookies until the edges are golden brown, about 15 minutes. Cool on the cookie sheets on wire racks. **MAKES 30 COOKIES**

Brownies

We were almost finished with this book when we realized
it didn't have a recipe for brownies. We couldn't have a
book of American cooking without a brownie recipe, so
we added the one we've been making for years. Don't
worry too much about how long to bake it: If you pull the
pan out of the oven early, then cut into it, the brownies
will simply taste like molten chocolate cake.

½ pound (2 sticks) unsalted butter,
    cut into small cubes
20 ounces semisweet chocolate, coarsely chopped
1 cup granulated sugar
1 teaspoon finely ground coffee or instant espresso powder
1 teaspoon vanilla extract
7 large eggs, lightly beaten
1 cup all-purpose flour, sifted
½ teaspoon salt
1 cup chopped walnuts, hazelnuts, or pecans (optional)

Melt the butter and chocolate in a double boiler over hot,
not simmering, water, stirring occasionally until the mixture is smooth. Transfer the chocolate to a large bowl, stir
in the sugar, coffee, and vanilla extract, and let cool to
room temperature.

Preheat the oven to 350°F. Lightly grease and flour a
12 x 9 x 2-inch baking pan.

Stir the eggs into the chocolate mixture until mixture is
thoroughly combined. Stir in the flour, salt, and nuts, if
using, mixing just until combined. Pour the batter into the
prepared baking pan, spreading it evenly with a spatula.

Bake until a toothpick inserted into the center of the
brownies comes out clear, 40 to 45 minutes. Let cool completely, then cut into 12 bars.   **MAKES 12 BROWNIES**

Chocolate-Pecan Squares

These bar cookies are like miniature pecan pies.

FOR THE CRUST

1½ cups all-purpose flour

⅔ cup granulated sugar

½ teaspoon salt

12 tablespoons (1½ sticks) unsalted butter, cut into
    pieces, chilled

FOR THE FILLING

8 tablespoons (1 stick) unsalted butter, softened

1 cup (packed) light brown sugar

2 large eggs

¼ cup all-purpose flour

1 teaspoon vanilla extract

3 cups chopped pecans

1 (12-ounce) bag semisweet chocolate chips

Preheat the oven to 350°F.

For the crust, combine the flour, sugar, and salt in a large bowl. Add the butter and stir or cut it in with a pastry blender until the mixture resembles coarse meal. If it's too soft, chill it for 30 minutes. Press the mixture into the bottom of an ungreased 12 x 9 x 2-inch baking dish. Bake the crust until golden brown, about 18 minutes. Let cool.

For the filling, in a medium bowl, with an electric mixer, beat the butter and brown sugar until light and fluffy. Add the eggs one at a time, beating well after each addition. Beat in the flour, then beat in the vanilla extract. Stir in the pecans and chocolate chips.

Spread the filling over the baked crust. Bake until the top is golden brown, 30 to 35 minutes longer. Let cool completely on a rack before cutting into squares.

MAKES 24 SQUARES

Lemon Bars

Like our Chocolate-Pecan Squares (page 417), these bar cookies are a portable version of a pie, or, this time, actually a tart, with a pastry base made of shortbread.

FOR THE CRUST

1½ cups all-purpose flour

½ cup confectioners' sugar

12 tablespoons (1½ sticks) unsalted butter,
    cut into pieces, softened

FOR THE FILLING

4 large eggs

1½ cups granulated sugar

1 tablespoon all-purpose flour

1 tablespoon grated lemon zest

½ cup fresh lemon juice

Confectioners' sugar, for dusting

Preheat the oven to 350°F. Lightly butter a 12 x 9 x 2-inch baking pan.

For the crust, combine the flour and confectioners' sugar in a medium bowl. Add the butter and stir or cut it in with a pastry blender until the mixture resembles coarse meal. If it's too soft, chill it for 30 minutes. Press the mixture into the bottom and up the sides of the pan. Bake until golden brown, about 18 minutes. Let cool.

For the filling, whisk together the eggs, sugar, flour, lemon zest, and lemon juice in a medium bowl. Pour the filling into the baked crust. Skim off any bubbles from the surface of the filling.

Bake until the filling is set, about 20 minutes longer. Let cool on a rack, then cut into 24 bars. Sift confectioners' sugar over the bars before serving. Store in the refrigerator.

MAKES 24 BARS

DESSERT TOPPINGS

Bourbon–Hot Fudge Sauce

We think of this as an indulgence for grown-ups who still eat banana splits—like us.

8 ounces semisweet chocolate, chopped

1 tablespoon unsalted butter

¼ cup granulated sugar

⅓ cup light corn syrup

½ cup hot water

½ cup unsweetened cocoa

1 teaspoon finely ground coffee

½ teaspoon ground cinnamon

¼ teaspoon ground nutmeg

⅓ cup Kentucky bourbon

Melt the chocolate and butter together in a double boiler over hot, not simmering, water, stirring occasionally. Remove from the heat.

Combine the sugar, corn syrup, hot water, cocoa, coffee, cinnamon, and nutmeg in a medium saucepan, bring to a rolling boil over medium heat, and boil for 5 minutes.

Remove the saucepan from the heat and whisk in the melted chocolate mixture. Whisk in the bourbon. Serve immediately, over ice cream or your favorite dessert. The sauce can be stored in an airtight container in the refrigerator for up to 1 month. Reheat over low heat before using.   **MAKES ABOUT 1 1/4 CUPS**

Creamy Caramel Topping

When you make your own caramel sauce, you get to decide how dark you want it to be. The darker you cook the sugar, the deeper the flavor will be. But don't go too far, or the caramel will become bitter.

1 cup heavy cream
8 tablespoons (1 stick) unsalted butter
1 cup granulated sugar

Combine the heavy cream and butter in a small saucepan over low heat and stir occasionally until the butter melts. Remove the pan from the heat.

Place the sugar in a large saucepan over low heat and cook until the sugar melts and turns a rich caramel color. Immediately whisk the hot cream mixture into the caramelized sugar. The mixture will bubble up in the pan. Remove from the heat and continue whisking until the caramelized sugar has totally dissolved. Strain into a bowl and refrigerate to thicken. The sauce can be stored in an airtight container in the refrigerator for up to 1 month. Reheat over low heat until the caramel comes to a pourable consistency. **MAKES 2 CUPS**

INDEX

index

ginger:
-buttermilk dressing, 93
grilled quail with orange,
marjoram, and, 229–30
roasted mushrooms with
mustard seeds and, 111
salami or pepperoni with,
277–79
goat cheese:
and cornmeal pudding, 284
eggplant roll-ups, 292
truffles, 291
graham crackers, 312
grain(s), 133–52
three-, salad with cucumber
and tomato, 137
see also bulgur wheat;
corn(meal); couscous;
oatmeal; rice
grape leaves:
porgies wrapped in, 175–76
preserved, 357
gravy:
mushroom, 226
our green olive, Mom Page's
skillet-fried chicken with,
213–14
greens, garlic, 107
griddle cakes:
bacon-oregano, 174–75
grilled trout with lemon
dressing and, 173–75
grilled cheese sandwiches:
blue, with apple, 295
Dry Jack, smoked chicken, and
caramelized onions, 296
Wisconsin Asiago, ham, and
overnight tomatoes, 297
grits, cheese, 285
gumbo, shrimp and andouille
sausage, 196–97

Ham:
black bean soup with sherry
and, 35–36
and chicken casserole with
artichokes, creamy,
219–20
country, parsley salad with
overnight tomatoes and,
84–85
country stuffing with, 223–24
grilled Wisconsin Asiago
sandwiches with overnight
tomatoes and, 297
roasted fresh, 257–58
hash, spring mushroom and
sweet pea, 108
hasty pudding, 139
herb bread, 302–3

herb purées and pestos,
21–25
basil purée, 21–22
see also pesto
hominy and shrimp stew,
195–96
honey:
grilled duck breasts with a
glaze of lavender, merlot,
and, 235–36
pumpkin pie, 394–95
roast rack of lamb with mint
and, 263–64
honeydew fruit salad, 406
horseradish:
cocktail sauce, warm, pan-
smoked shrimp with,
193–94
dressing, fresh, smoked fish
salad with, 181
hot fudge–bourbon sauce, 419

Ice wine dressing, oysters on
the half shell with, 184

Jams, 323–35
blueberry-cinnamon, 335
Mom Page's strawberry, 333
peach, 331
raspberry, 330
rose hip, 334
see also butters, fruit; conserves;
jelly; preserves
jelly, 328–29
mint, 336
see also butters, fruit; conserves;
jam; preserves
jicama and smoked trout
slaw, 93

Kebabs, lobster, 200–201
ketchup:
apricot, 10–11
famous tomato, 11–12

Lagniappe, 26–27
Home spice mix, 26
seasoned bread crumbs, 27
lamb, 263–69
with honey and mint, roast
rack of, 263–64

index

index